IMAGES
*of America*

# PARK RIDGE

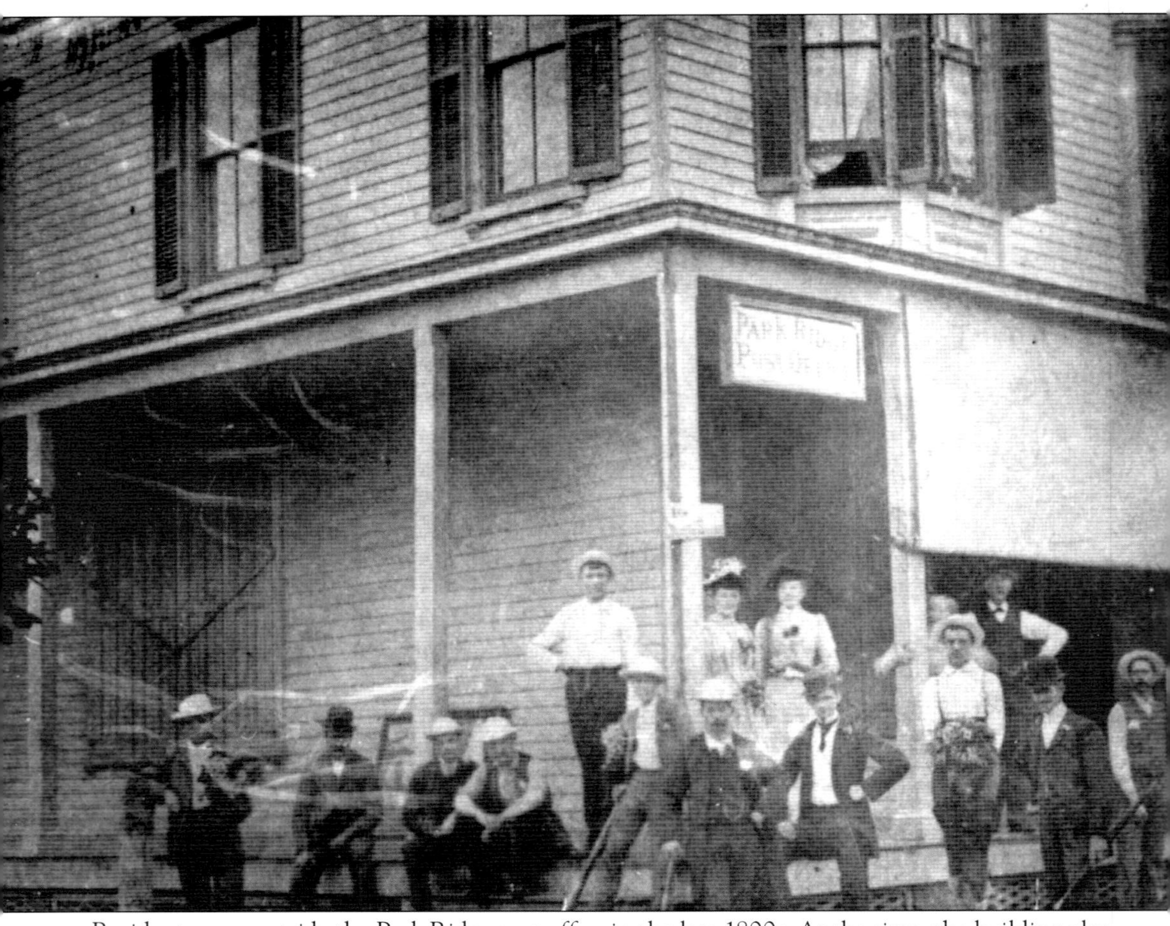

Residents pose outside the Park Ridge post office in the late 1800s. At the time, the building also housed hardware and groceries. It still stands today, much the same as it appears here.

*On the cover*: In 1912, local officials and members of the Park Ridge Volunteer Fire Department take part in the dedication of the firehouse on Park Avenue. The building was erected in 1911. (Courtesy Park Ridge Fire Department.)

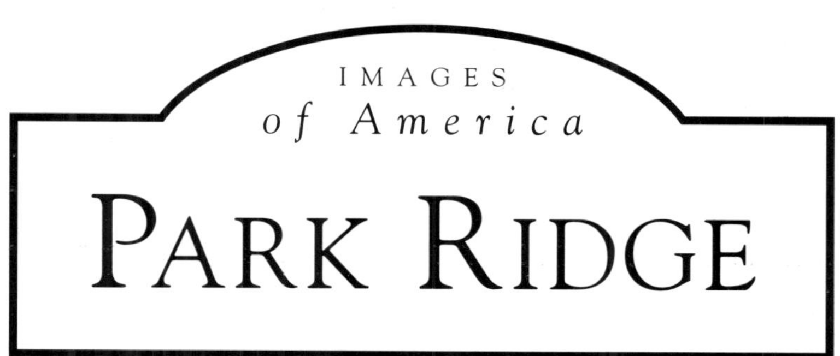


Chris Sagona

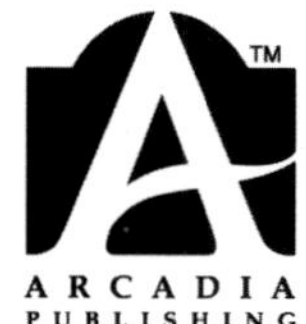

ISBN 0-7385-4611-9

Published by Arcadia Publishing
Charleston SC, Chicago IL, Portsmouth NH, San Francisco CA

Printed in the United States of America

Library of Congress Catalog Card Number: 2006928529

For all general information contact Arcadia Publishing at:
Telephone 843-853-2070
Fax 843-853-0044
E-mail sales@arcadiapublishing.com
For customer service and orders:
Toll-Free 1-888-313-2665

Visit us on the Internet at www.arcadiapublishing.com

*For Steve, Katie, Ken, my parents, the families of those who died in the events of September 11, 2001, and for all who have ties to Park Ridge.*

# Contents

# ACKNOWLEDGMENTS

This book was truly a community effort. When residents and neighbors heard that I needed photographs for this book, they rallied around me unbelievably. I am profoundly grateful to councilwoman Tammy Levinson; Barbara Martine, Park Ridge historian and councilwoman; historian Helen Whalen; Park Ridge assistant fire chief Jim Strabone, Park Ridge mayor Donald Ruschman; the Park Ridge Council; Park Ridge police chief Richard Oppenheimer and Capt. Joseph Madden; Larry Coslow and Park Ridge Water and Electric; Anthony Rizzo; Don Smith; the Quackenbush family; Neil Giovanniello; Dana Mendelson; Linda Salib and Jim Giens; Charles and June Bertini; Walter and Carolyn Noller; and everyone who lent me a photograph and told me a story for this book. Thank you, thank you, thank you.

# INTRODUCTION

From the comfort given to the pastor of the Pascack Reformed Church after his wife and seven children were murdered, to a doctor hurrying along in a horse and buggy to bring his self-made pills to a heal a sick patient in the night, to volunteer firefighters rushing along the roughest road in Bergen County to douse a fire with buckets of water, to a miller figuring out how to make wampum, Park Ridge has a history of altruism, perseverance, and brains.

I had always heard about the wampum machine and William Campbell, who had made the device that could drill holes in conch shells, producing hundreds of wampum in a day. I always assumed it was a myth or that it was exaggerated. But on the very first day of a world financial history course taught by John Lanza, vice president of a major bank in downtown Manhattan, I heard the name Park Ridge mentioned. I was shocked. Lanza explained that Campbell moved early American history past the stage of barter and into the world of finance when he created currency with the American Indians. The impact that the wampum machine had reached far outside the community's borders. Many pioneers had come up with the idea of making wampum, but Campbell was the one to move it to the point of producing a mint.

The strong faith of the early settlers affected daily life. At Leach's Chapel on Ridge Avenue, a friend of the Leaches spoke of abolition. He spoke not only to those in the North but also to people in the South, commanding slave owners to adhere to the Emancipation Proclamation and release their slaves.

A look at the cemetery indicates the good health of the residents, as the tombstones indicate many people died in their 80s and even 90s. Dr. Neer's meticulous journal, which includes medicine he made himself, is still available today.

Park Ridge has always been a progressive town with a small-town look. In his later years, the Bear's Nest in Park Ridge was home to former Pres. Richard M. Nixon, who, on April 22 after suffering a stroke, was taken to the hospital by volunteers of the Park Ridge Ambulance Corps. He later died. Park Ridge was home to James Gandolfini, who plays Tony Soprano in the television show *The Sopranos*, and it is also the hometown of the Roches, a singing trio.

Long ago, Park Ridge vacationers purchased postcards and wrote messages to friends and family about the beauty of Park Ridge and Atkin's Glen. More than 150 years later, the words written on the back of one of those postcards holds true: "In Park Ridge I have found a place of beauty, that is at the same time surprisingly progressive. Here one can warm oneself by fire in winter and cool oneself in summer. A fine place—Wish you were here."

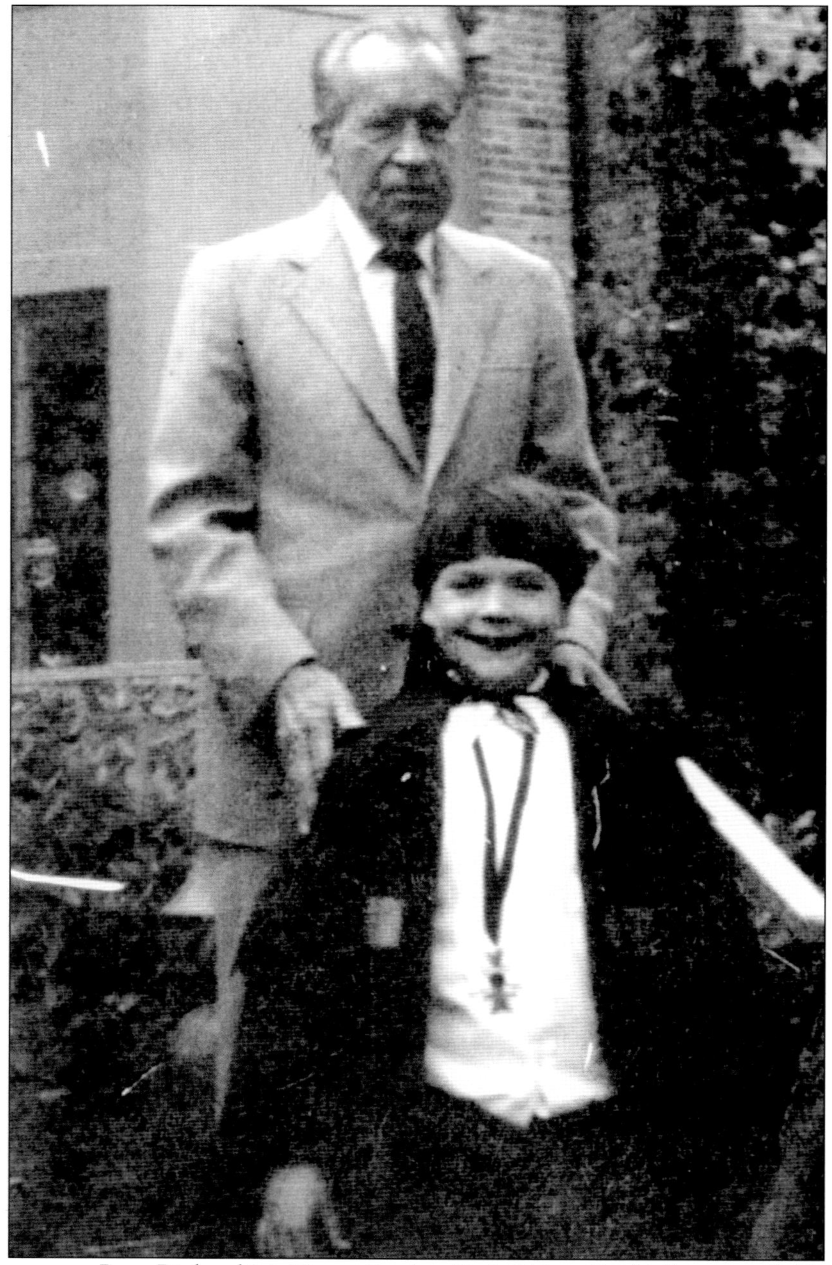

In his later years, Pres. Richard M. Nixon lived in Park Ridge. On Halloween, children would trick or treat in front of his home. Here he is shown on one Halloween with young Park Ridge resident James Bertini.

# *One*

# Pioneers and Wampum

The earliest recorded history of Park Ridge mentions American Indians and pioneers who traded for bear and deer meat in winter and summer.

Given the bountiful land and the hunting skills of the American Indians, early pioneers were anxious to trade. This keen interest inevitably sparked the pioneers' idea of finding a way to make wampum. Wampum, made from polished shells, was highly esteemed by the American Indians, and the first American Indian trading post, called the Block House, was built in the 1600s in Park Ridge.

As the years went by, one local settler excelled at making wampum, and thus he and Park Ridge eventually became part of financial history. In an upstairs room of a mill along the Pascack Brook, John Campbell produced hundreds of wampum per day, making himself rich and moving early American pioneer days from barter to currency, as wampum was accepted at trading posts as a form of payment.

The trading post on Pascack Road brought commerce to Bergen County. The same natural beauty that brought American Indians and pioneers to the area also soon attracted vacationers, especially after the railroad was established. The growth of Park Ridge was inevitable.

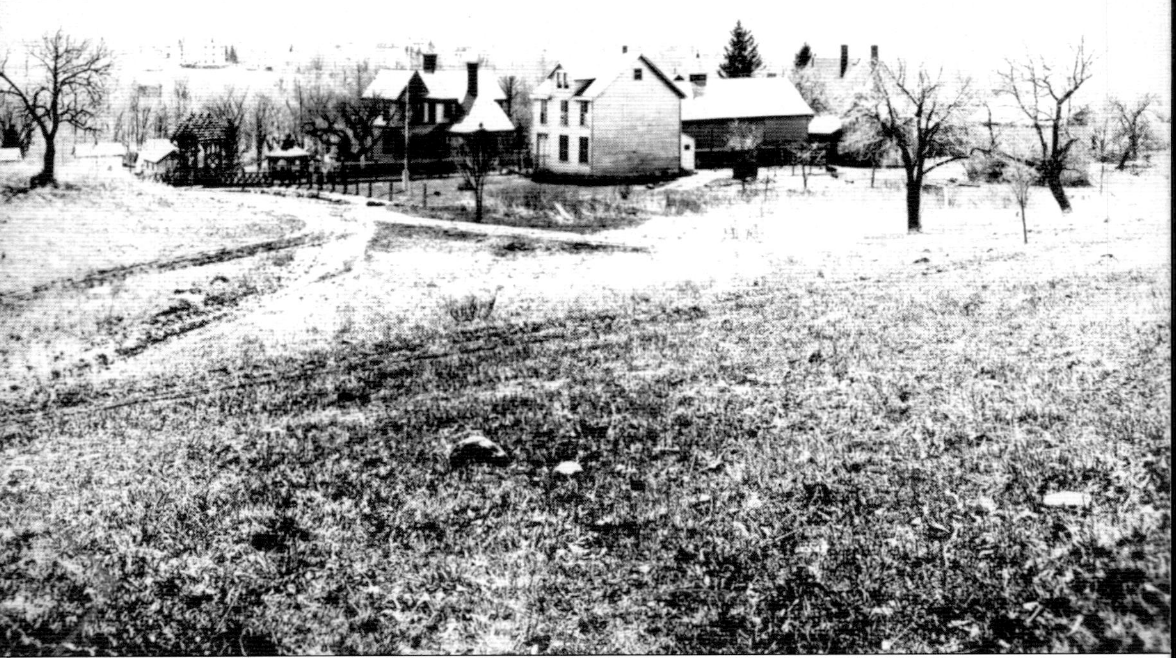

Park Ridge was still known as Pascack and arguably considered by some as a part of New York State when this photograph was taken in 1836. With only a few houses, the area consisted mostly of woods. American Indians had left the area in the mid-1700s, and it is said that a cave in Atkin's Glen, which was used by Native Americans as a hiding place when they were passing through the area, later became a hiding place for outlaws.

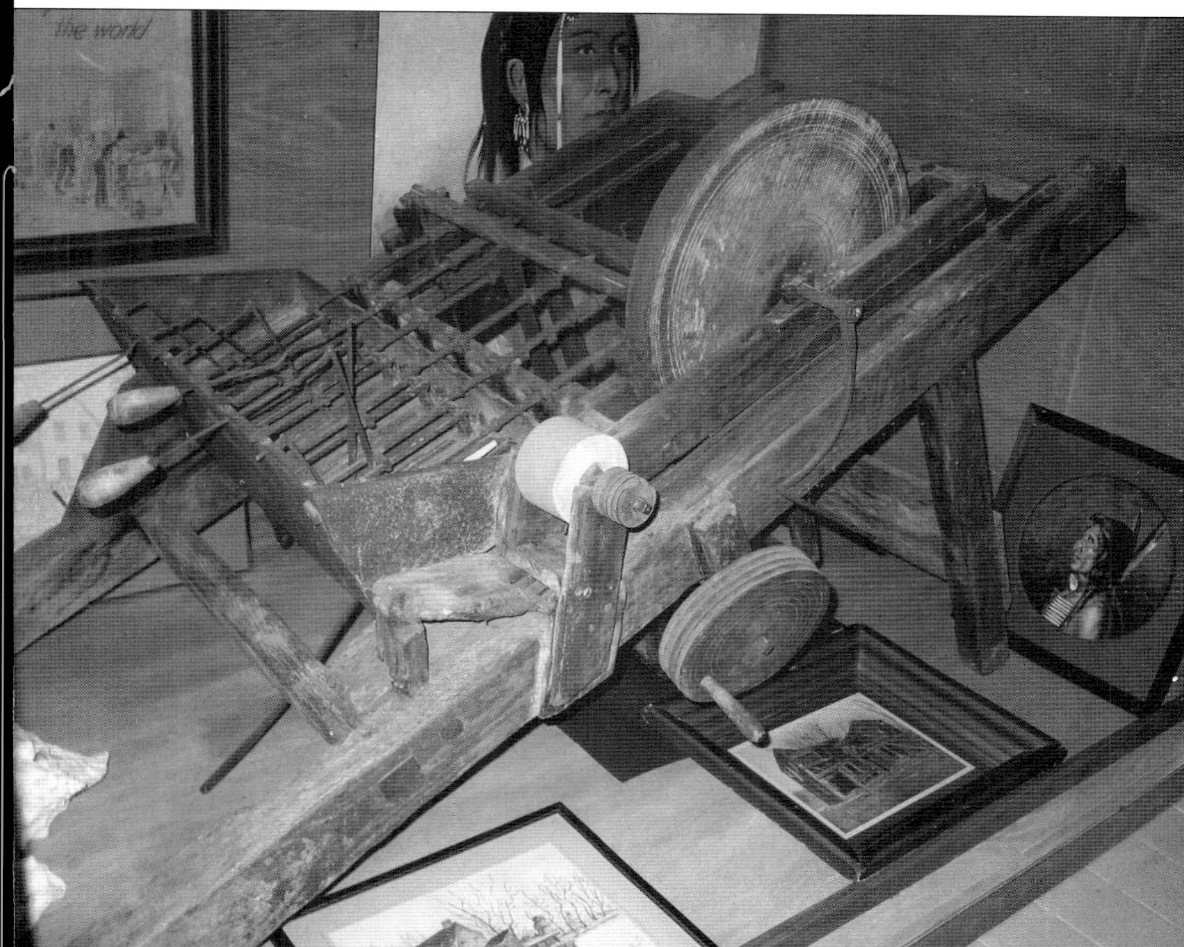


The wampum machine is a wooden structure with six prongs used to drill holes through six seashells at one time. The machine was the brainstorm of John Campbell, whose father, William, came to Bergen County in 1735 and soon thereafter began making wampum. John moved the business to Park Ridge, then known as Pascack, in 1789, using water from the Pascack Brook to turn the wheel that smoothed the wampum beads.

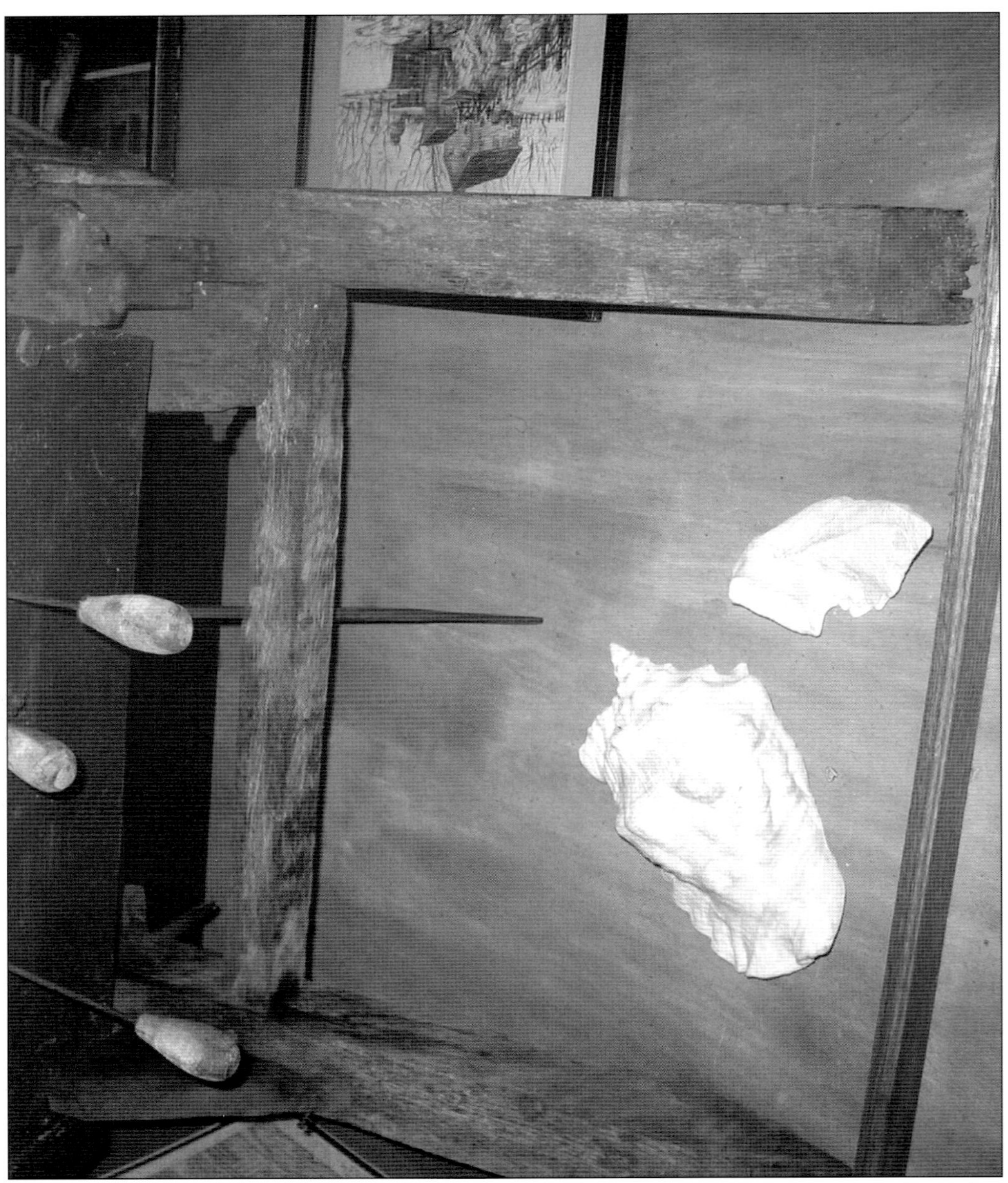

Since the Dutch and English were prohibited from making coinage in America, early settlers had a need for currency, which wampum filled. Settlers not only used the wampum for trade with American Indians, they used it to trade with one another. The U.S. government, in fact, purchased wampum for negotiations with American Indians, and it played a significant role until the 1880s. John Jacob Astor was one of the settlers who made the most of wampum and investments. Arriving in America penniless, he became the richest American of his time.

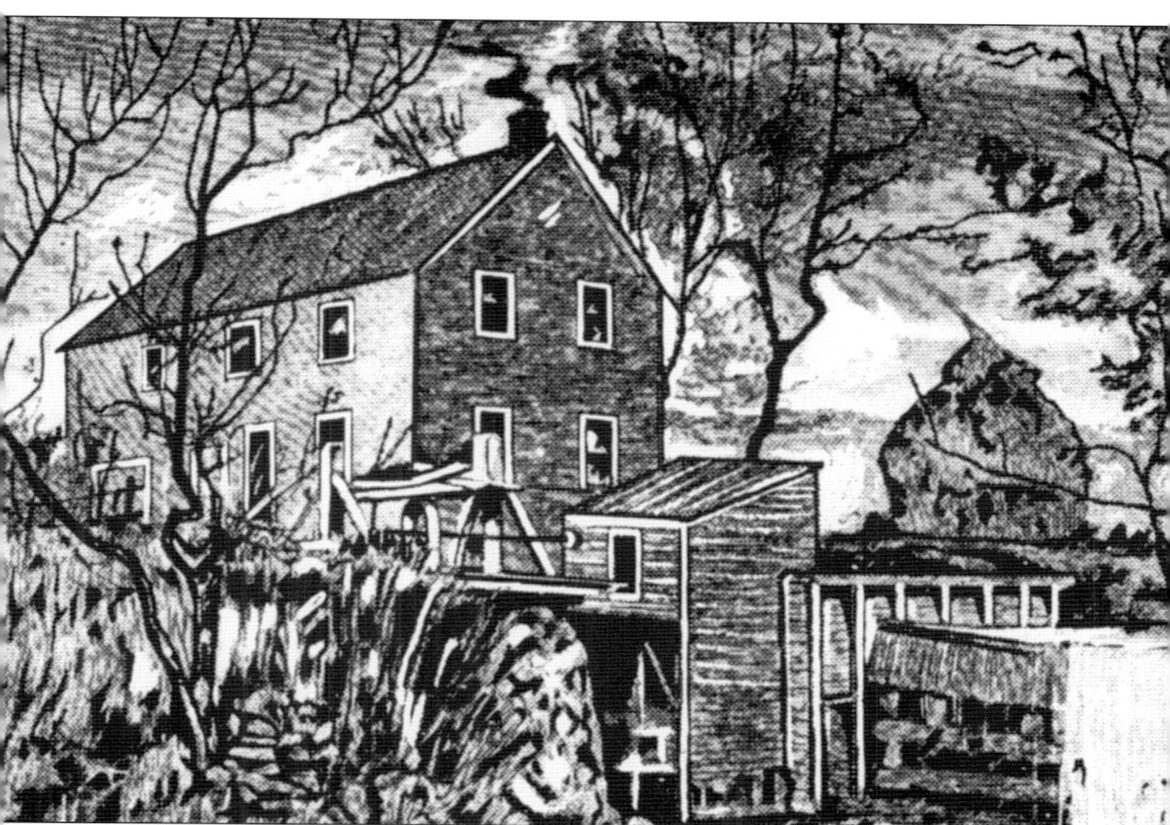

John Campbell was aware that his idea of making six wampum at a time enabled him to produce wampum much faster than other settlers who painstakingly made wampum by hand. He, in fact, is said to have tried his best to keep the machine secret and did not keep ready access to the mill's second level, where the machine was kept. Records show Astor purchased wampum from Campbell and traded at the trading post on Mill Lane and Pascack Road. Wampum made by Campbell is exhibited in the Smithsonian Institution in Washington, D.C.

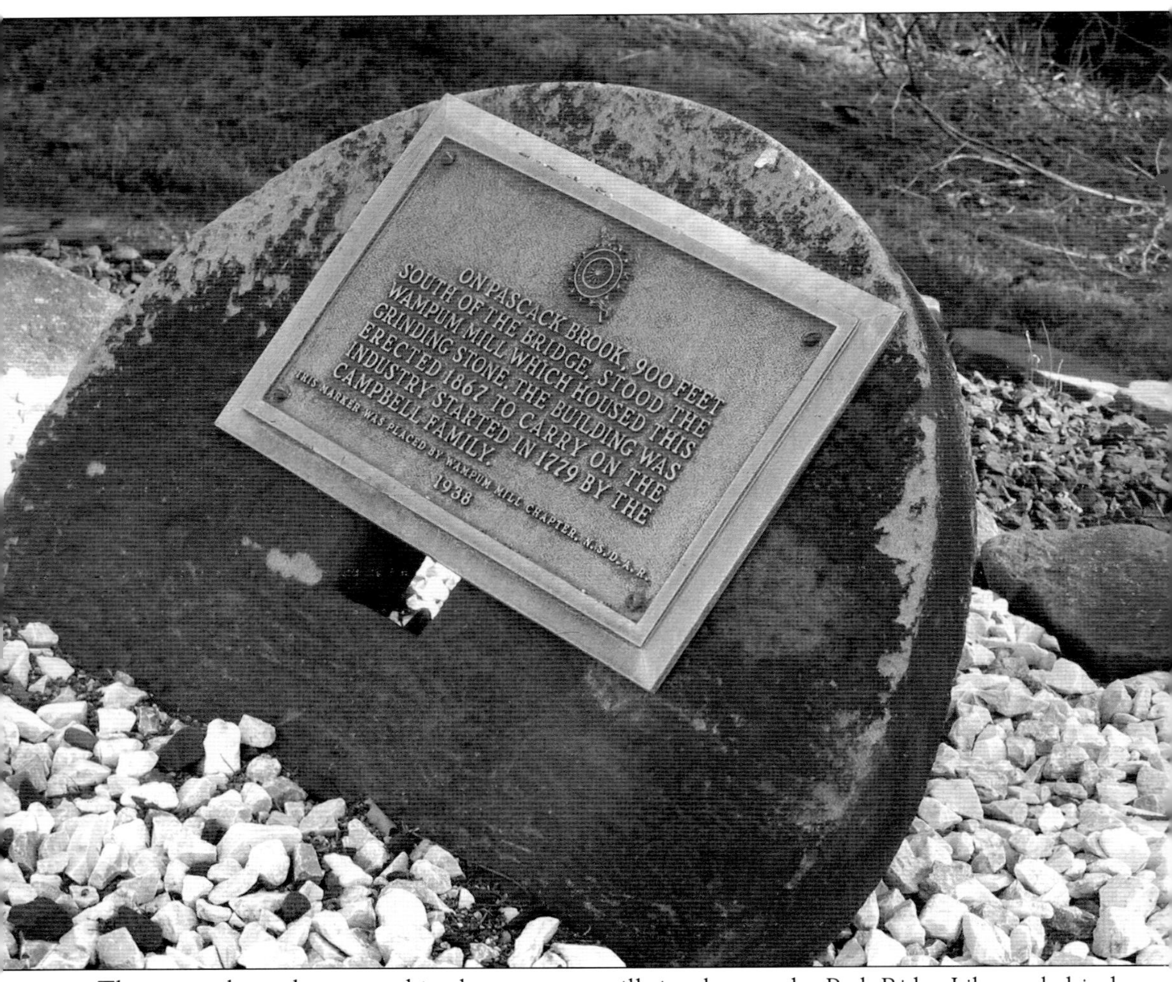


The original grindstone used in the wampum mill sits close to the Park Ridge Library, behind borough hall. The plaque, dedicated in 1938, states that the mill, which housed the grindstone, stood 900 feet south of the bridge over the Pascack Brook. The building was erected in 1867 to carry on the industry started in 1779 by the Campbell family.

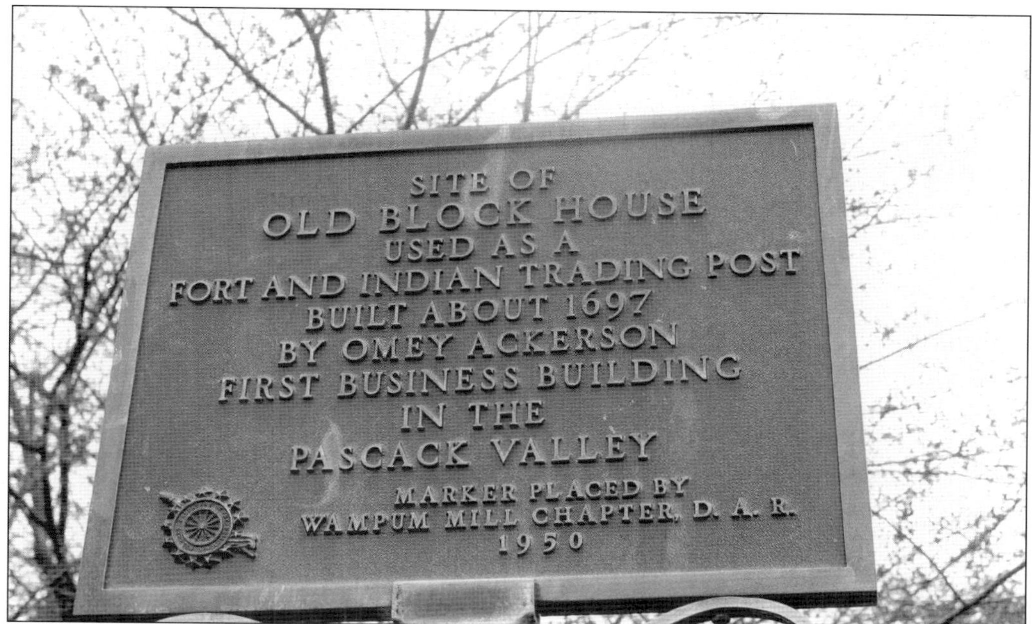


The Old Block House, built by Omey Ackerson around 1697, once stood on this Pascack Road site. It was used as a fort and a trading post, and was the first business building in the Pascack Valley. Today a ranch-style home is located here, and under its front lawn are the remains of the Block House's foundation. While gardening, the owner of the present-day house often unearths intriguing old bottles and other items from the trading post.

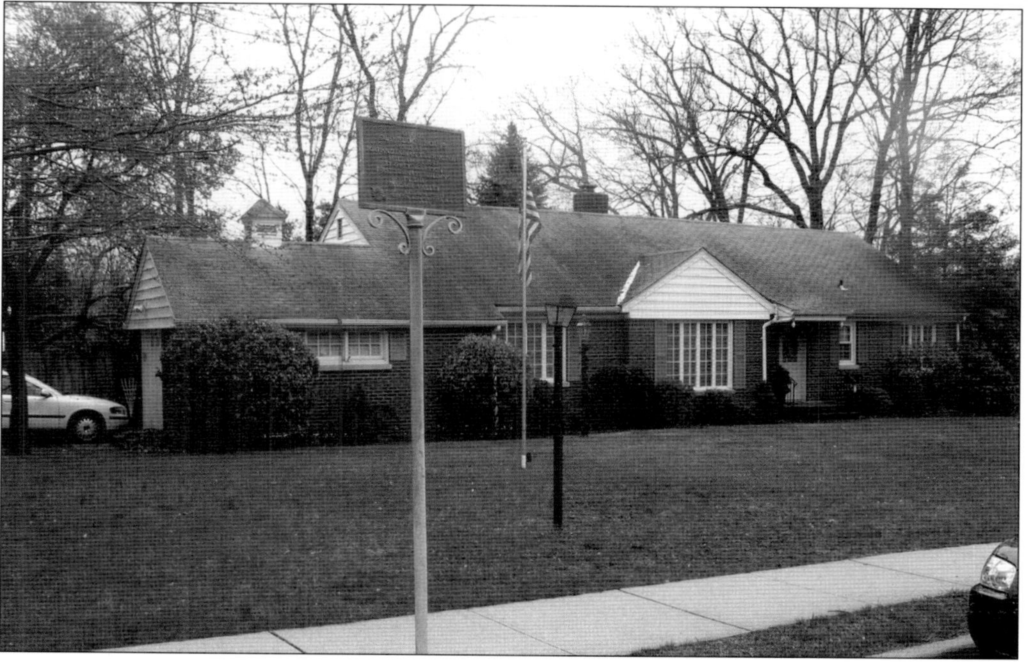

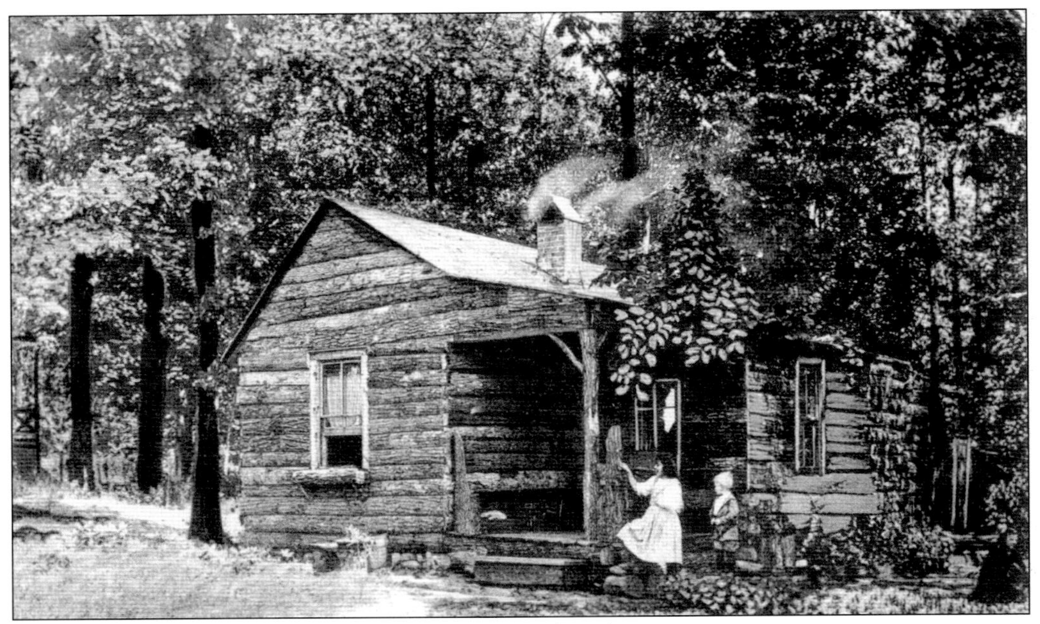

Pictured is a log cabin, located in the woods of Park Ridge.

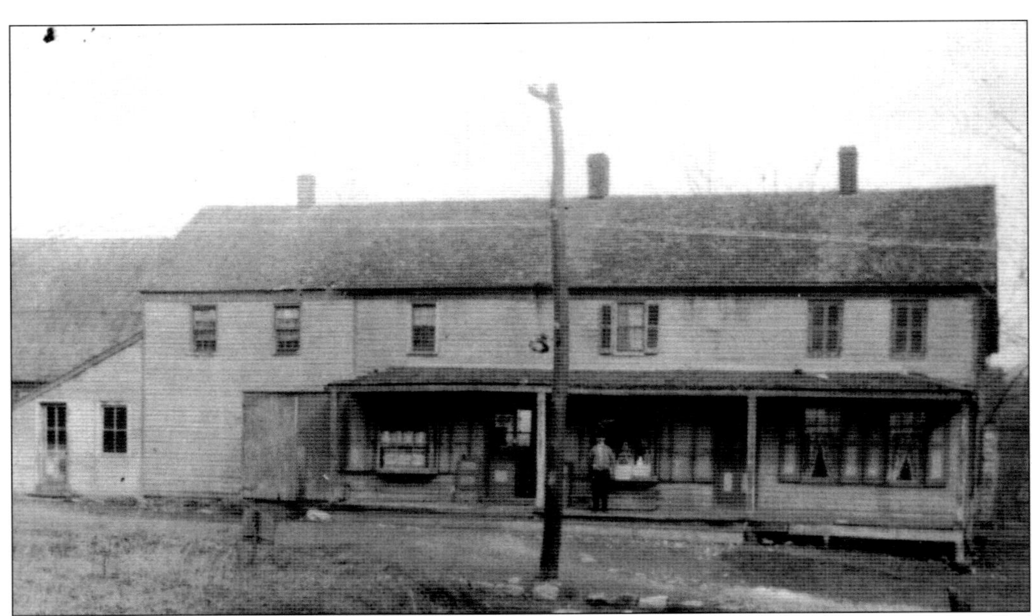

The Pascack trading post, on Mill Lane and Pascack Road, was first owned by the Ackerson family. It was the first commercial structure known in the area since the Block House of the 1600s. The trading post was eventually sold to another owner who was murdered by a man named Cisco during what was called a political argument. The alleged murderer was tried and sentenced to death. It was the last execution in Bergen County.

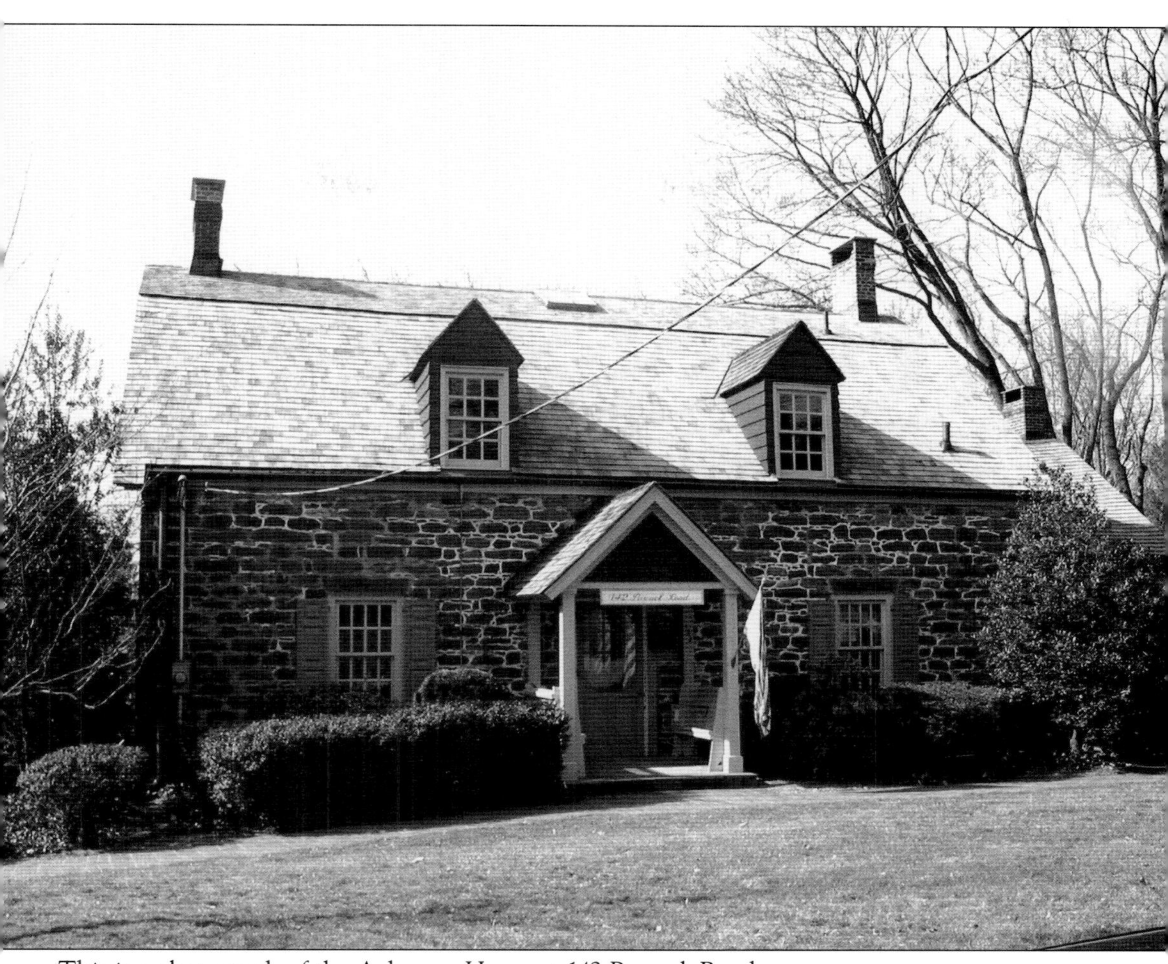

This is a photograph of the Ackerson House at 142 Pascack Road.

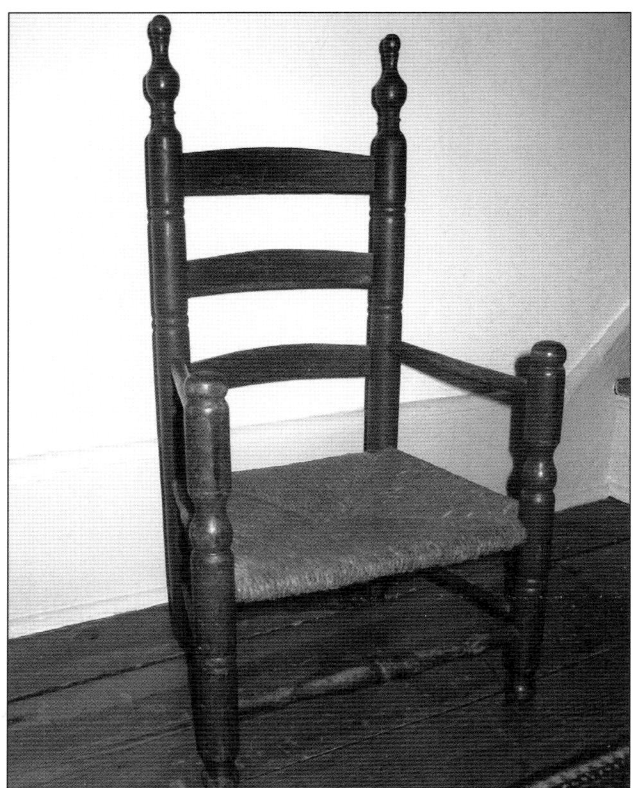

The current owners of the Ackerson house are antique collectors, specializing in locally made items. Pictured is a child's chair. The unique style of the finials indicates that this is a Bergen County chair.

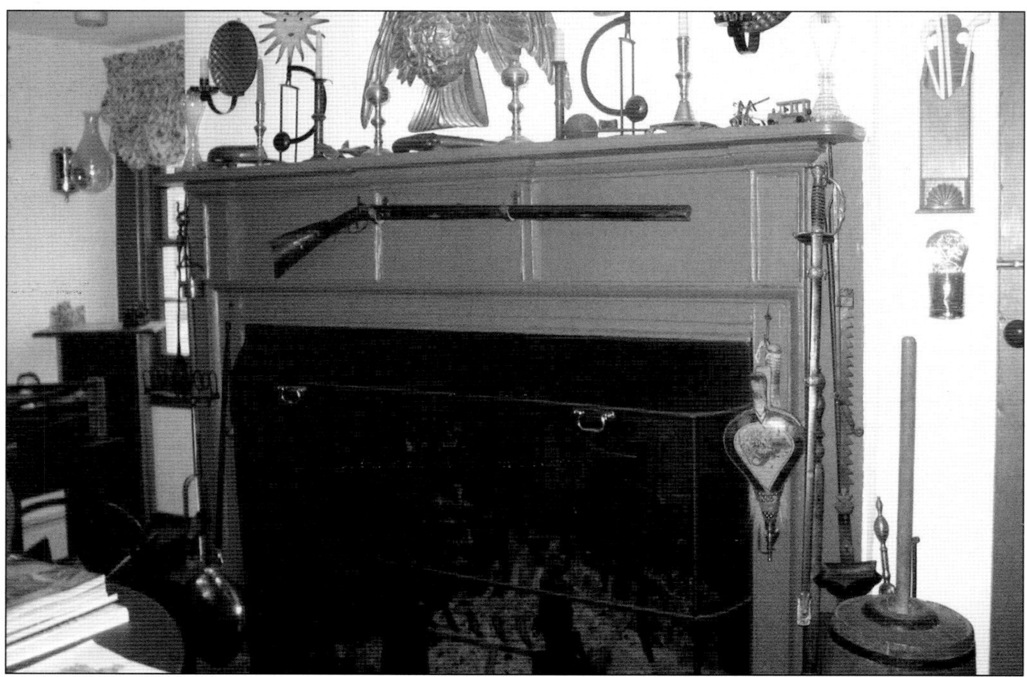

This fireplace is in the Ackerson House. The Bergen County bed warmer (hanging on the left side) was filled with embers and placed in the bed to momentarily warm it before turning in on a chilly night.

# *Two*

# PUBLIC SERVICE

The first fire company was organized in 1898. It ordered a fire engine from Muskegon, Michigan. The engine was first housed in an old lumber shed, at Park and Magnolia Avenues, until the firehouse on Hawthorne Avenue was ready. The building was accidentally set on fire during a late night of cigars and drinking. The next, more fireproof house was built on Willet Street and Park Avenue, using concrete slabs from the Mittag Company in Park Ridge. It was the beginning of a long tradition of volunteerism by the fire department.

The police department began unofficially with a man who rode through town giving out tickets. Thereafter, Anthony Salimone was appointed chief of police, beginning a long line of chiefs, with Richard Oppenheimer serving as the current chief.

The borough of Park Ridge was incorporated in 1894, with very well-attended meetings in the early days. The mayors of Park Ridge are remembered with street names such as Sibbald Drive, Siebert Court, and Shaw Place.

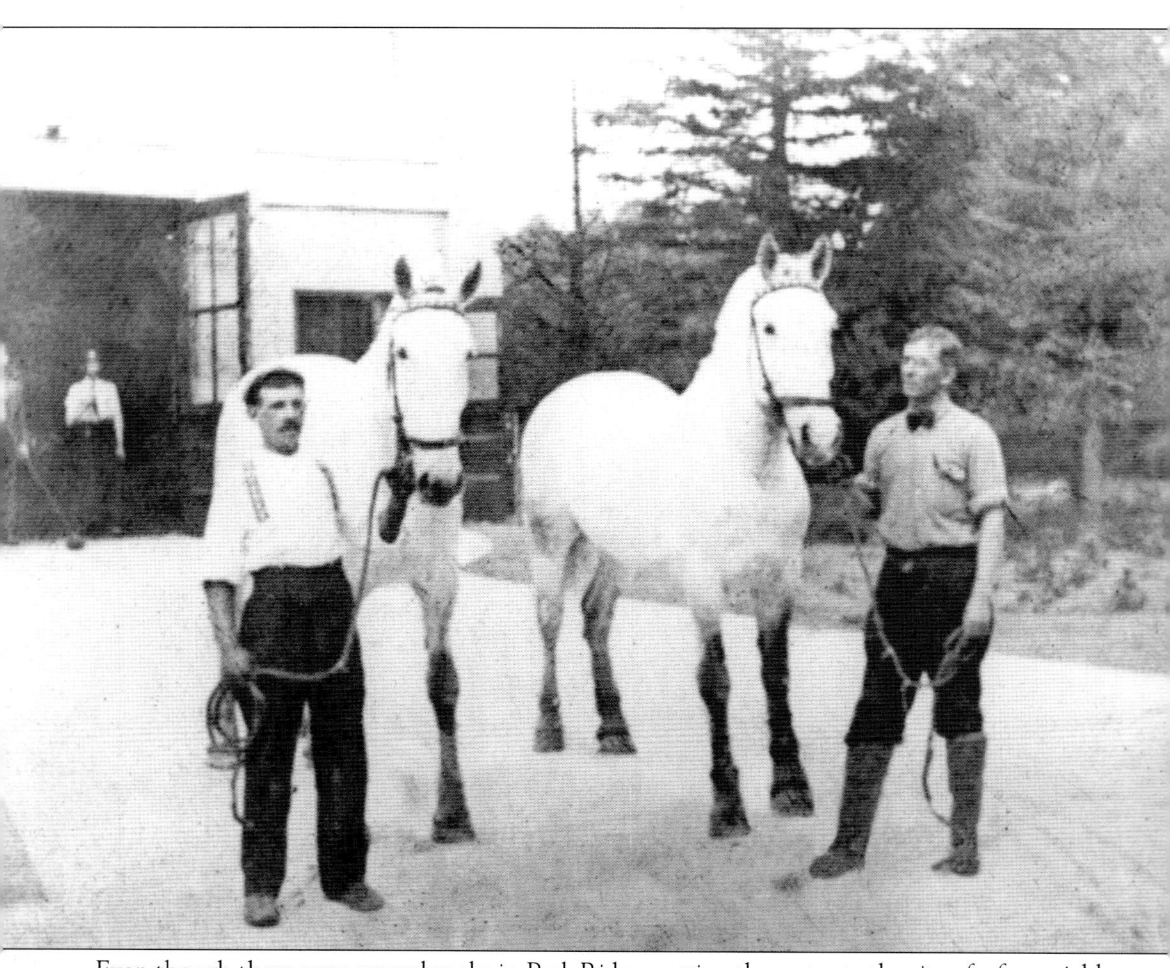

Even though there were many brooks in Park Ridge, getting the water to the site of a fire quickly presented a challenge. After several fires ravaged buildings, volunteers got together to form a fire department. Horses were rented from a nearby stable. Firefighters pose with horses that pulled their engine to fires.

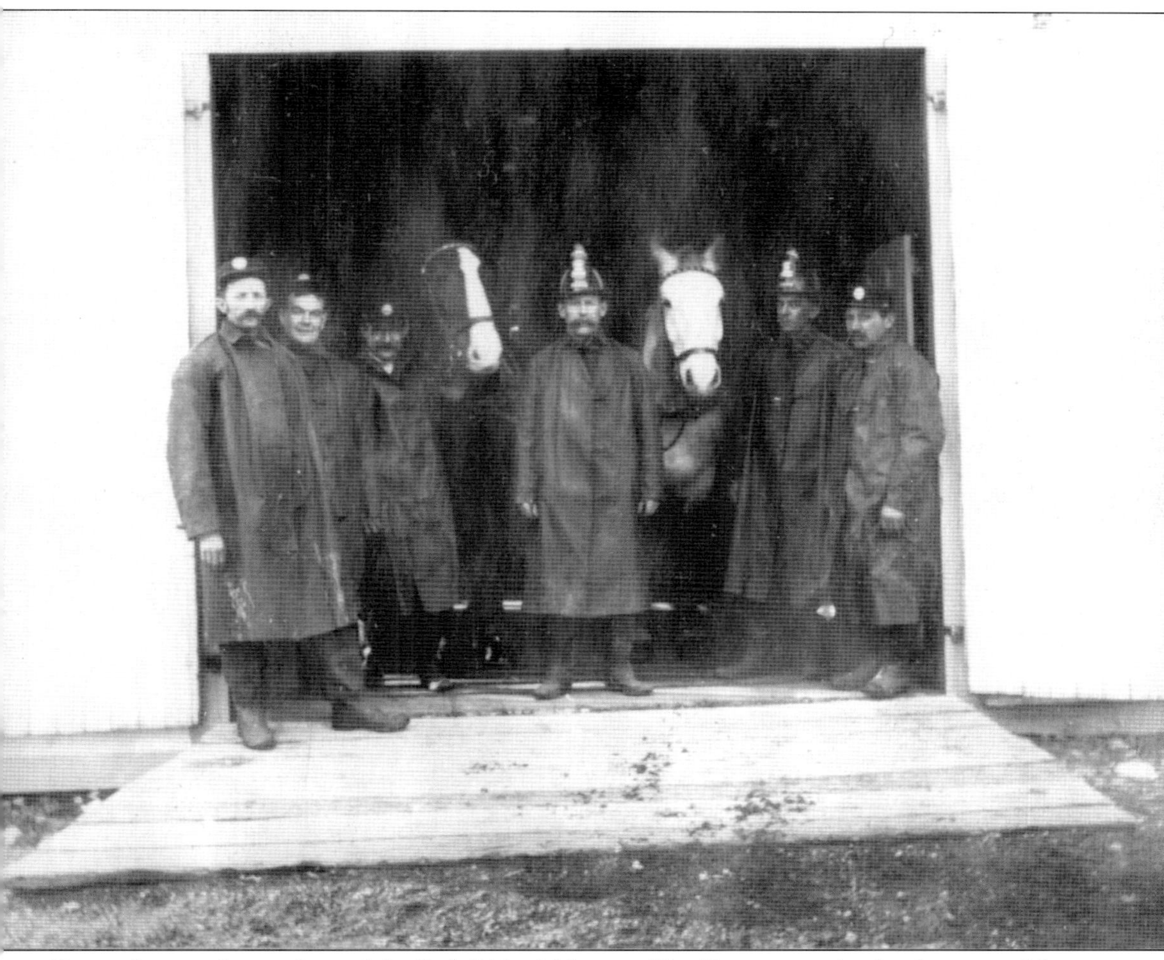

Pictured are early members of the Park Ridge Volunteer Fire Department in the doorway of the firehouse on Hawthorne Avenue. The white horse was called Old Betsy, and in later years, when the department purchased its fire truck, it was named "Old Betsy."

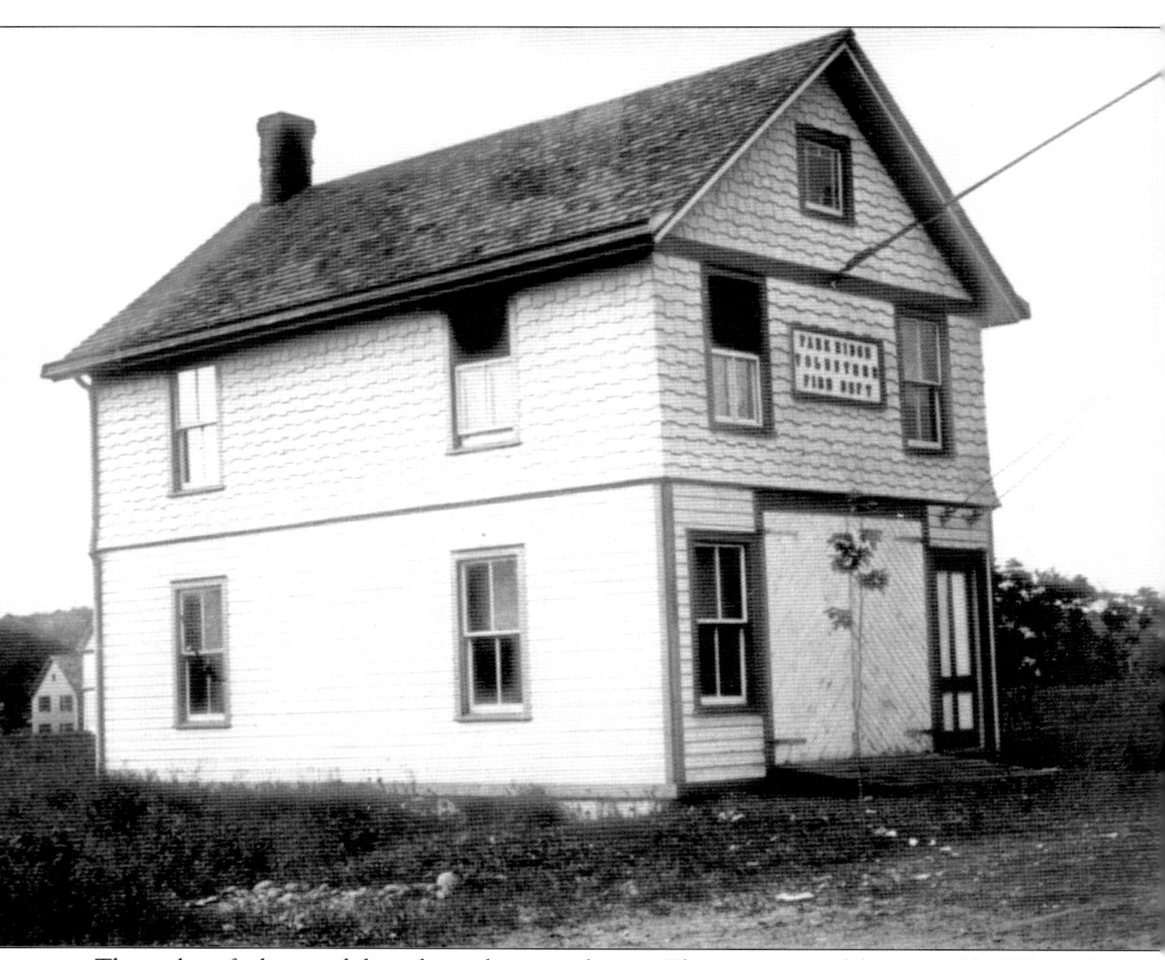

The earliest firehouses did not have their own horses. They were rented from a stable. When the fire alarm sounded, the livery person would take the horses to the firehouse, where they would be met by firefighters who would then hitch the horses to a wagon, carrying a huge vat of water and many buckets, and make their way to the fire.

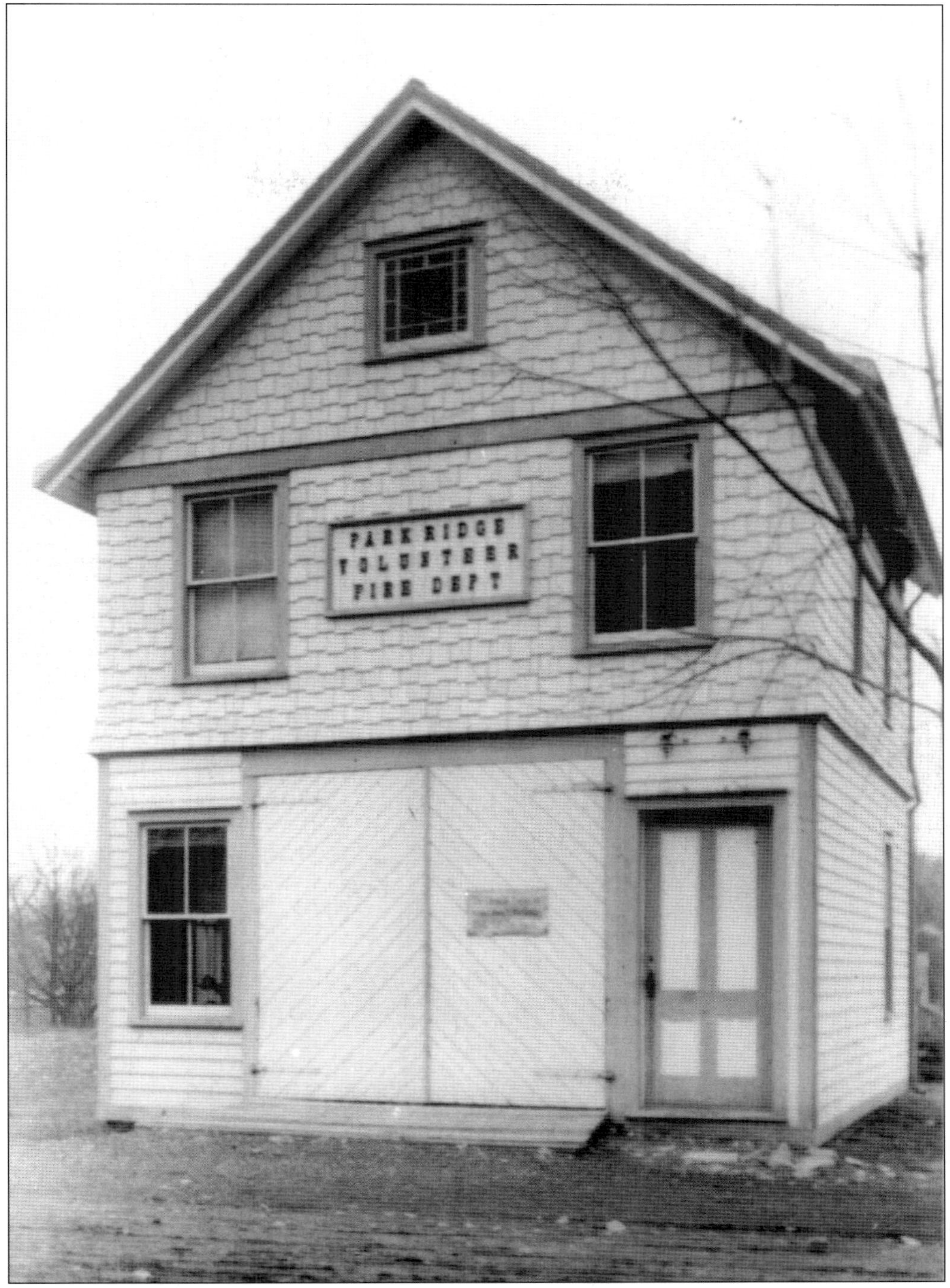


When the fire department bought an engine—basically a wagon with the ability to carry a lot of buckets and a copper vat of water—it needed a place to store it. For a time it was housed in an old garage. Later it was moved to the borough's first firehouse, the Park Ridge Volunteer Fire Department on Hawthorne Avenue.

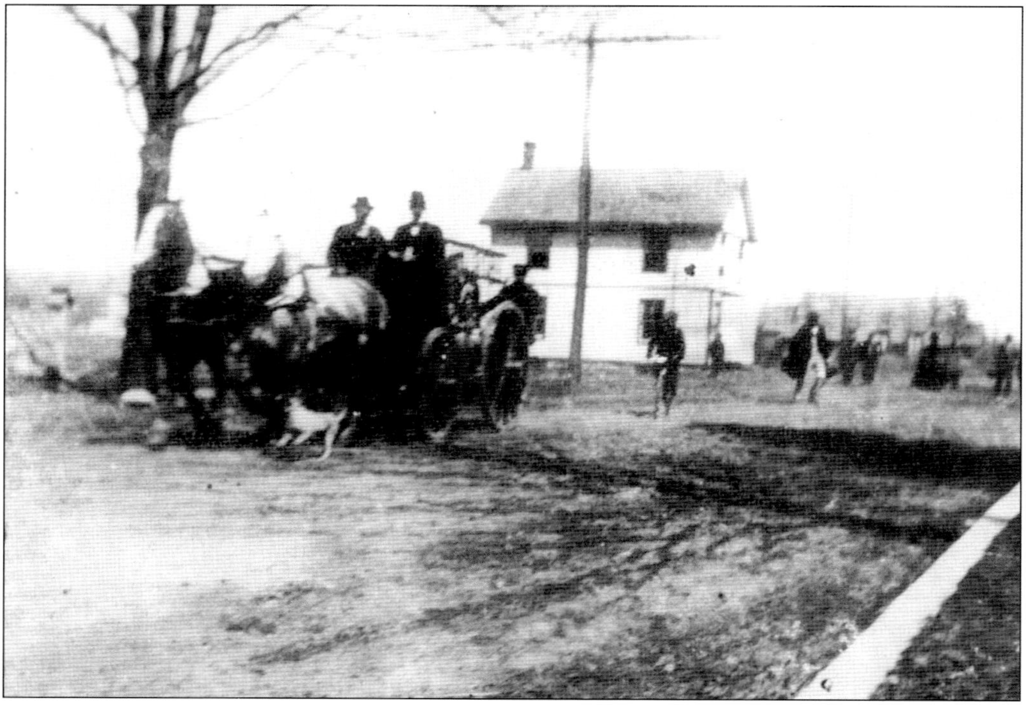

Volunteer firefighters rush from the Hawthorne Avenue firehouse to the scene of a fire in the late 1800s. Residents rush behind the truck, and a dog jumps out in front of the fire engine. The firehouse still stands today as an apartment house.

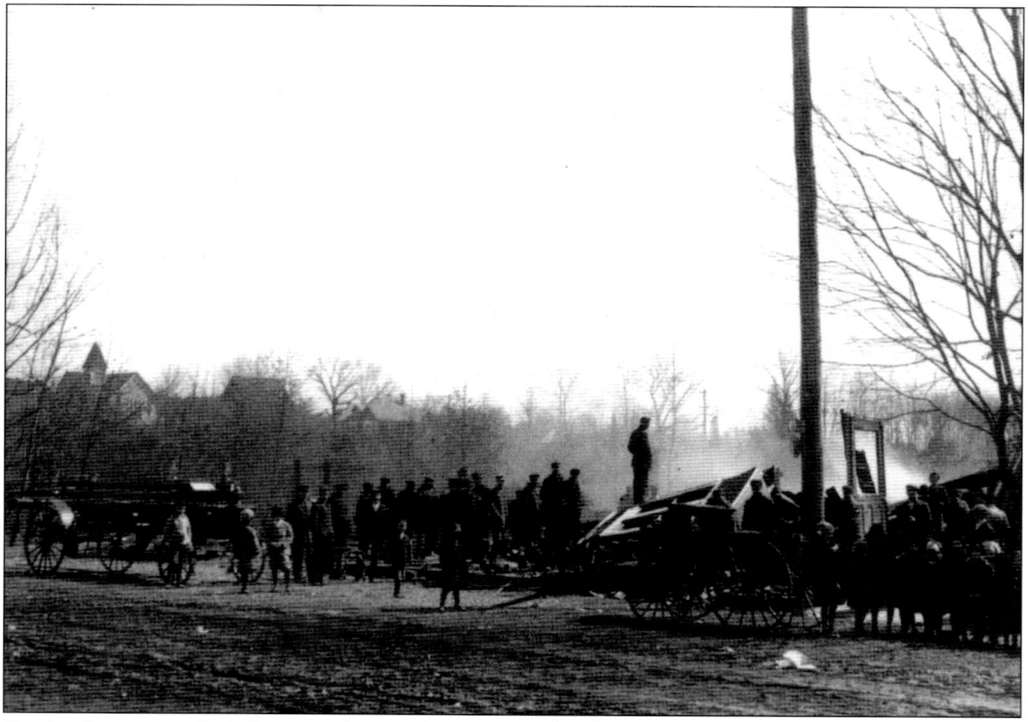

At the fire scene, firefighters and onlookers survey the damage.

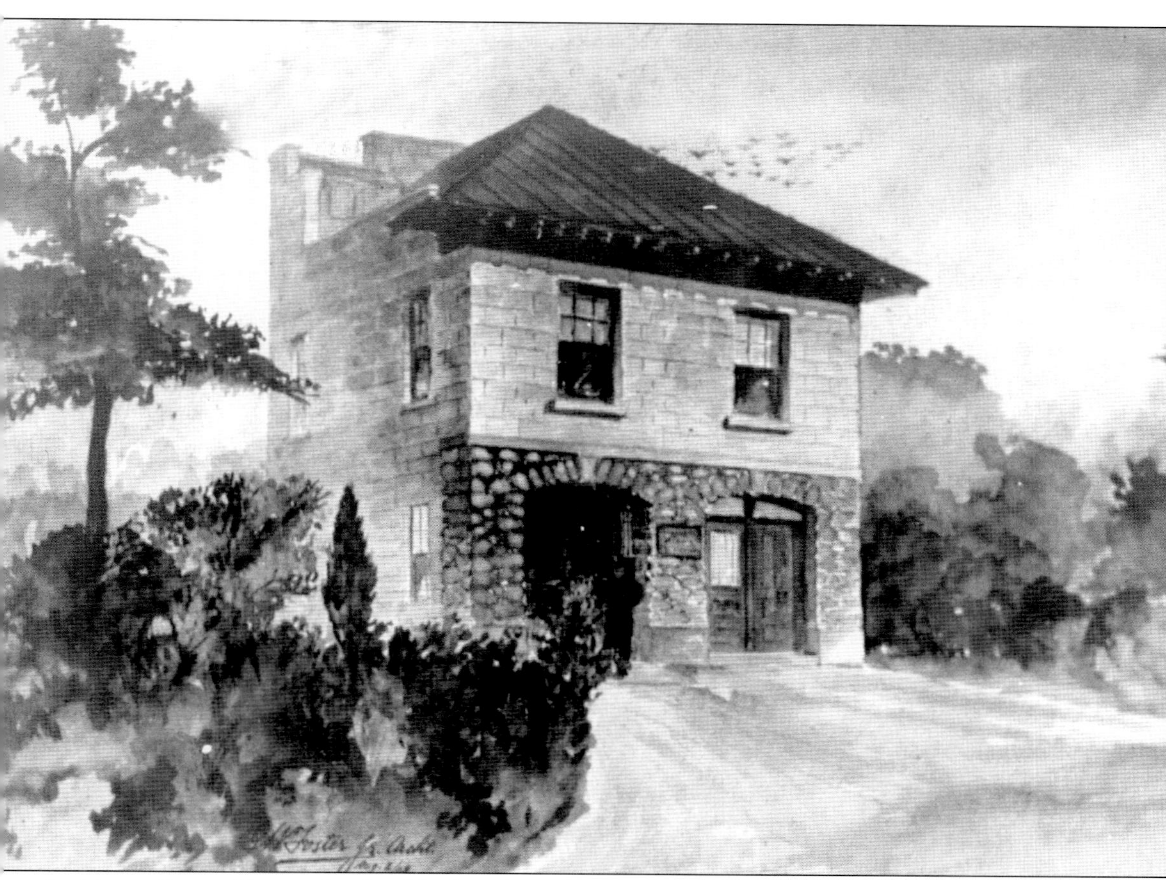

Architect George Foster, the first black architect licensed in the state of New Jersey, designed and sketched this firehouse for the Colony Hose Company, which formed in 1907 on the west side of town. The first meeting was held at A. C. Patton's Colony Avenue house, and the first engine, designed to be pulled by firefighters rather than horses, was purchased secondhand from the Nanuet Fire Company. It was originally housed in James A. Heale's garage, on Colony and Lafayette Avenues, across from James Mittag's house. All three were fire company members, along with George Foster, Abram Odell, Charles Greisch, Martin Verbeyst, and John Brownsell. The firehouse still stands on Colony Avenue between Fifth Street and Brook Road. Foster's house still stands on Brook Road. Foster's daughter, Mercedes Foster Scharrenberg, reports that her father's ancestry includes a Blackfoot Indian and that Jefferson Davis was a relative of her paternal grandmother.

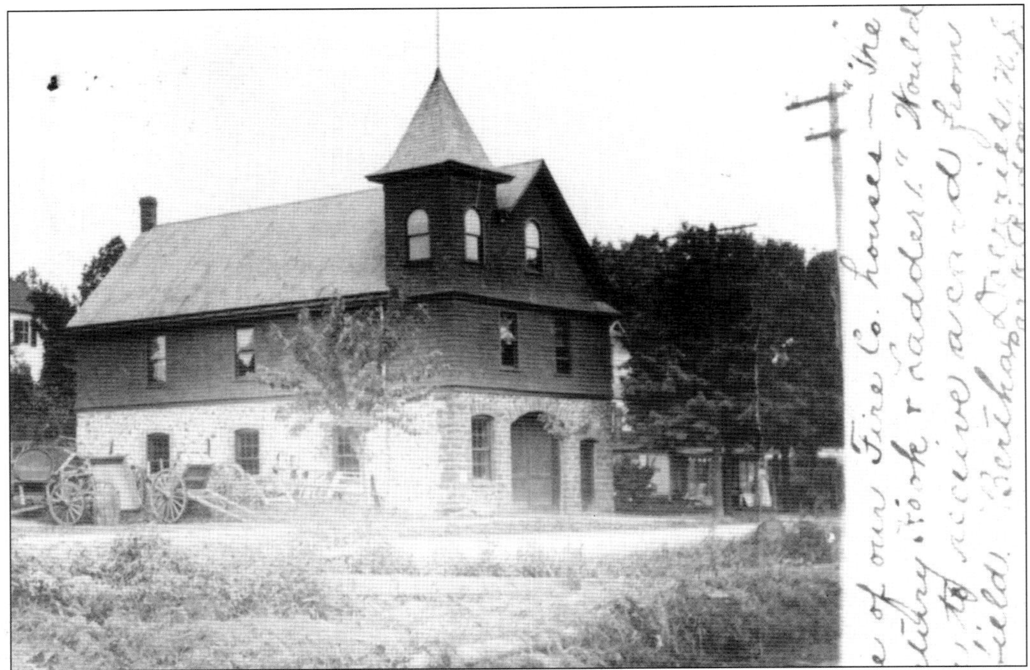

The Century Hook and Ladder Company was formed by 15 volunteer firefighters in 1900. The volunteers built a firehouse on Broadway near Perry Street. The building still stands, but the turret roof has been replaced. It was originally planned as an observation point before telephones and radios existed. The need for several firehouses in Park Ridge stemmed from the need for quick access to water. Wagons carried buckets, which were dipped into large containers of water and passed along a line of men, who then tossed the bucketful of water onto the fire.

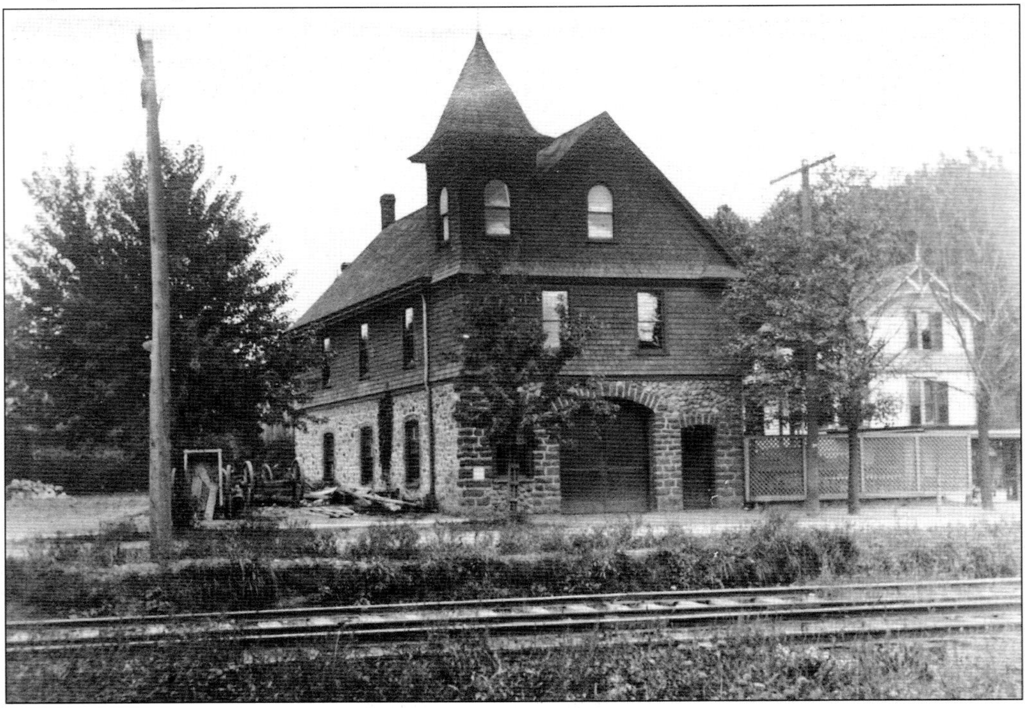

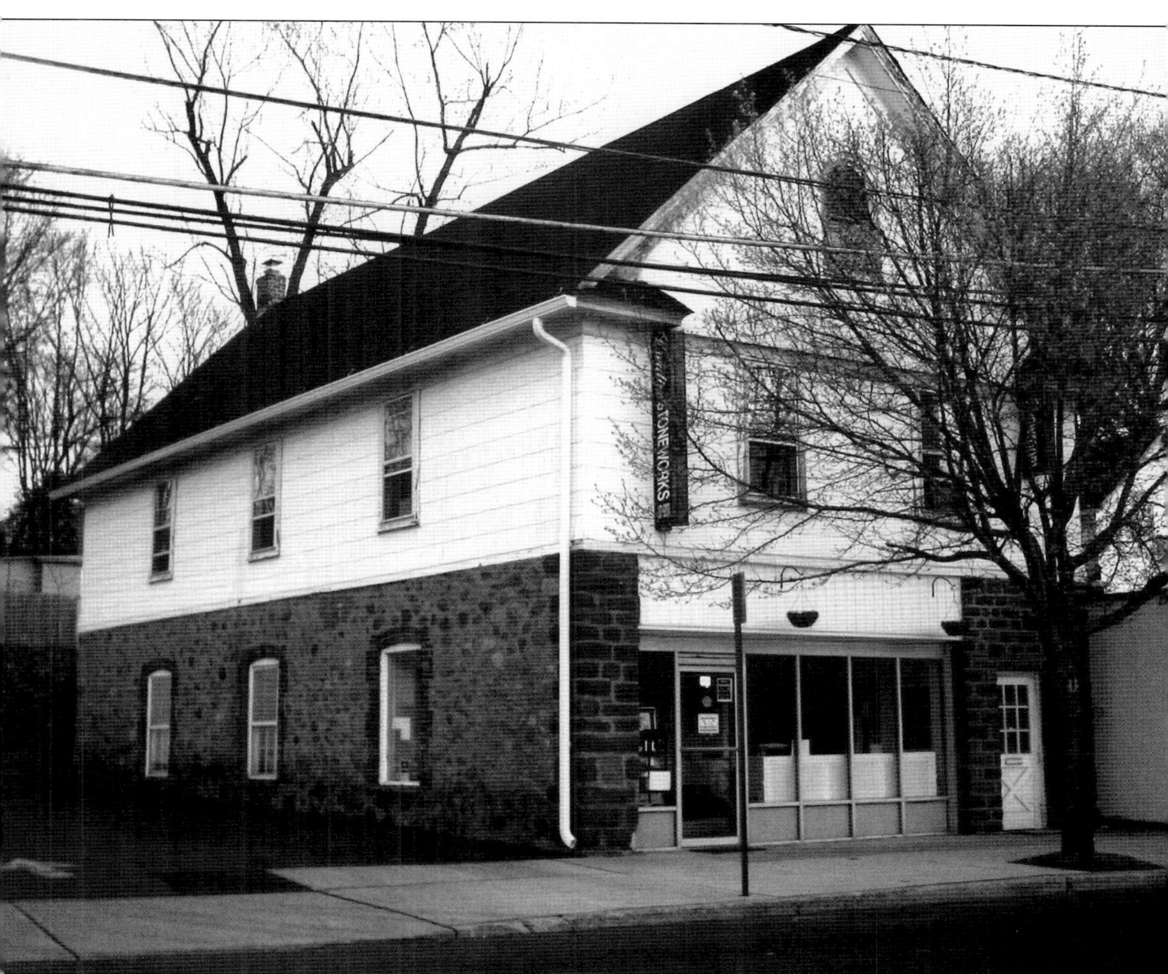


The hook and ladder company building eventually housed the Tri-Boro Ambulance Corps before it moved into its current home at Mill Pond. The original building now houses Stoneworks, a ceramic stoneware showroom.

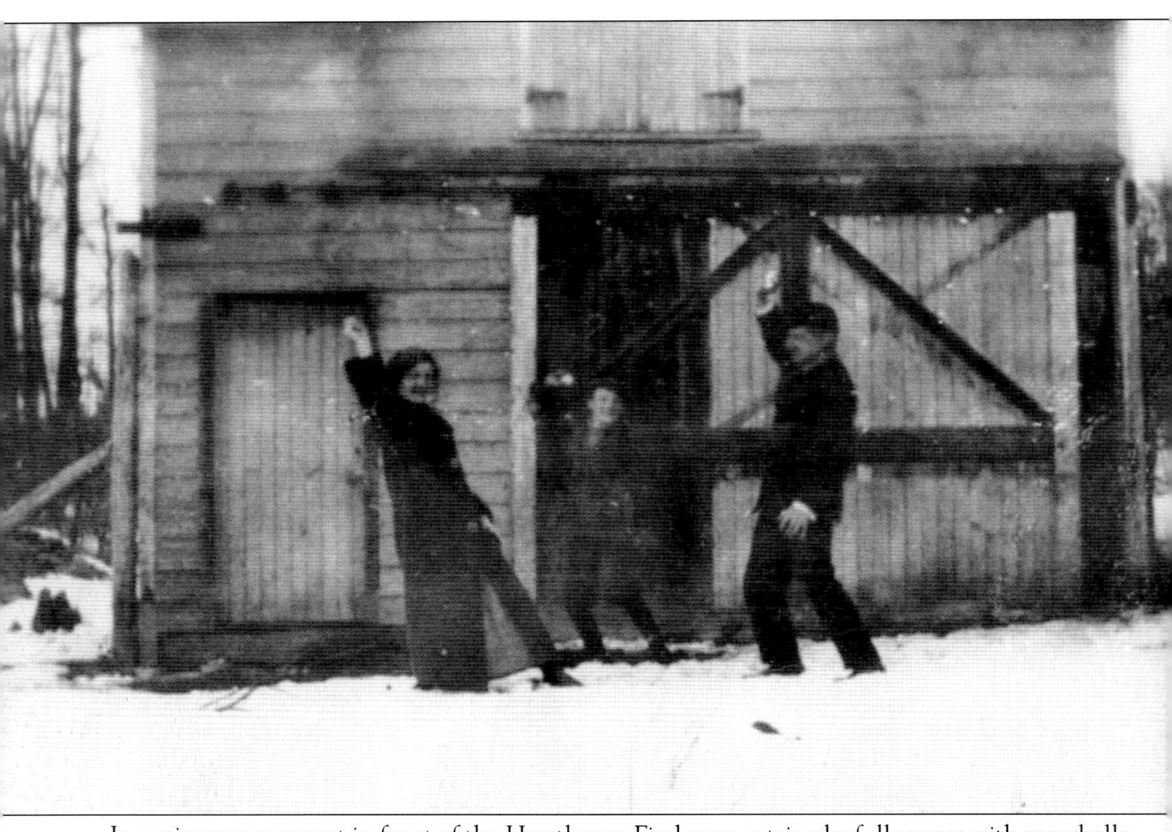

In a winsome moment in front of the Hawthorne Firehouse, a trio playfully poses with snowballs poised in midair. The photograph was taken in the 1800s.

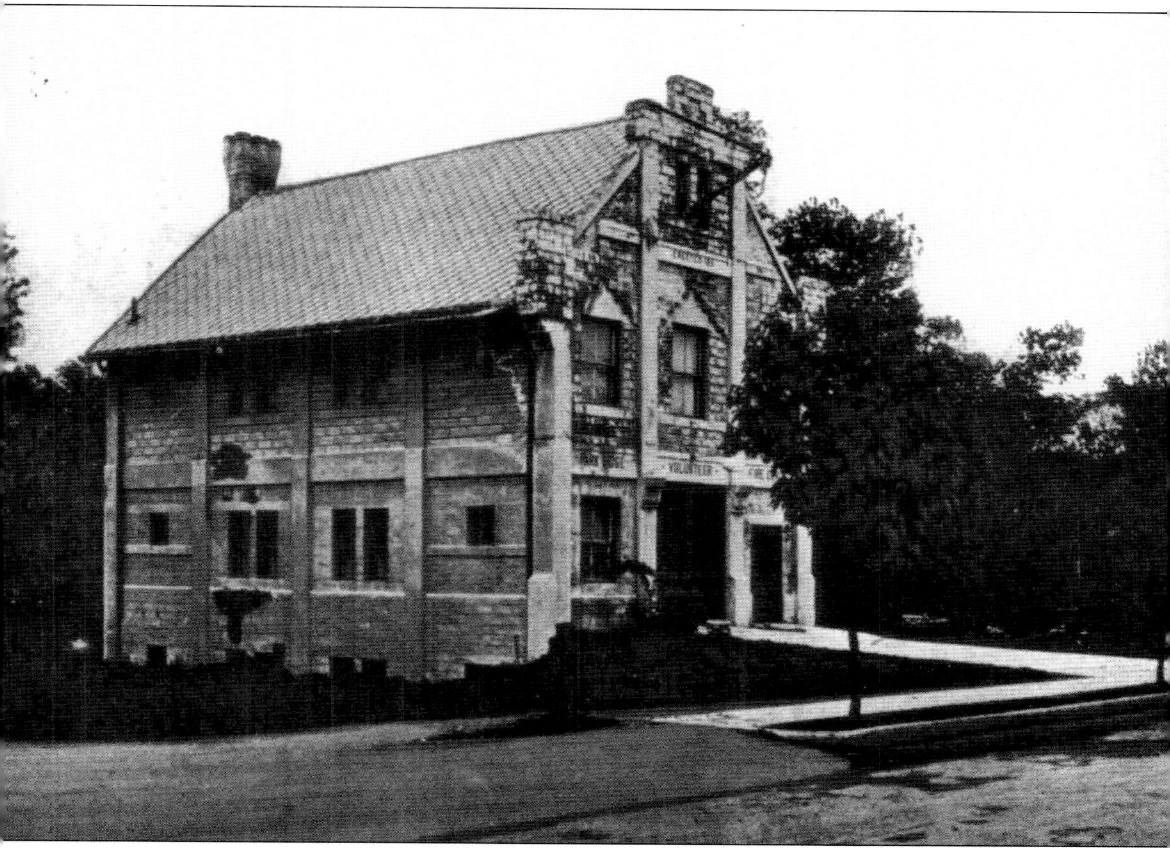

Pictured is the firehouse, built in 1912, before it was converted to the Park Ridge Garage in 1950. This firehouse on Park Avenue was a far cry from the first firehouse on Hawthorne Avenue. Sturdy and much larger, the building still stands today.

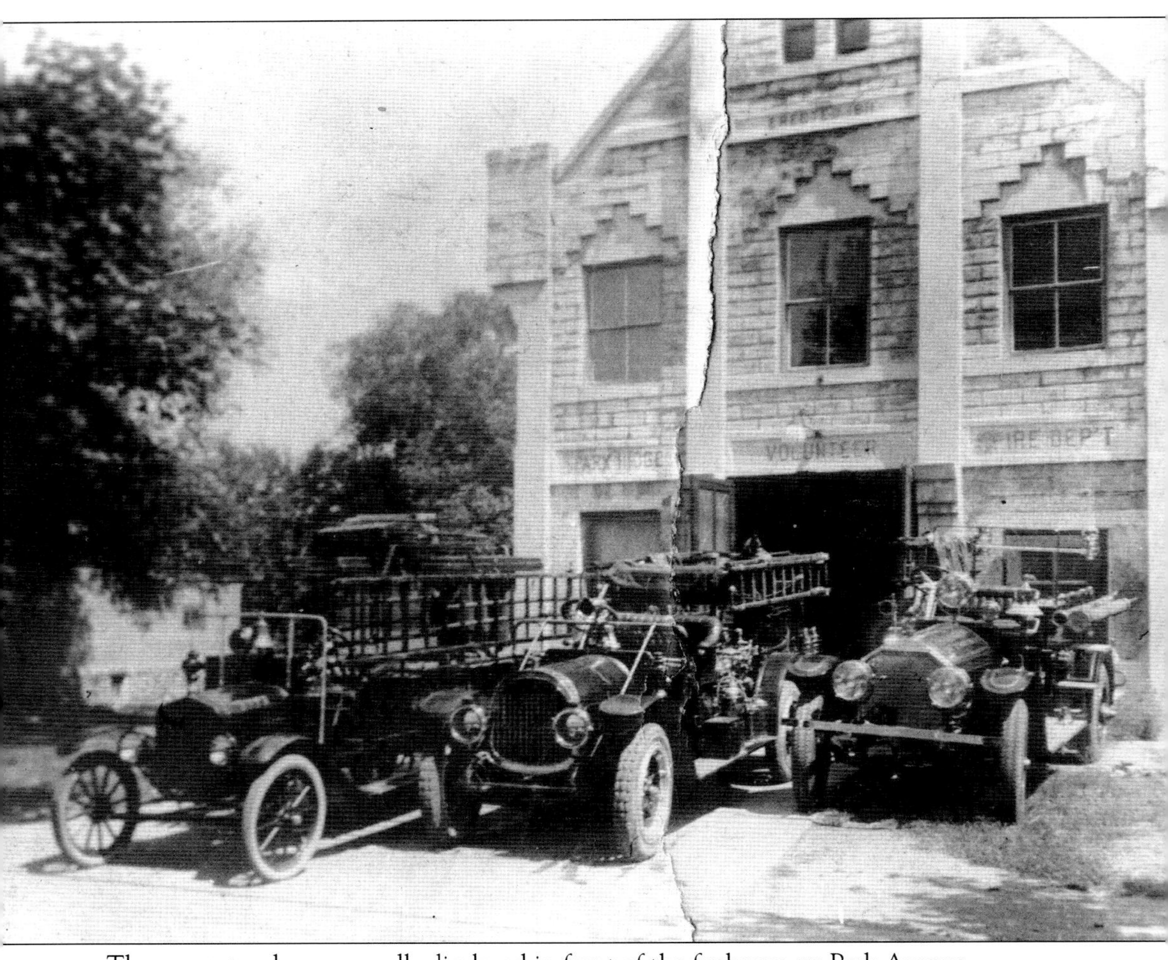


Three new trucks are proudly displayed in front of the firehouse on Park Avenue.

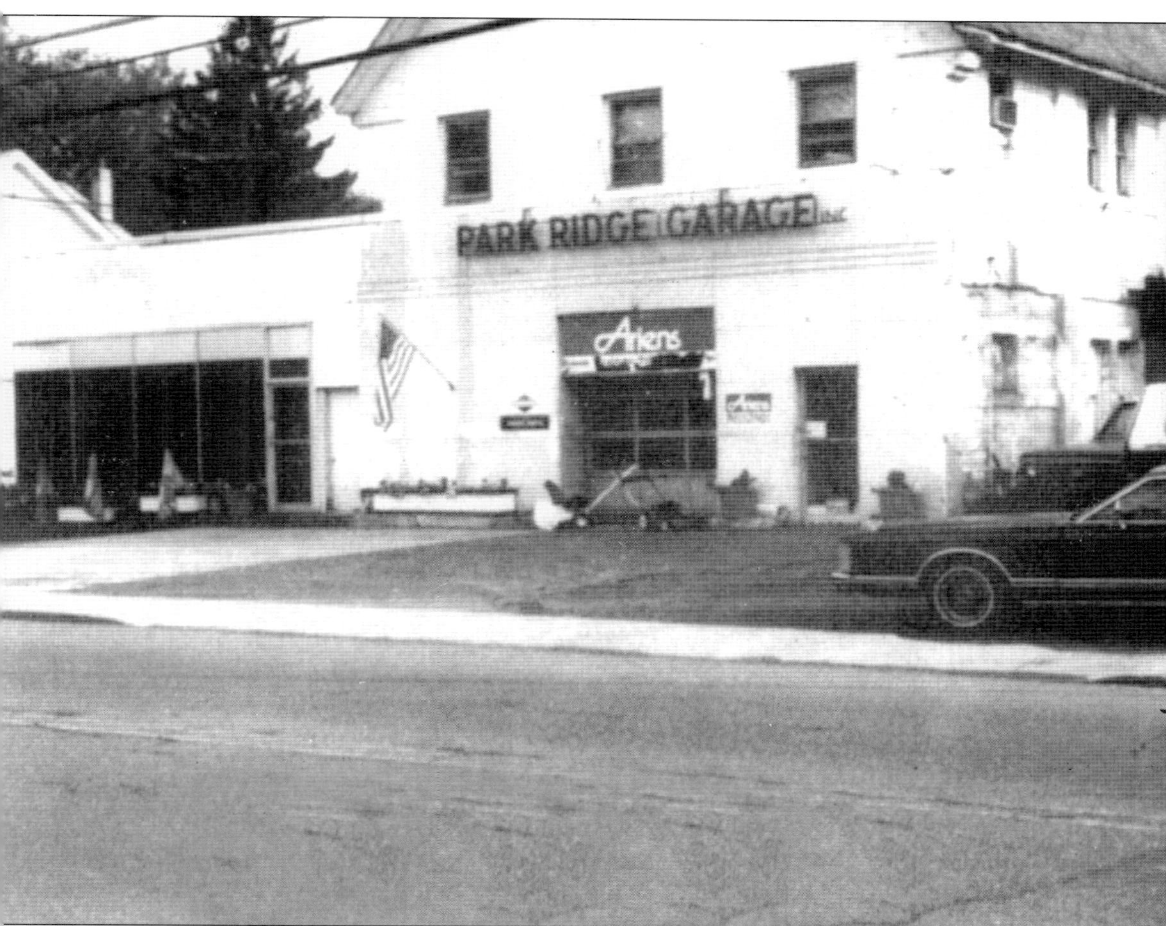


The building still stands today on Park Avenue, across from the post office and Park Ridge Police Station, next to Quackenbush Lumberyard. This photograph was taken in the 1950s.

MRS. H. P. CAMPBELL
PARK RIDGE
NEW JERSEY

Aug 14/29

o the Park Ridge Fire Department

Enclosed find a check for
ifty dollars as appreciation of the
oble work you did while my hou
was burning. I found some thin
hat were in the attic, to think th
ou Boys went in that blazing fir
am deeply impressed to think y
ook such a chance. I thank you o
nce more. I certainly am proud of
the Park Ridge Fireman

Sincerely Yours

Mrs H P Campbell

Park Ridge firemen received a grateful letter, which they framed and hung on the firehouse wall. The letter was written by a Mrs. H. P. Campbell on August 14, 1929. In it, she wrote, "Enclosed find a check for fifty dollars as appreciation of the noble work you did while my home was burning. To think that you boys went in that blazing fire. I am deeply impressed . . . I certainly am proud of the Park Ridge firemen."

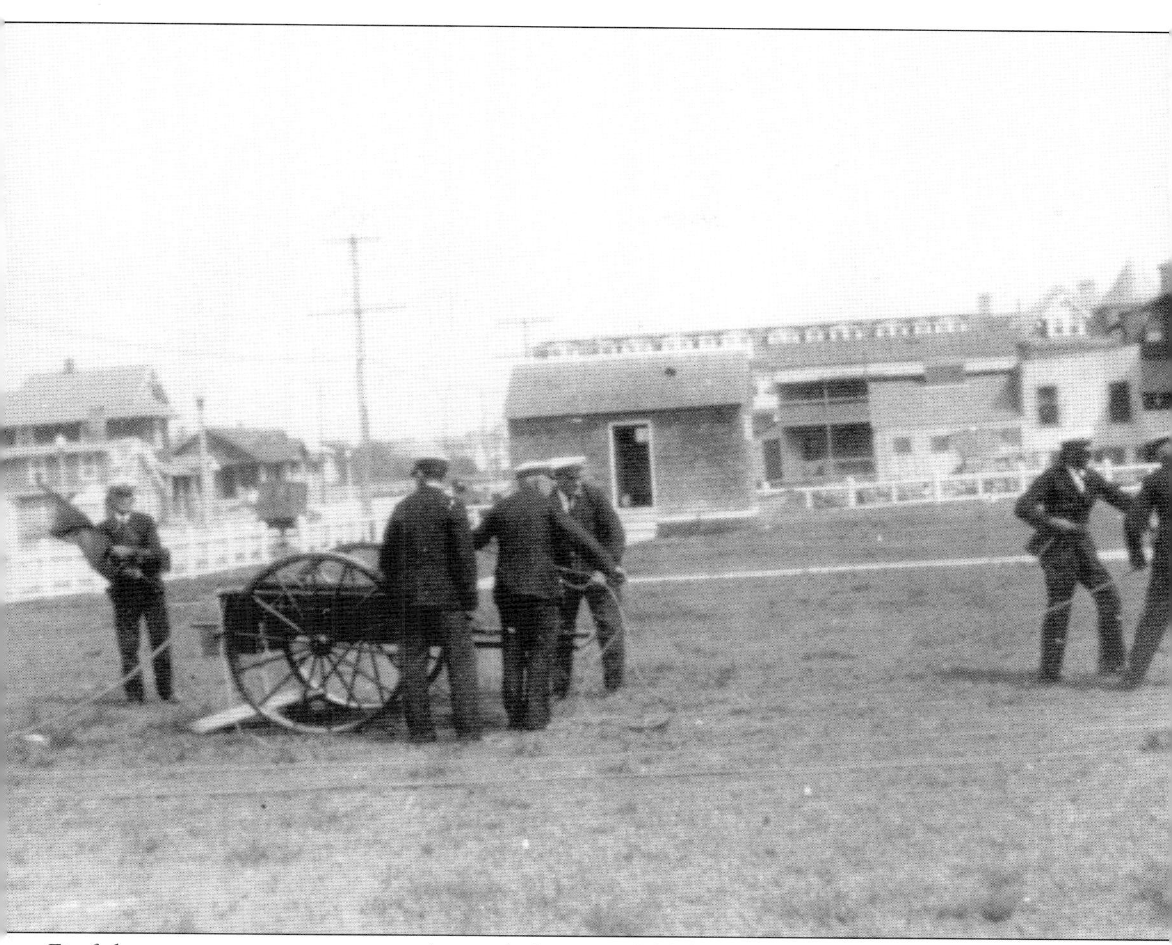

Firefighters set up games as a part of an early firemen's field day celebration.

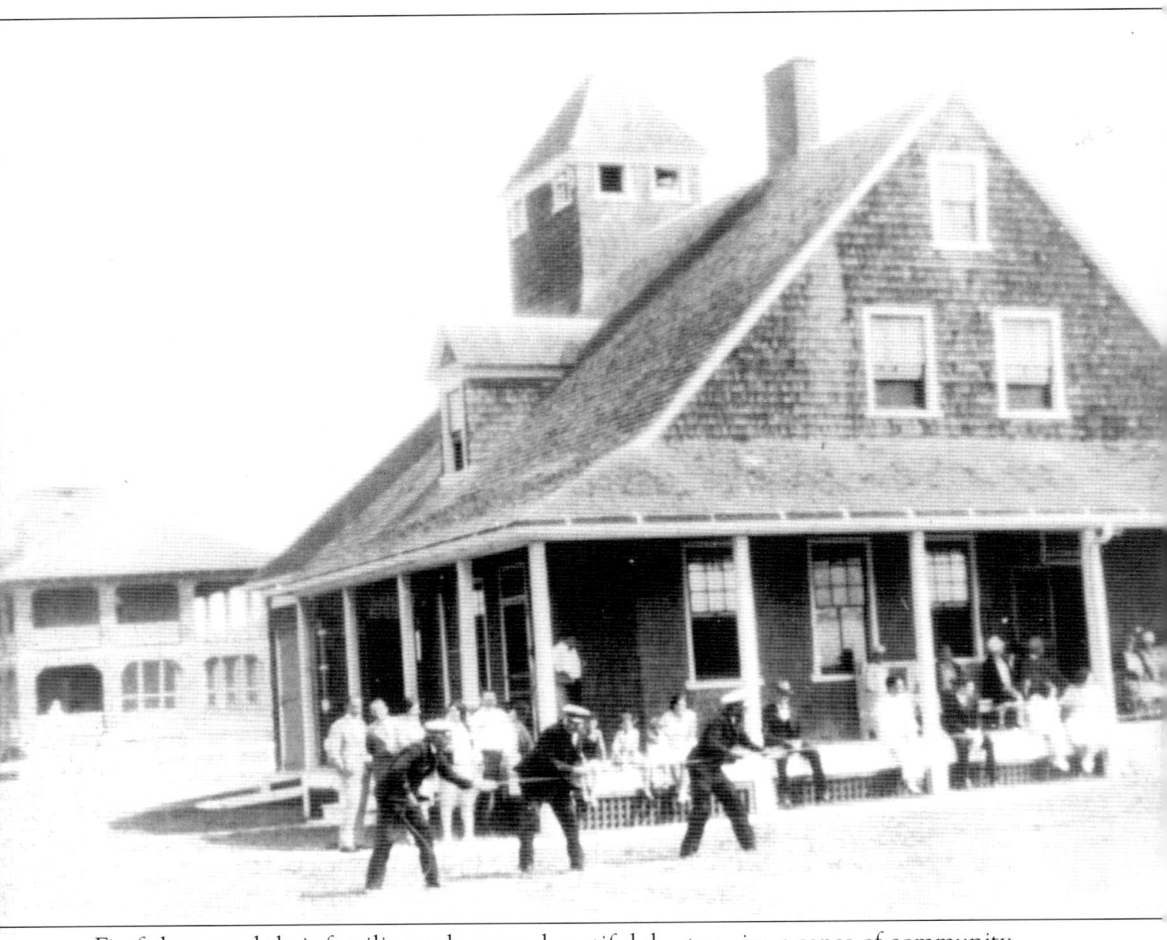

Firefighters and their families gather on a beautiful day to enjoy a sense of community.

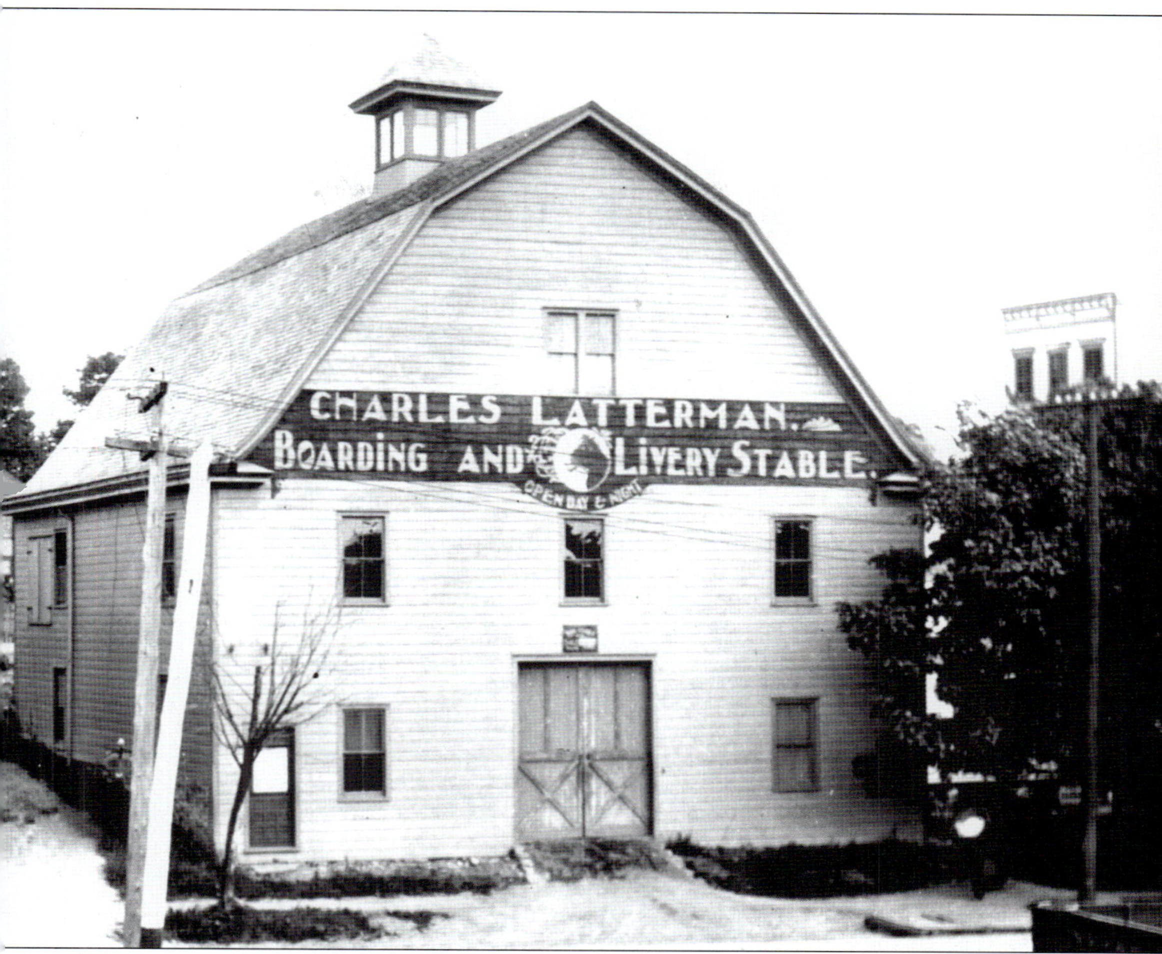


The livery stable kept horses, and when a fire occurred in the area, a livery worker would take two horses to the fire station, where they would be hitched to a wagon and carry a huge vat of water and many buckets to the site of the fire. The horses were available for anyone to rent. Occasionally when the firefighters needed one, no horse was available. Shown is the Charles Latterman Boarding and Livery Stable, "Open Day & Night."

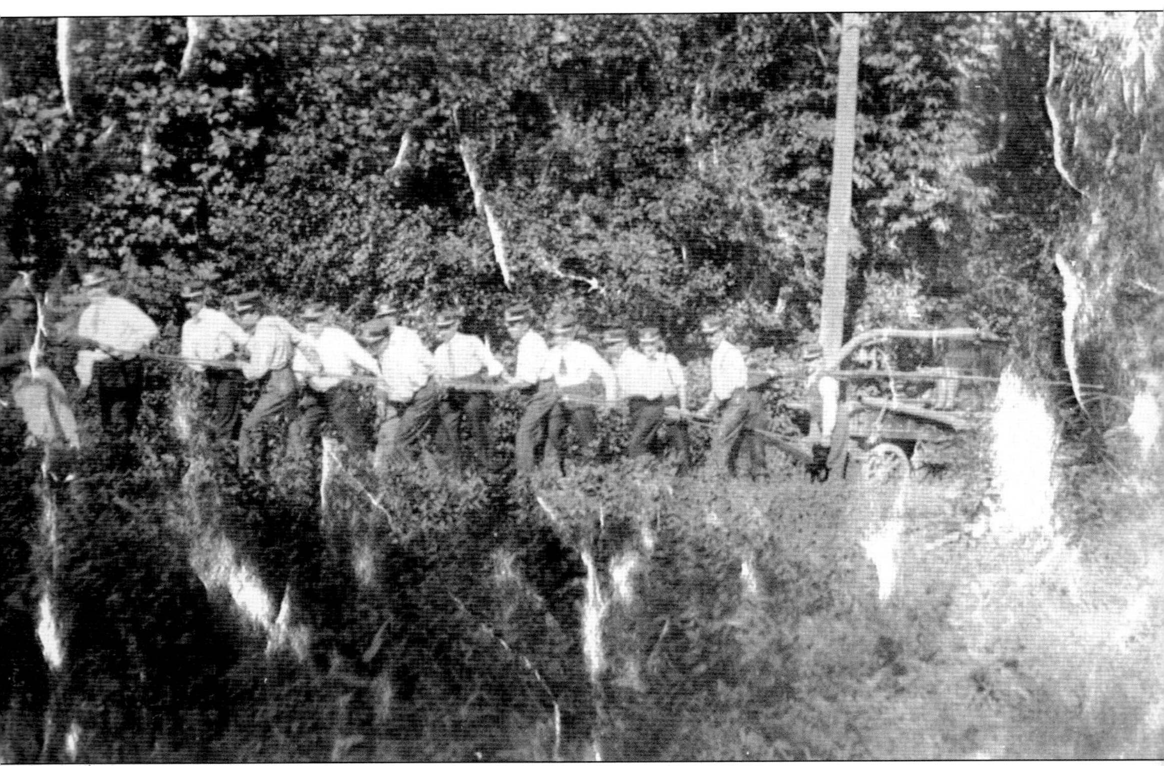

The volunteers of the Colony Avenue firehouse pull their engine by hand, as they did not have as much in the way of funding as the other firefighters in the area. The volunteers eventually raised funds so they too could rent horses at the livery stable.

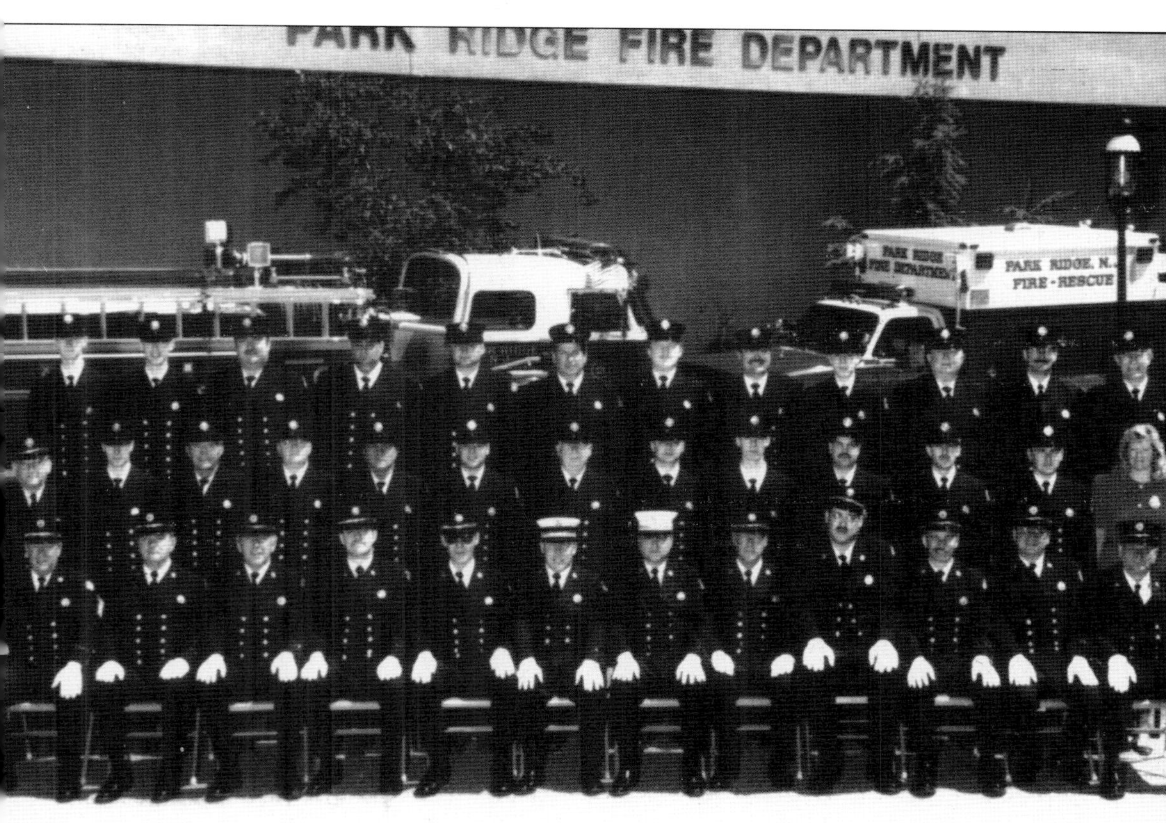


In this celebratory view, dated 1994, are the Park Ridge firefighters and fire commissioner and borough historian Barbara Martine. Firefighters, including the current chief, outgoing chief, and assistant fire chief, are pictured. The borough held its centennial in 2004.

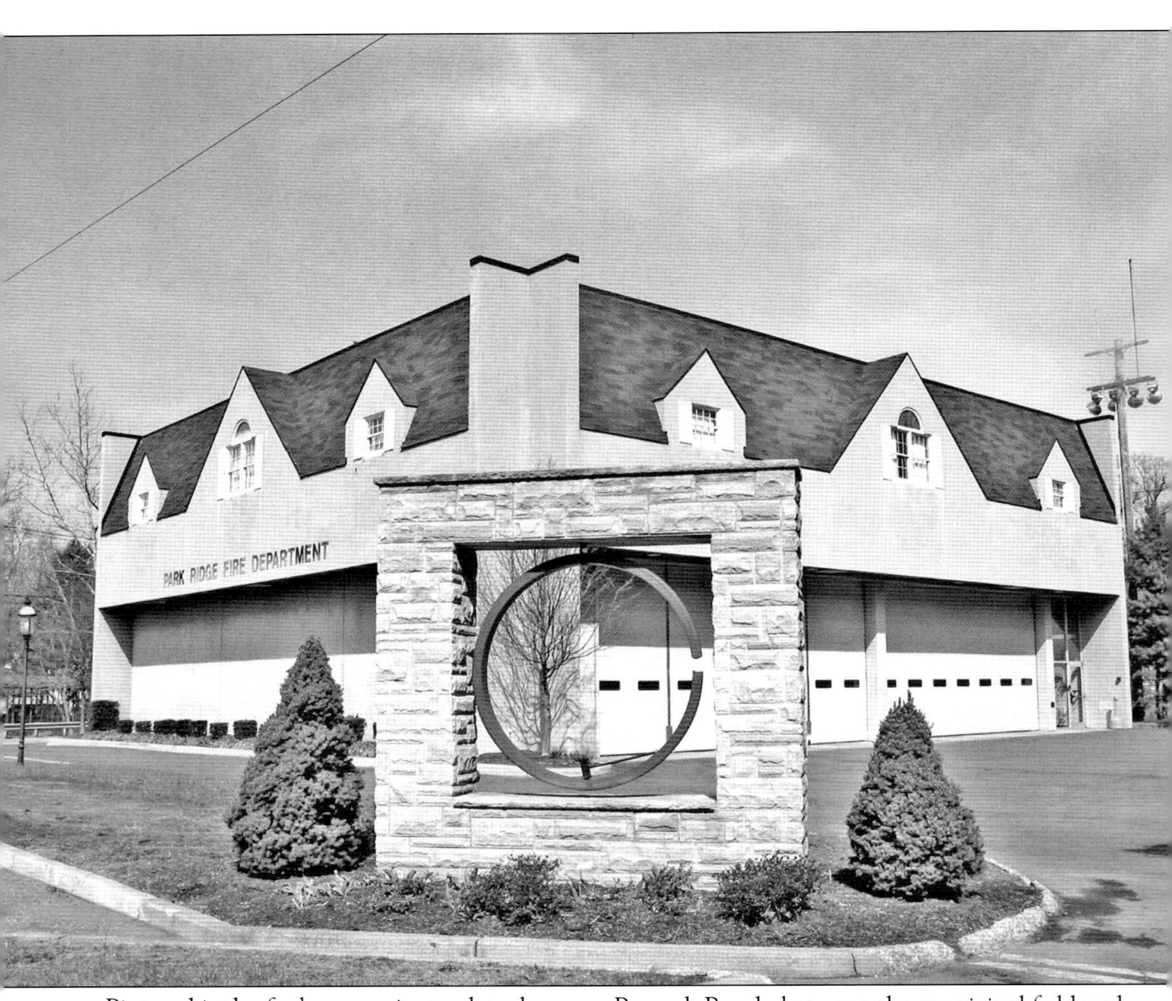


Pictured is the firehouse as it stands today, near Pascack Brook, between the municipal field and the library and borough hall.

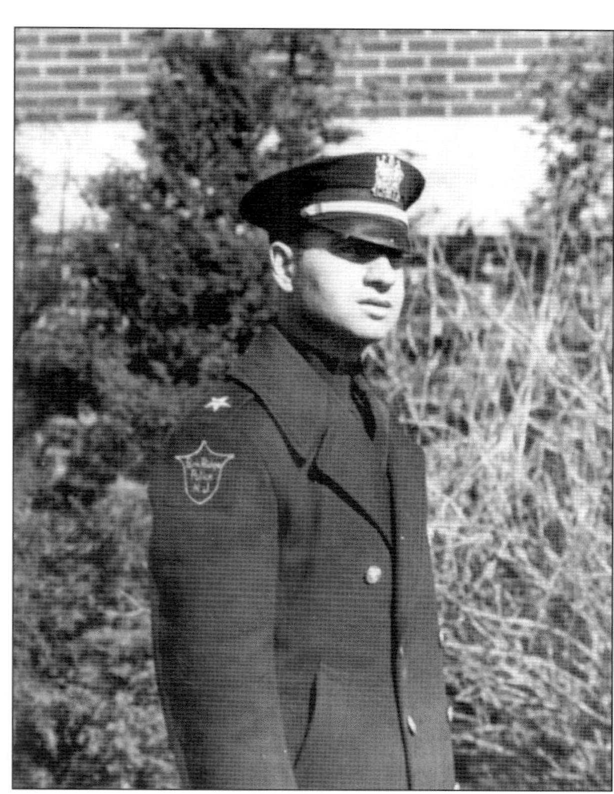

Anthony Salimone was the borough's first police chief.

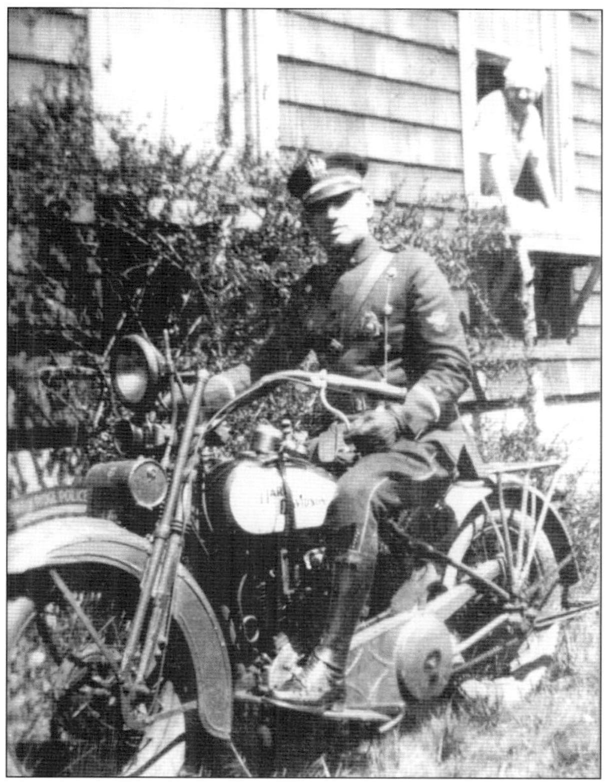

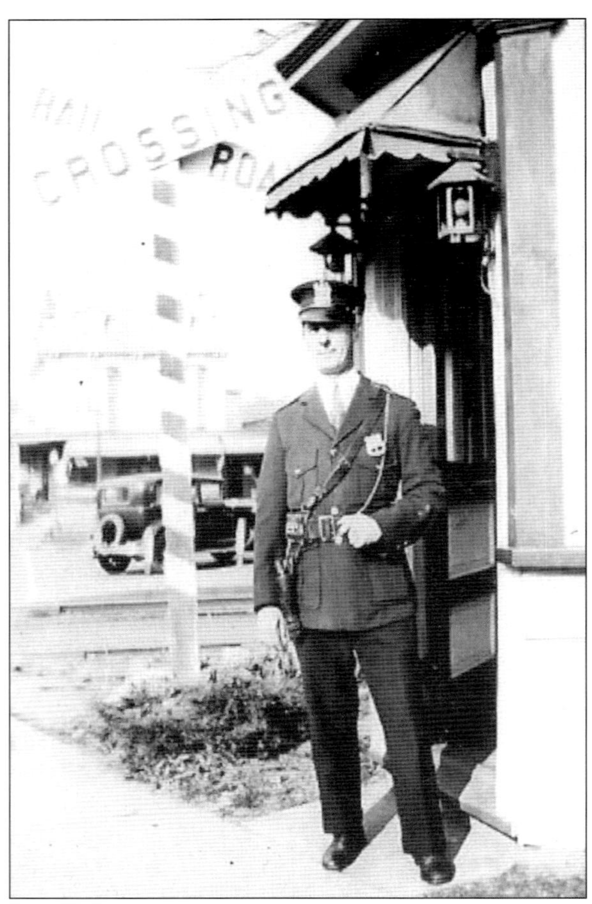


One of Park Ridge's finest poses in uniform on Park Avenue. Behind him is a 1920s automobile. He is standing just outside the doorway of the post office, which today is Cyclesport.

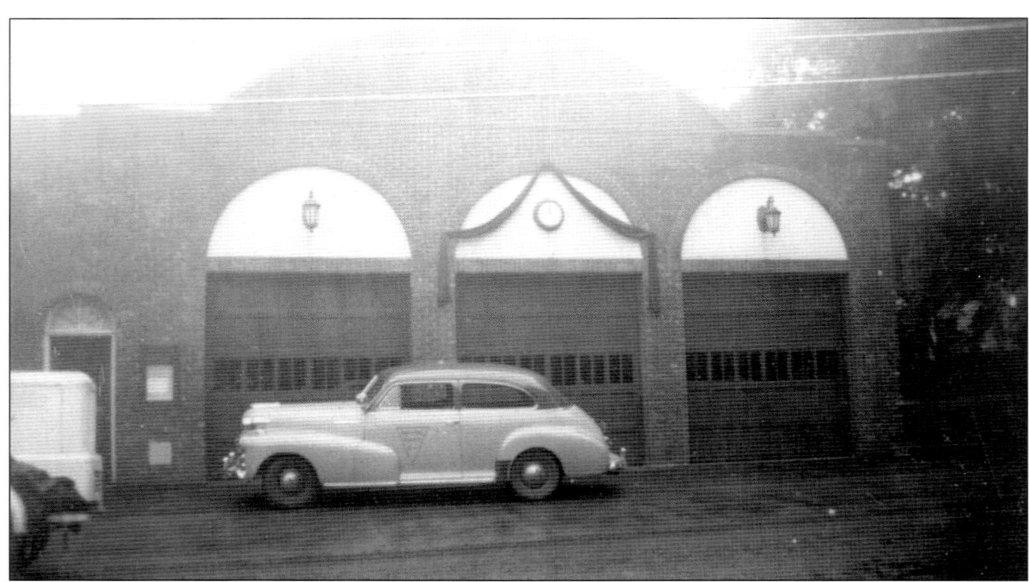

Pictured is one of the earliest Park Ridge police cars.

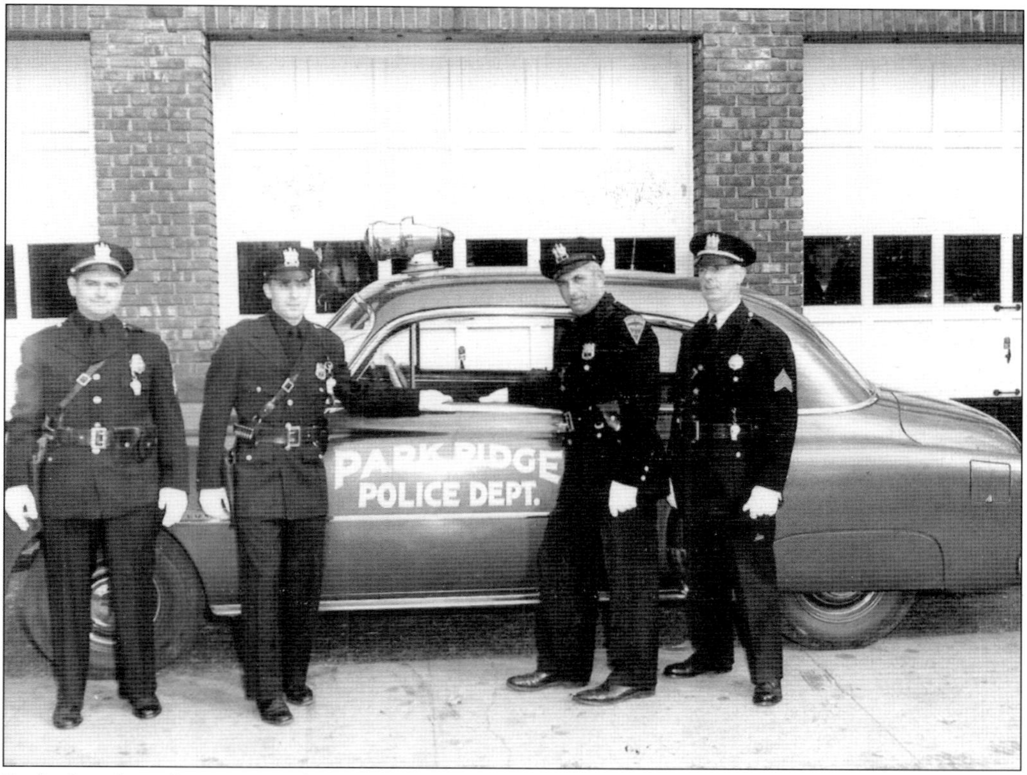

Parked and ready to serve the community is a newer police car. Looking it over are four local police officers.

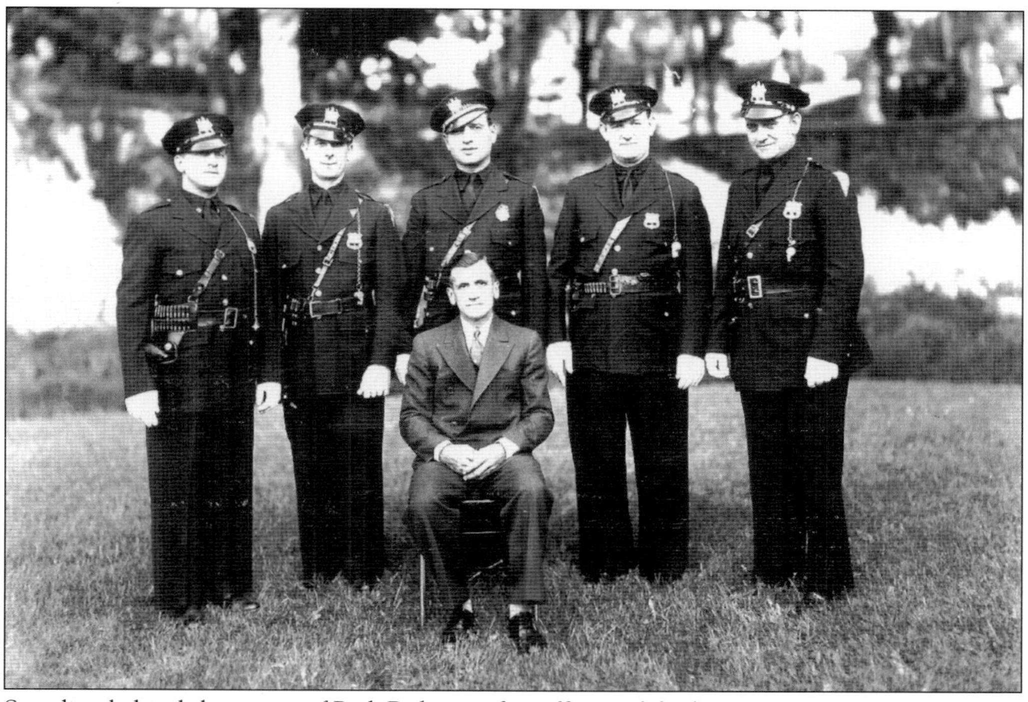

Standing behind the mayor of Park Ridge are five officers of the law.

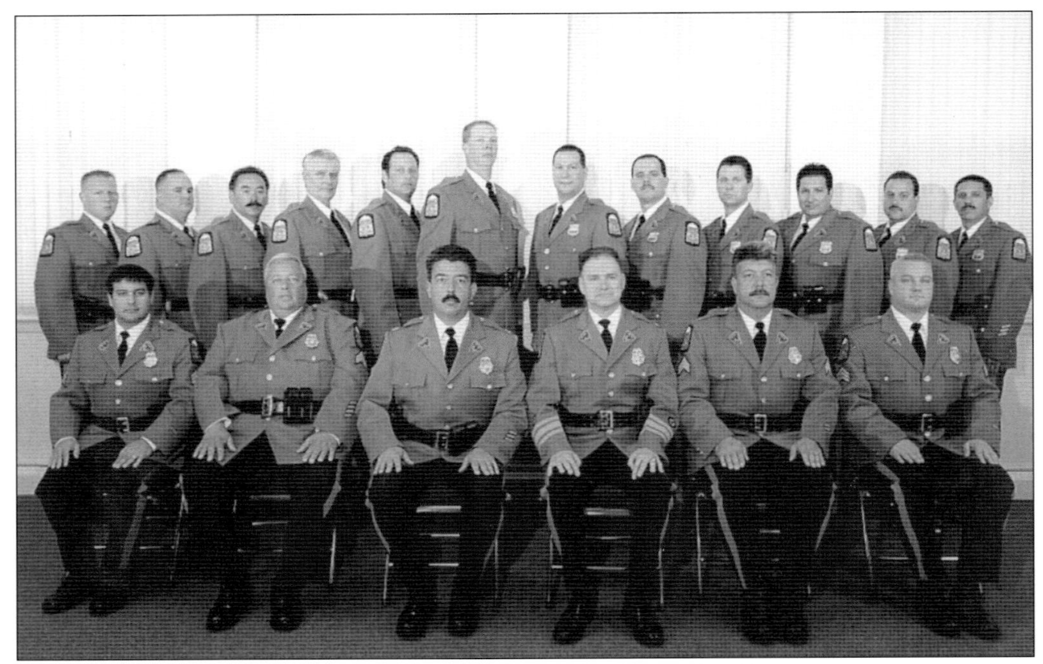

Posing in uniform in 2002 are 18 members of the Park Ridge Police Department.

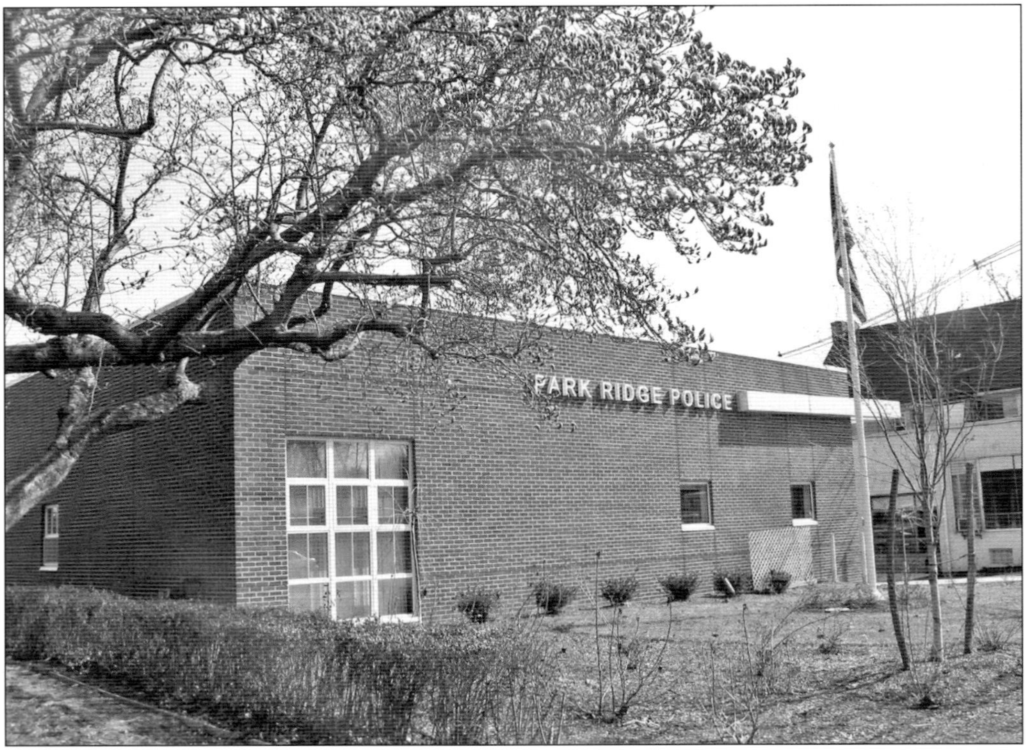

Shown is the Park Ridge Police Station of today.

# *Three*

# WATER AND ELECTRIC

History was made in the year 1903 when workers began to dig the deep hole that would bring Park Ridge to the forefront as far as lighting and electricity were concerned. It would also soon be able to supply water to residents, rather than their having to use the wells each house has nearby. The first hydroelectric plant was finished in 1904 and still stands today. Well No. 1, under borough hall, was drilled in 1924. In 1906, electricity lit Park Ridge for the first time. The electricity served as a drawing card to the area, as passersby on the train could marvel that Park Ridge was illuminated.

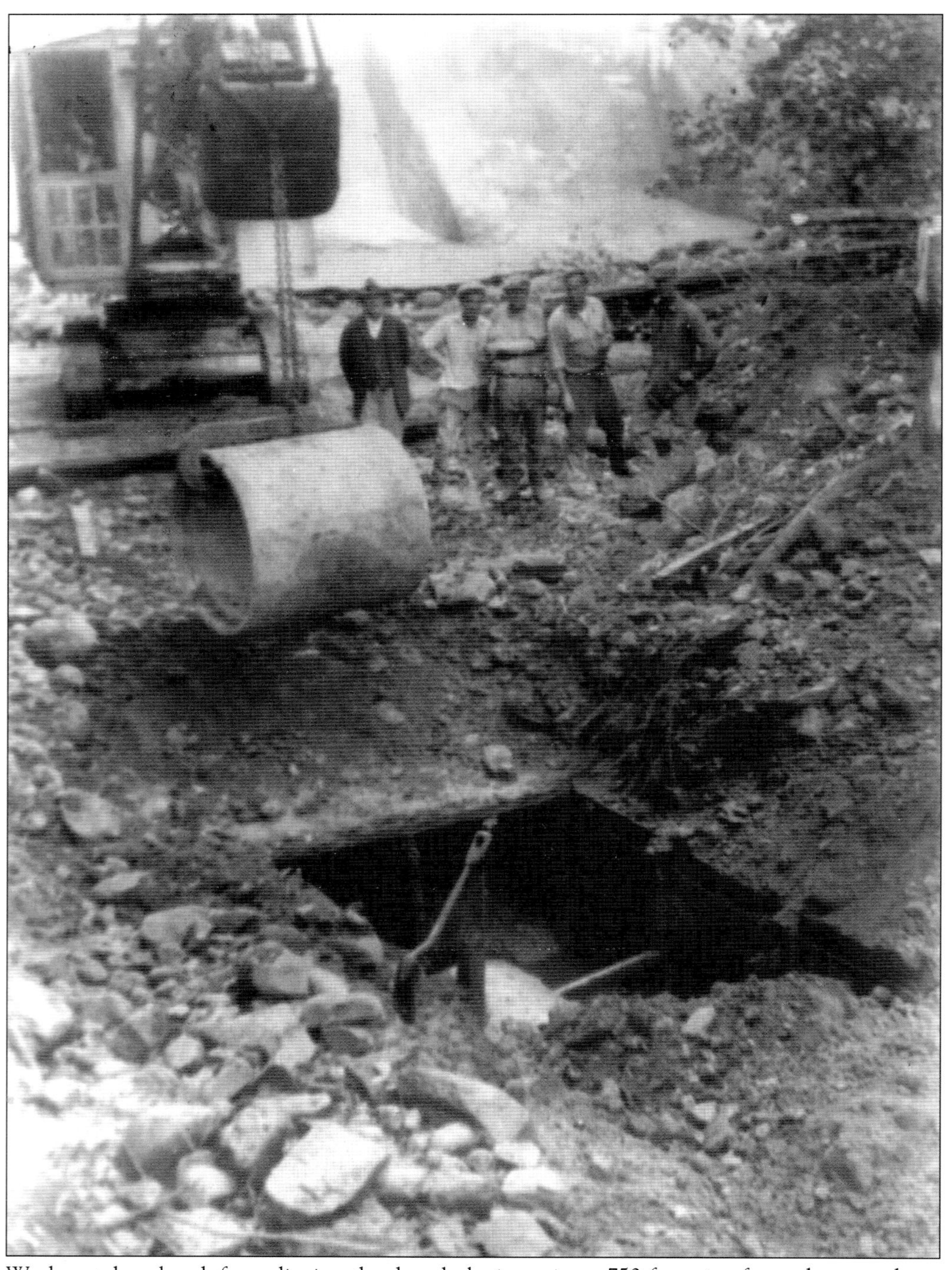

Workers take a break from digging the deep hole, inserting a 750-foot pipe far underground.

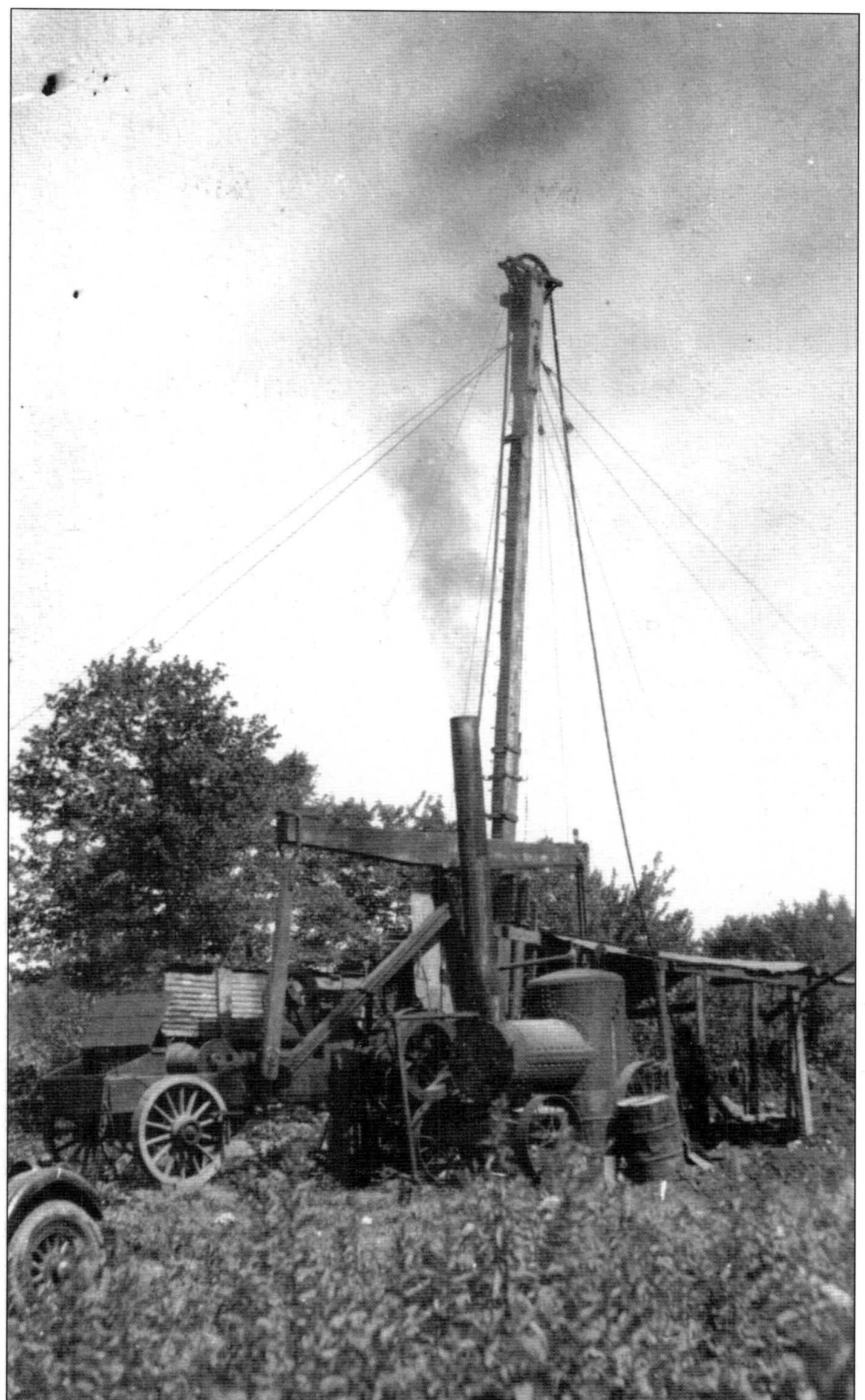

Well No. 3 was constructed next to the property where Lollipop Nursery School now stands on the west side of Park Ridge. As the population grew, the need for water grew, and more wells were dug. Today Park Ridge has 19 wells throughout the borough.

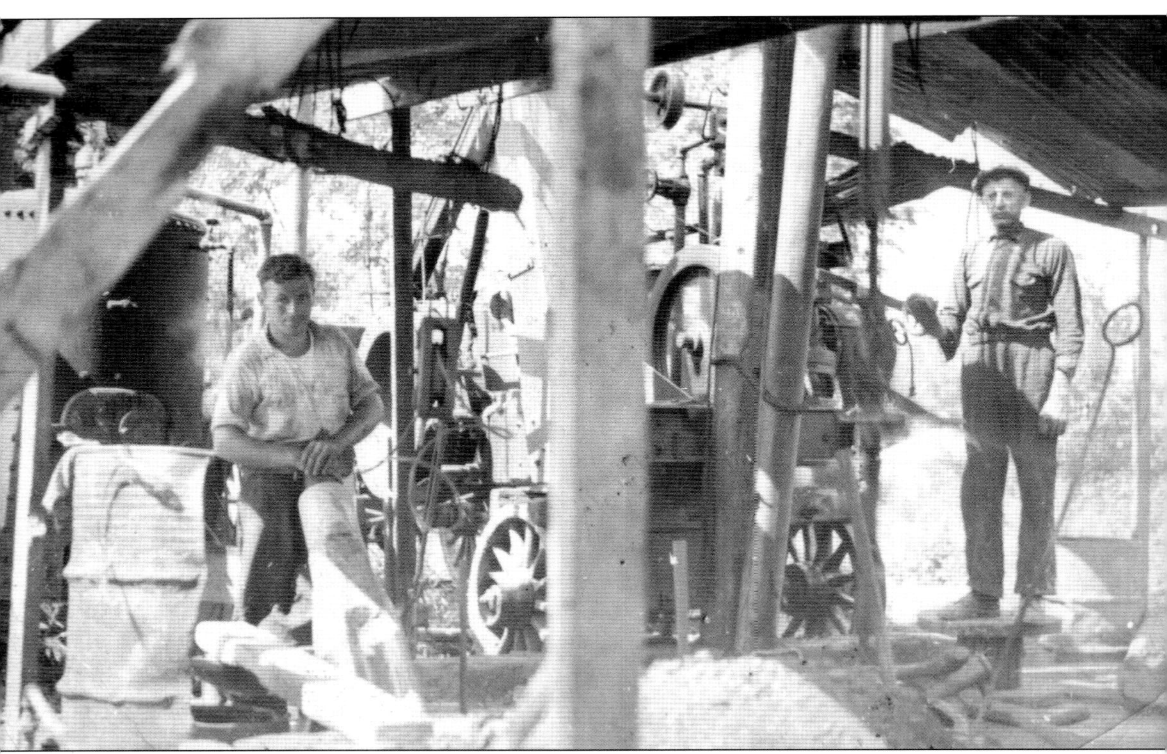

The concept of electricity was brought to Park Ridge by Meno Feddern, who sold his Colony Avenue house to move near Mill Brook, where he investigated the use of portable electric lamps. Pictured are well drillers at the site of Well No. 3, in 1934, next to where the Lollipop School now stands.

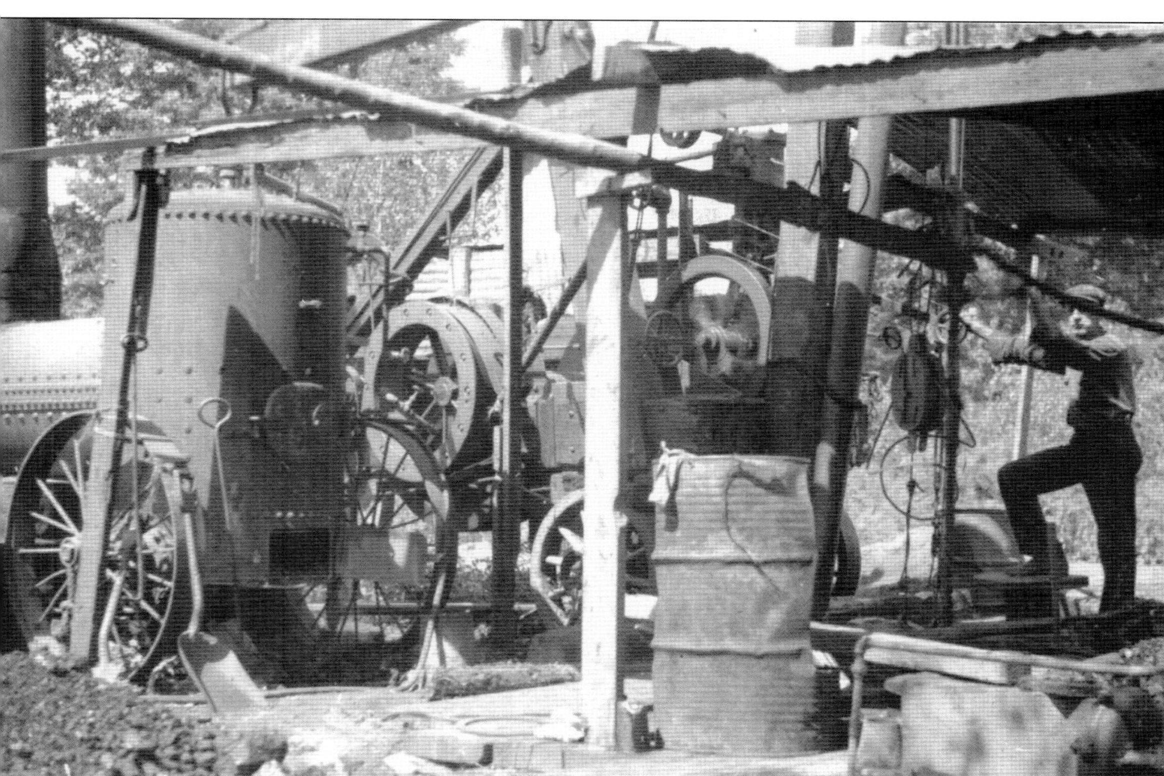

Feddern gave lectures on electricity. This is a photograph of the drilling of Well No. 3, at 59 Spring Valley Road.

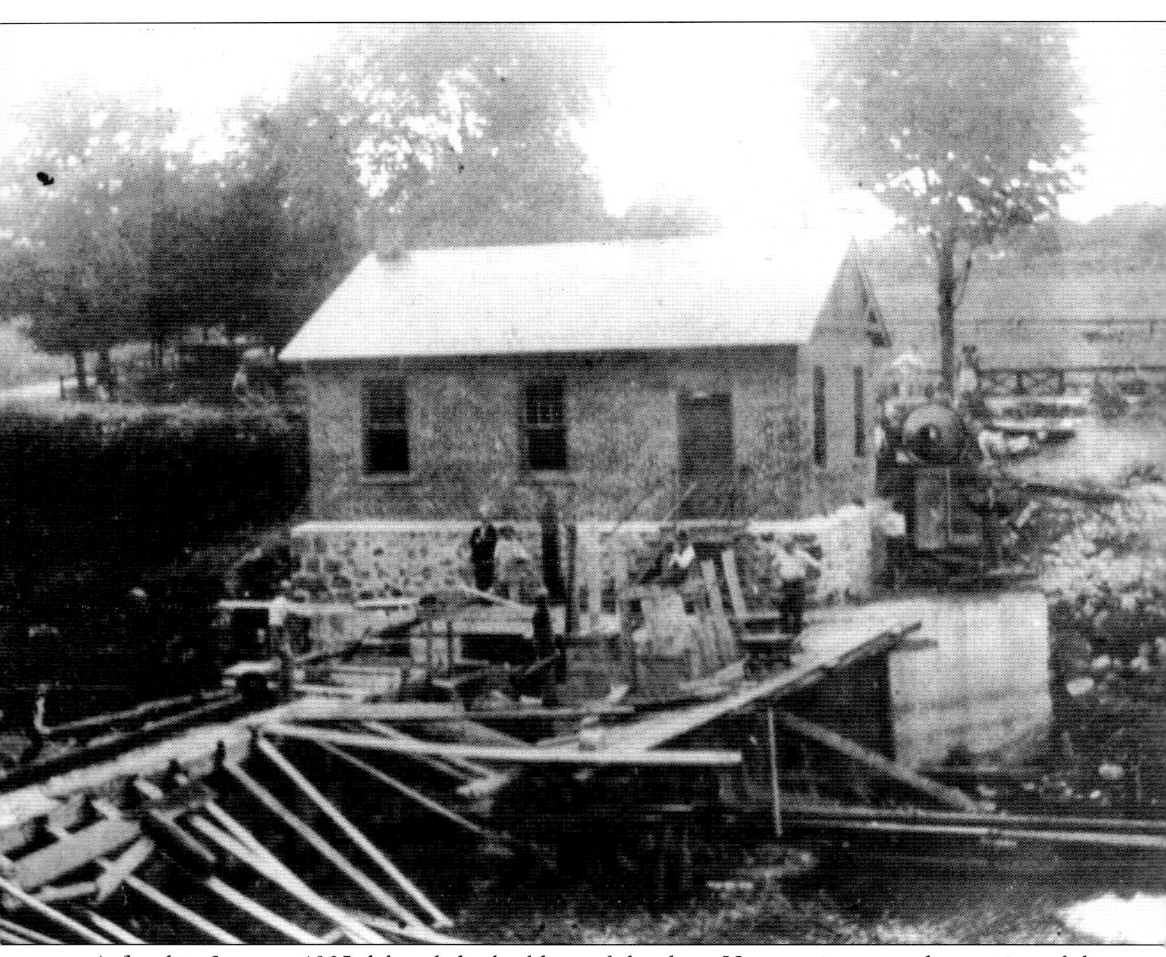

A flood in January 1905 delayed the building of the dam. Heavy rains caused a section of the dam to be carried away.

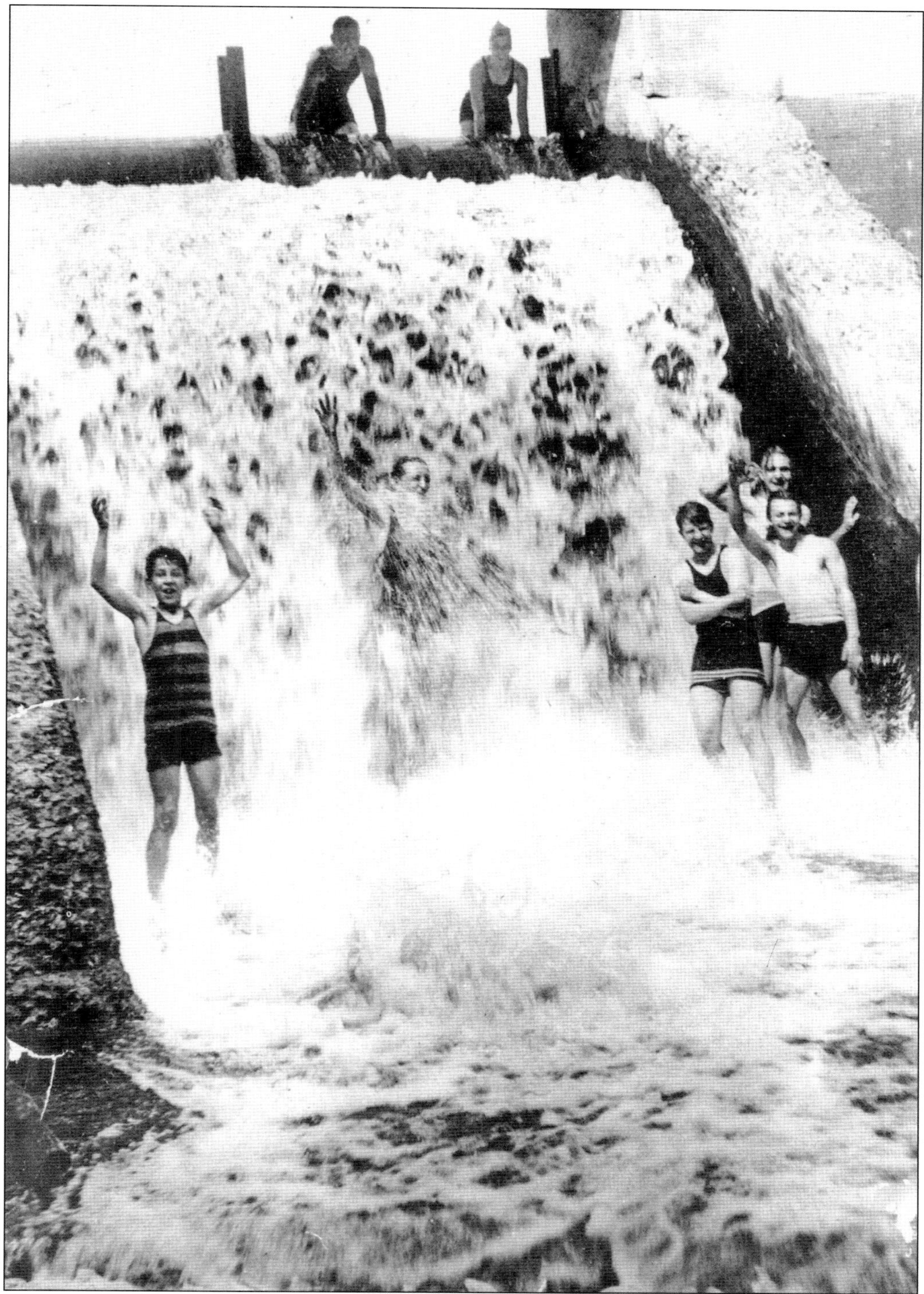

In the 1920s, vacationers could slip into the waters of the dam to cool off on hot summer days.

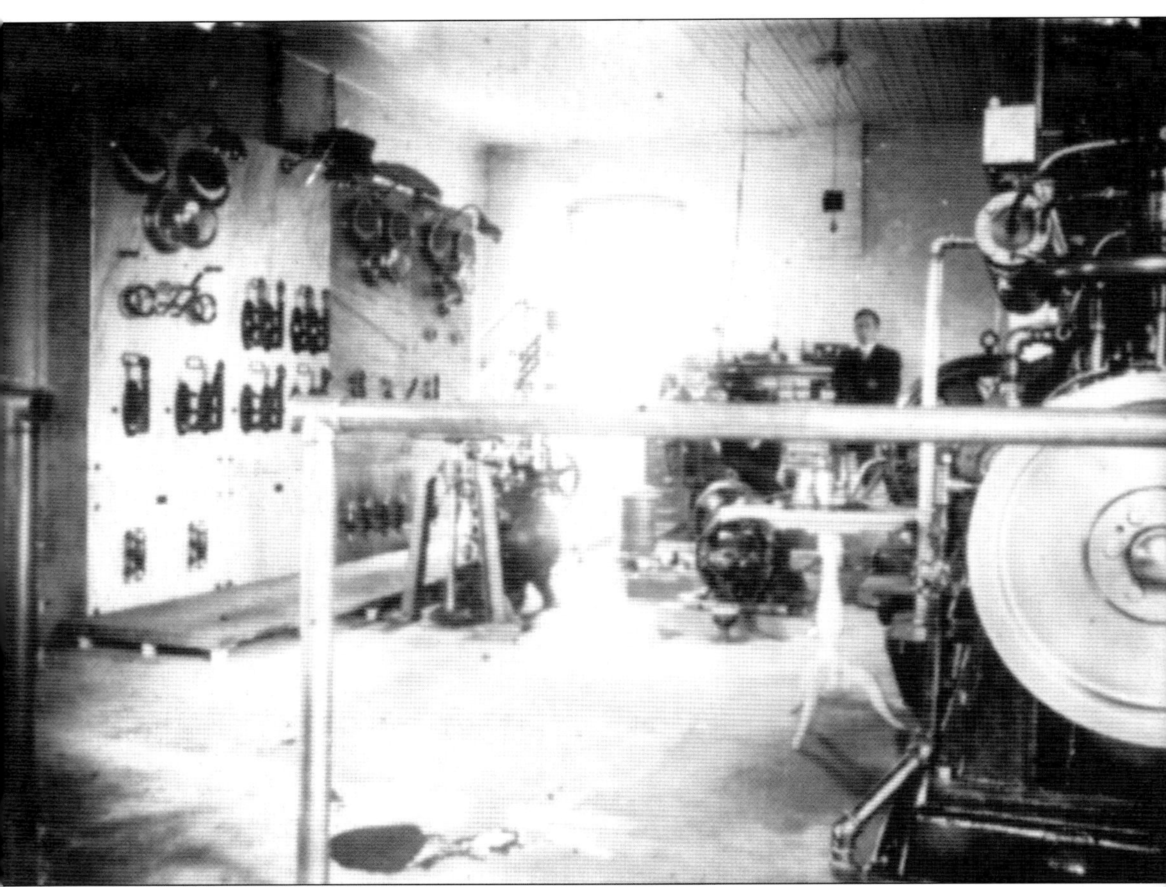

In 1919, a gasoline-fueled engine was brought in to help the water power. Pictured is the plant's turbo engine.

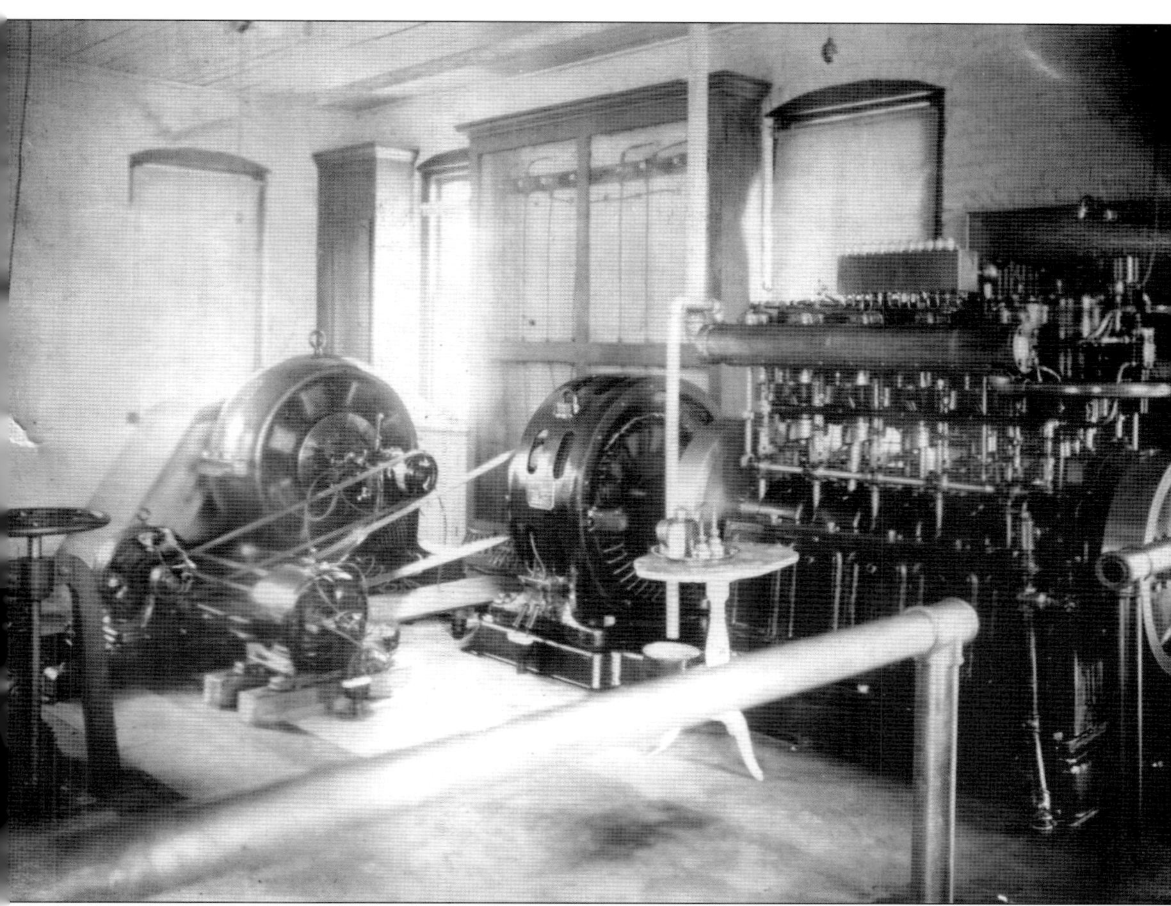

The inner workings of the hydroelectric plant were very modern for the time.

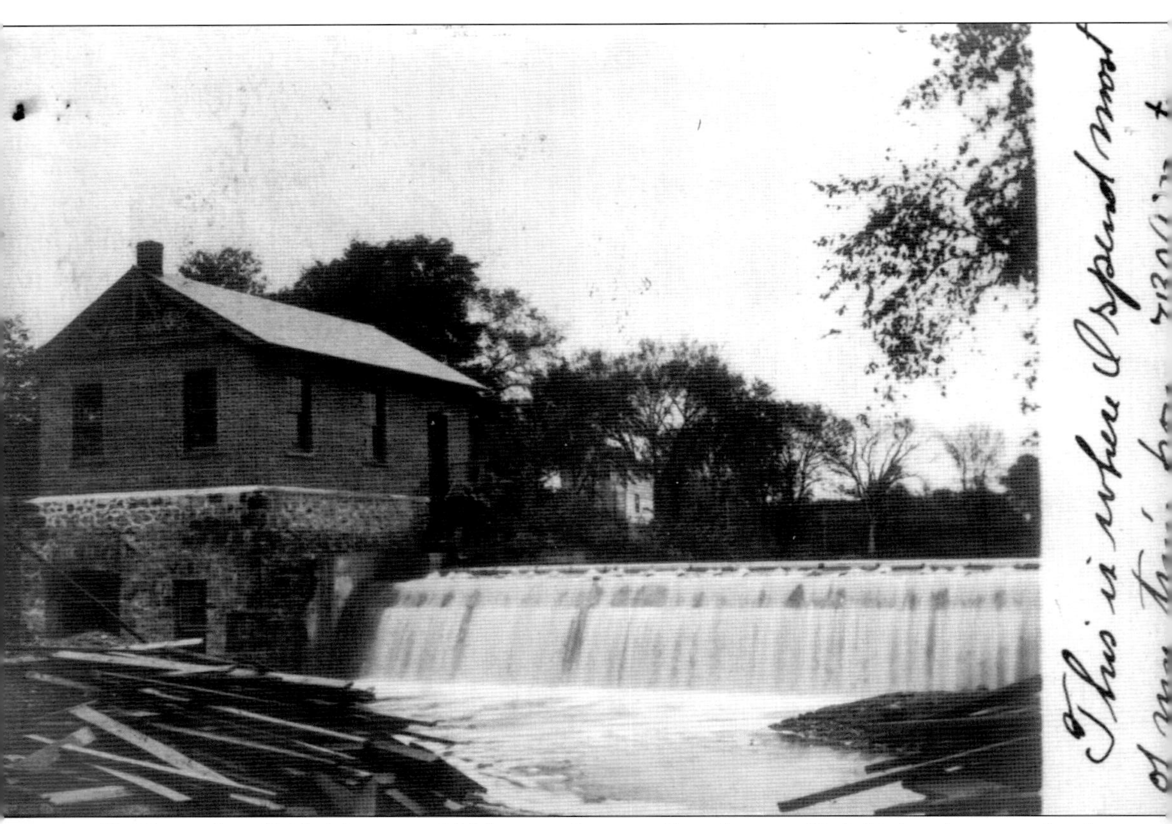


In November 1906, Mittag and Volger, a plant on Broadway in Park Ridge, became the first customer of the new plant, and by the end of the summer of 1907, there were 18 customers.

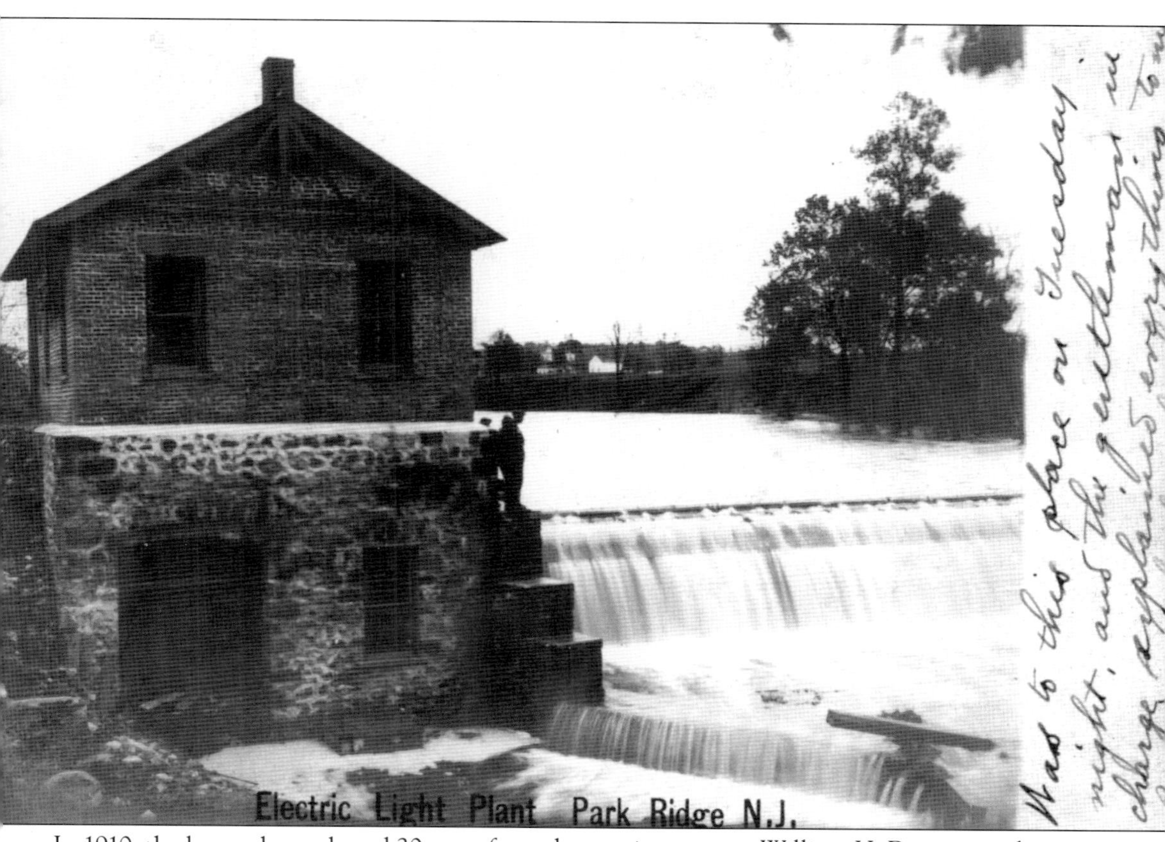


In 1910, the borough purchased 20 acres from the previous owner, William H. Dean, in order to maintain the water level at 18 feet.

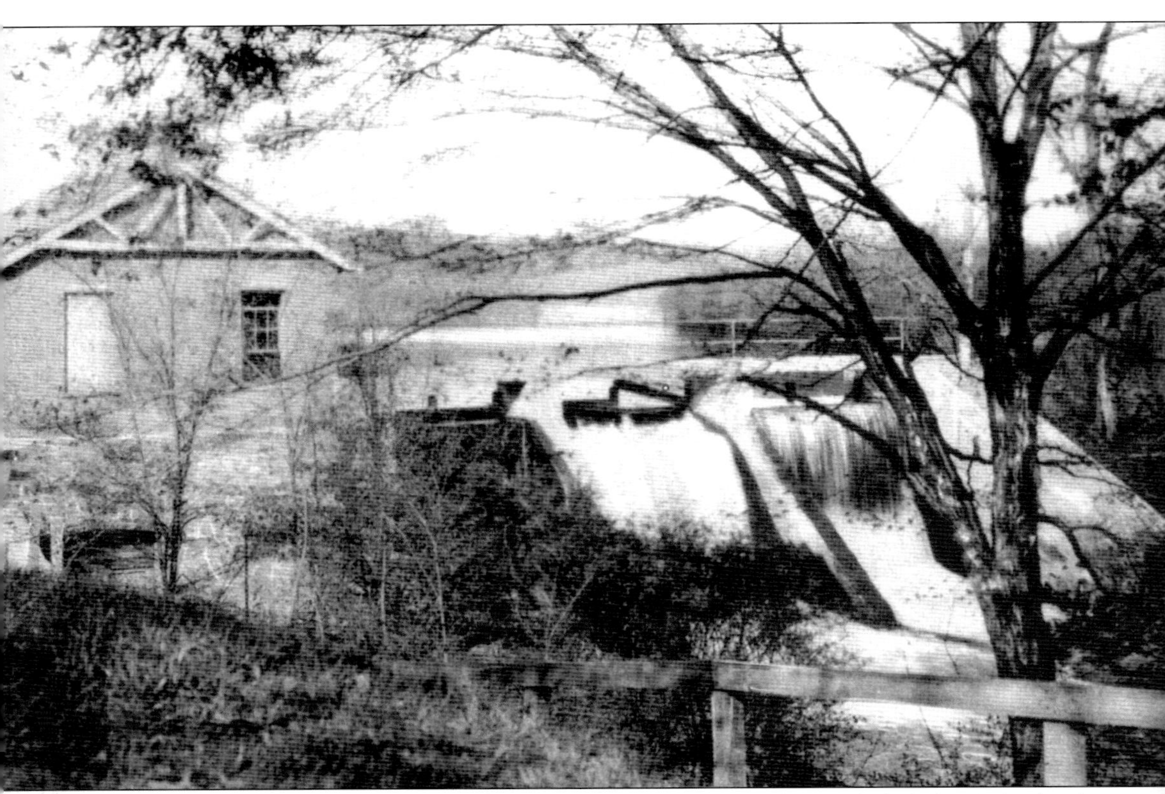

In this photograph, the site of the hydroelectric plant has changed slightly. A bridge has been added.

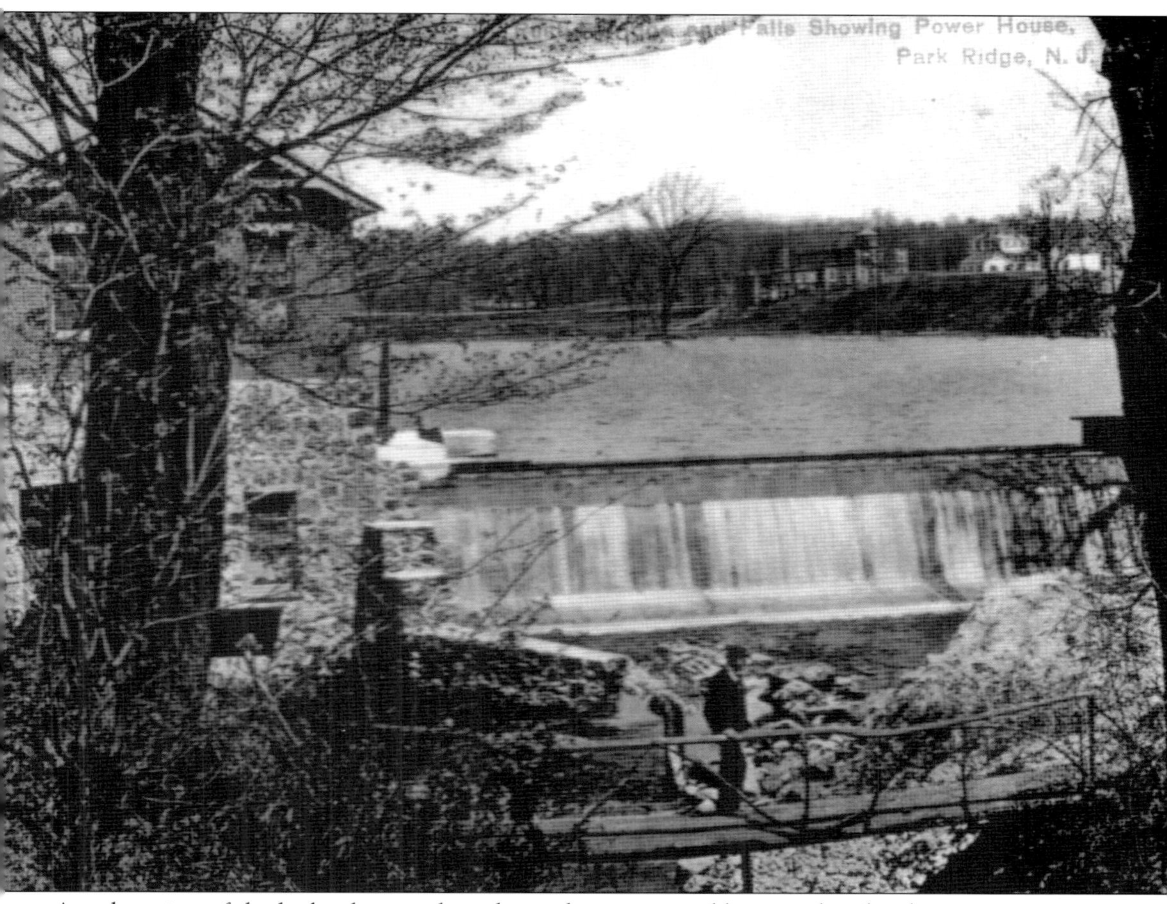


Another view of the hydroelectric plant shows that a post-and-beam railing has been put up.

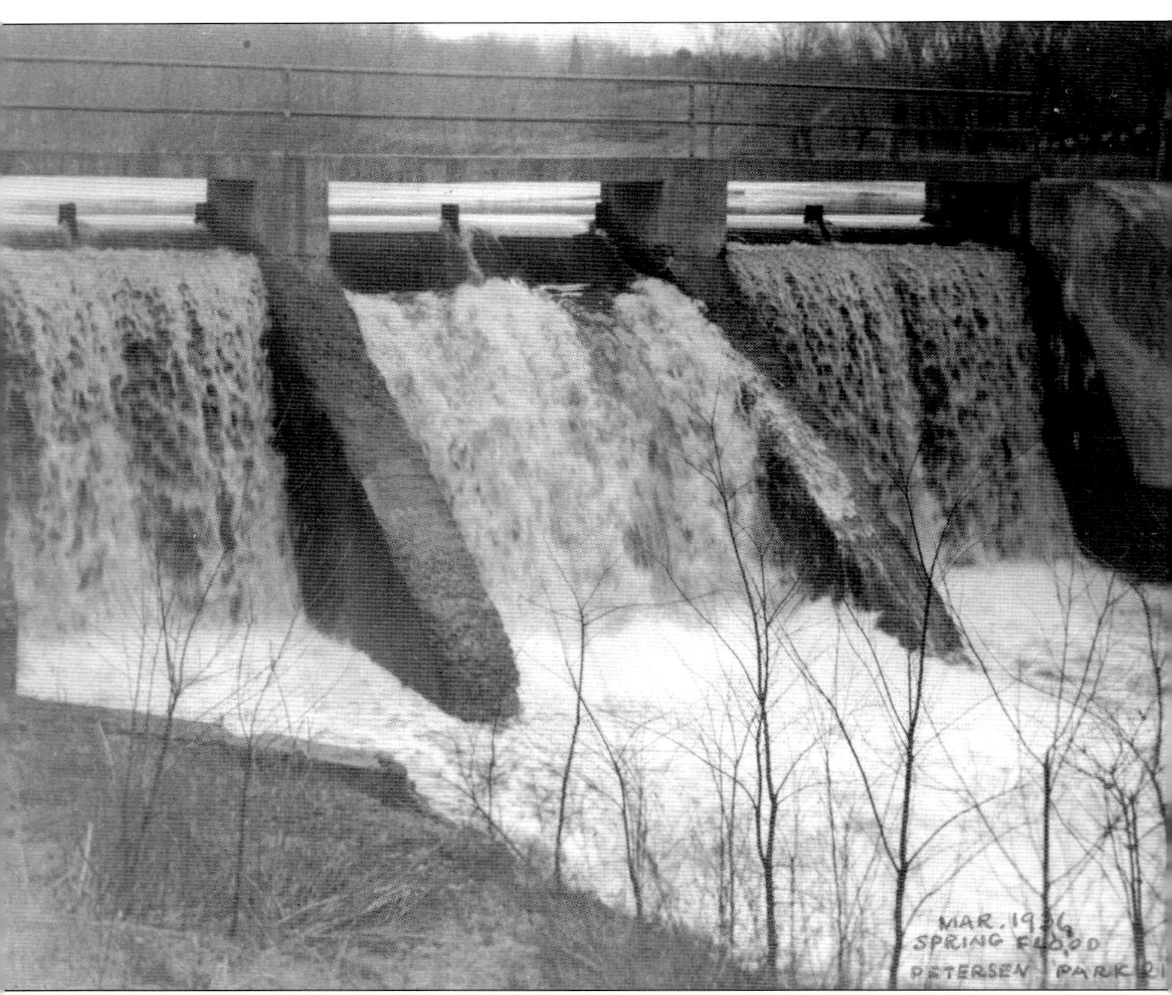


In the spring flood of March 1936, water pours over the dam at Electric Pond. It was first called Silver Lake, the Mill Pond, then Electric Lake. Now it is at times called Mill Pond once again.

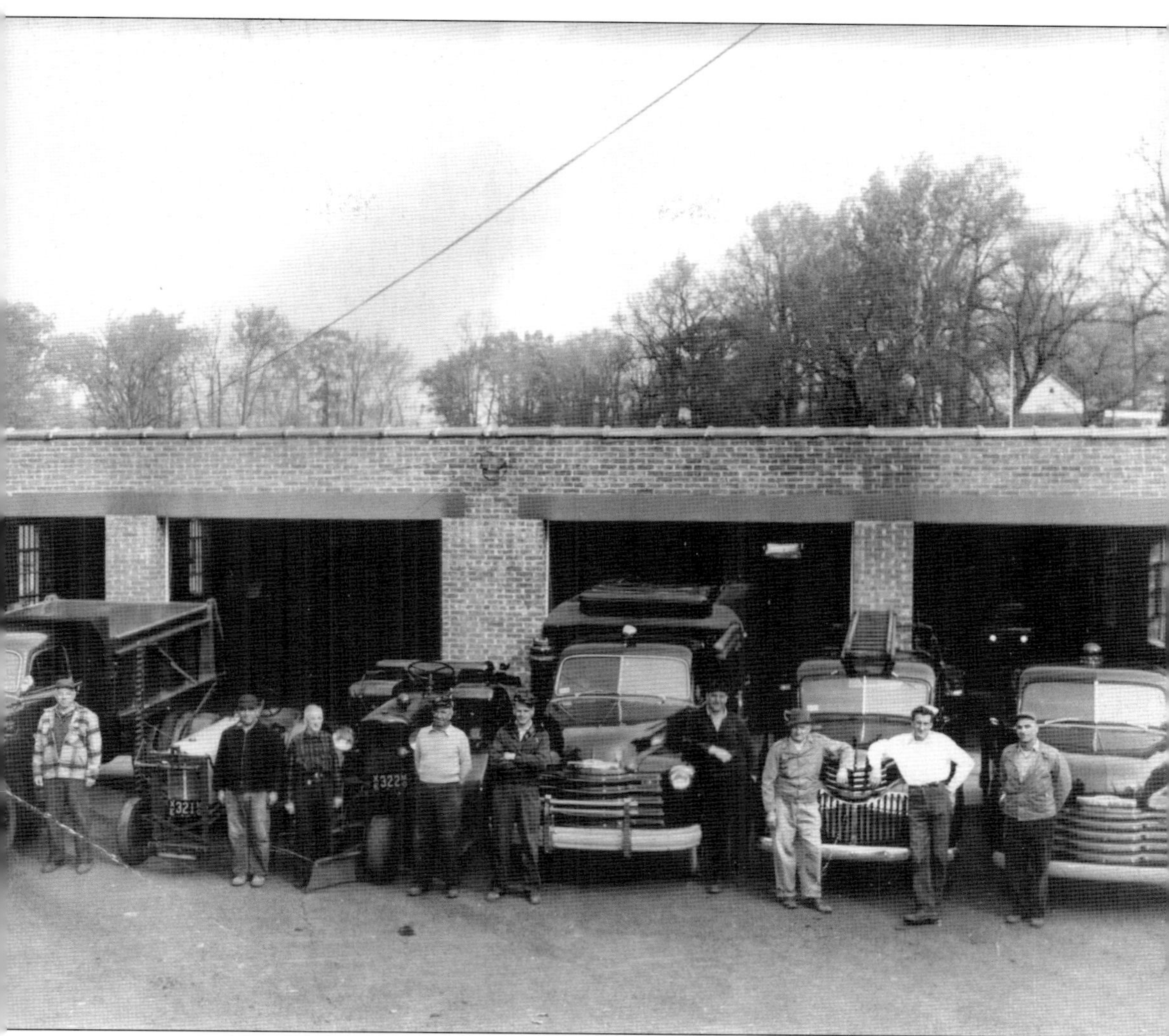

Members of the water department and the department of public works pose with their vehicles. At the time, the building was located where the Park Ridge Public Library is now. The department of public works has since moved to Sulak Lane.

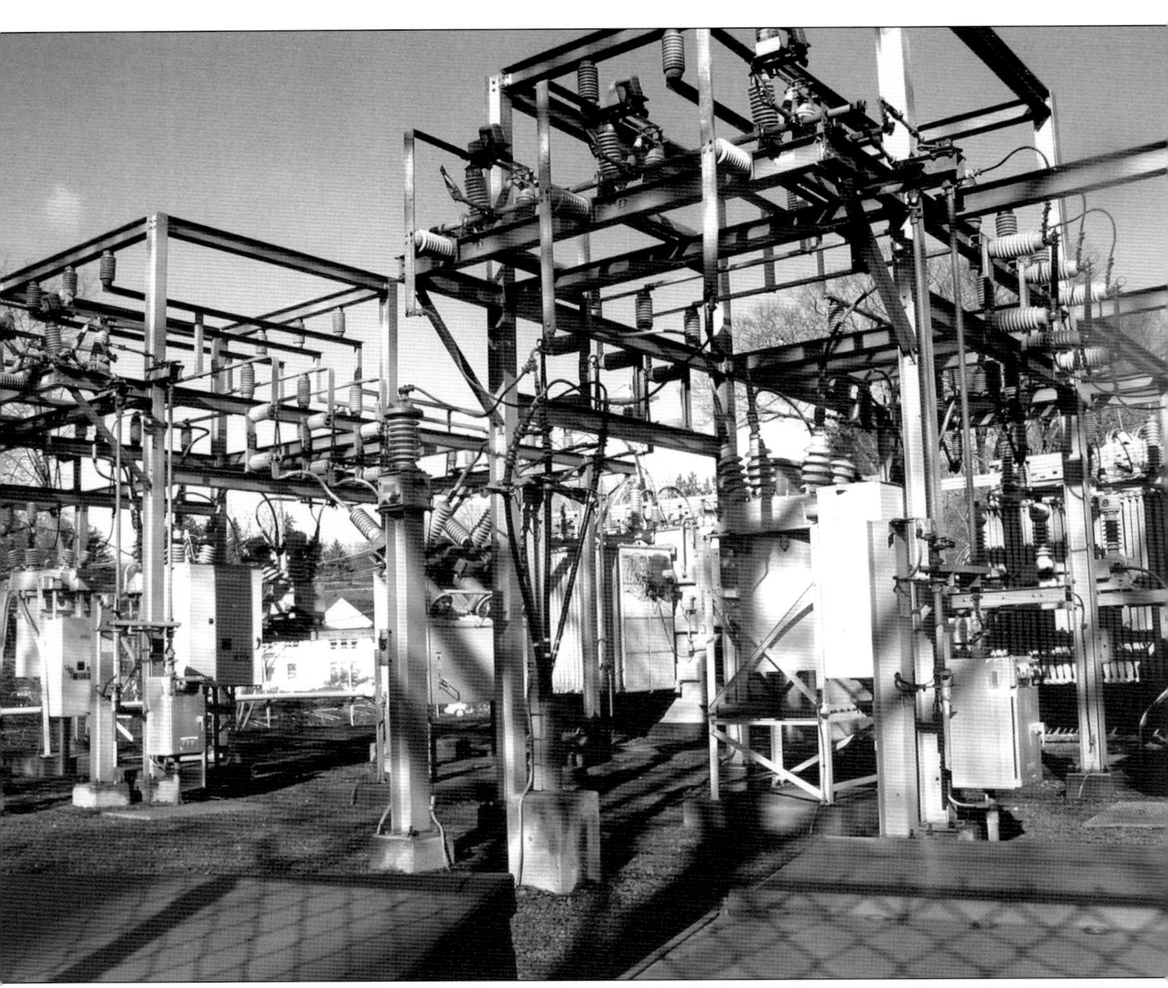

Pictured are the borough's electric lines today. While the borough now purchases its electricity wholesale, it remains the only municipality in Bergen County that has its own electric utility and residents' rates are lower than any other municipality in the county. The hydroelectric plant was closed in 1928. The borough purchased electricity from Rockalned Electric for awhile, then Public Service Electric and Gas Company (PSE&G).

# *Four*

# Building Up

In the late 1800s, the Quackenbush family came to Pascack. Charles Quackenbush had worked in the lumber business in the Netherlands and was at first casually helping out neighbors when they were building their new houses here. He began helping others more and more from his house, and then in 1896, he opened a lumberyard on Park Avenue. Originally delivering lumber by horse and carriage, the business eventually bought one truck, then many.

The lumberyard thrived right from the start, and the fourth generation of the Quackenbush family still operates the business at the same location today. The lumberyard's buildings appear the same as in 1896 and are located between the public library and the building that used to be the old firehouse on Park Avenue. Many of Pascack's earliest buildings were constructed using Quackenbush lumber, and the Quackenbush house and barn still remain as they were on Pascack Road and West Ridge Avenue.

Not all of the houses in the area were made from lumber, however. In the earliest days, there were some log cabins and quite a few houses and a few churches originally built using sandstone or fieldstone, which was quarried locally. A bit later, Italian artisans came to the area and quite a few houses had stone foundations or stone fences.

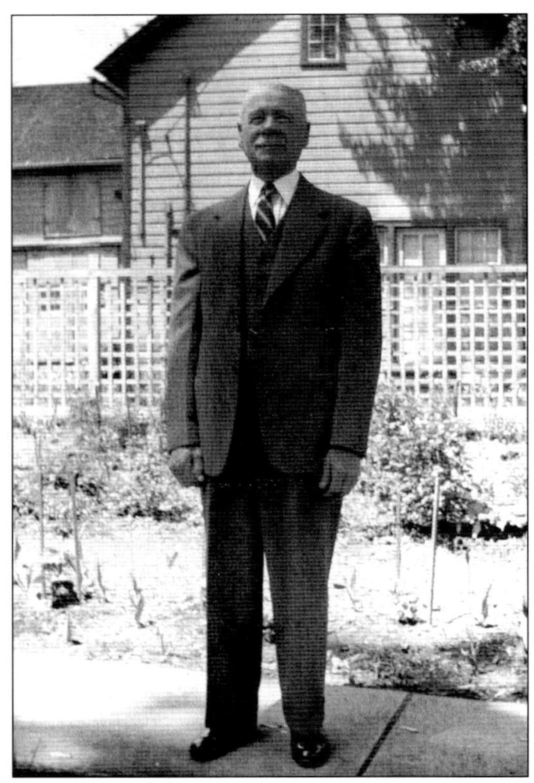

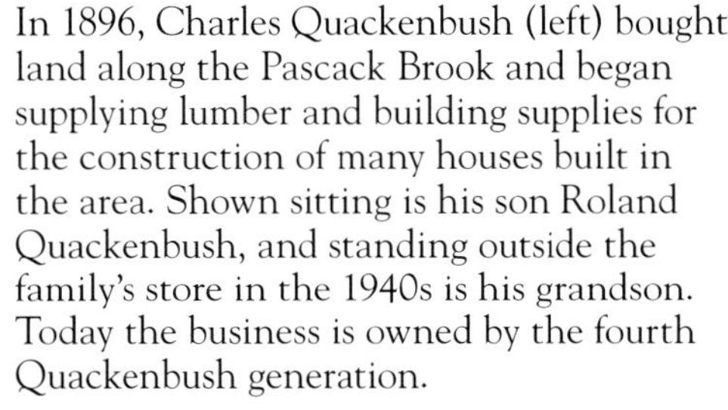

In 1896, Charles Quackenbush (left) bought land along the Pascack Brook and began supplying lumber and building supplies for the construction of many houses built in the area. Shown sitting is his son Roland Quackenbush, and standing outside the family's store in the 1940s is his grandson. Today the business is owned by the fourth Quackenbush generation.

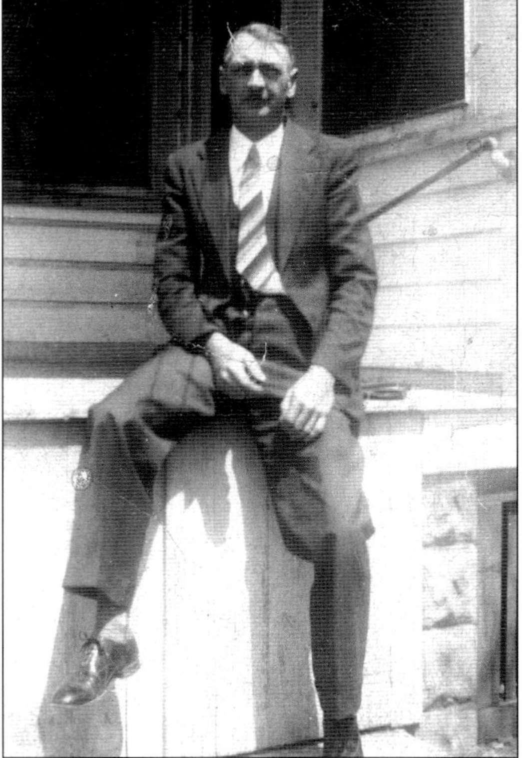

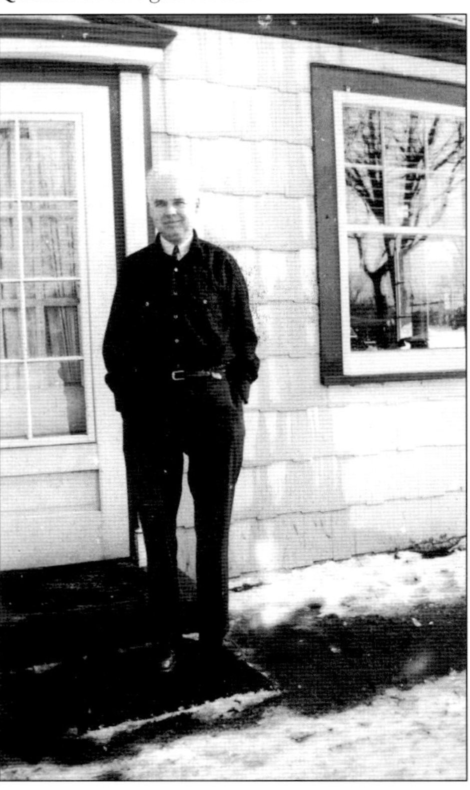

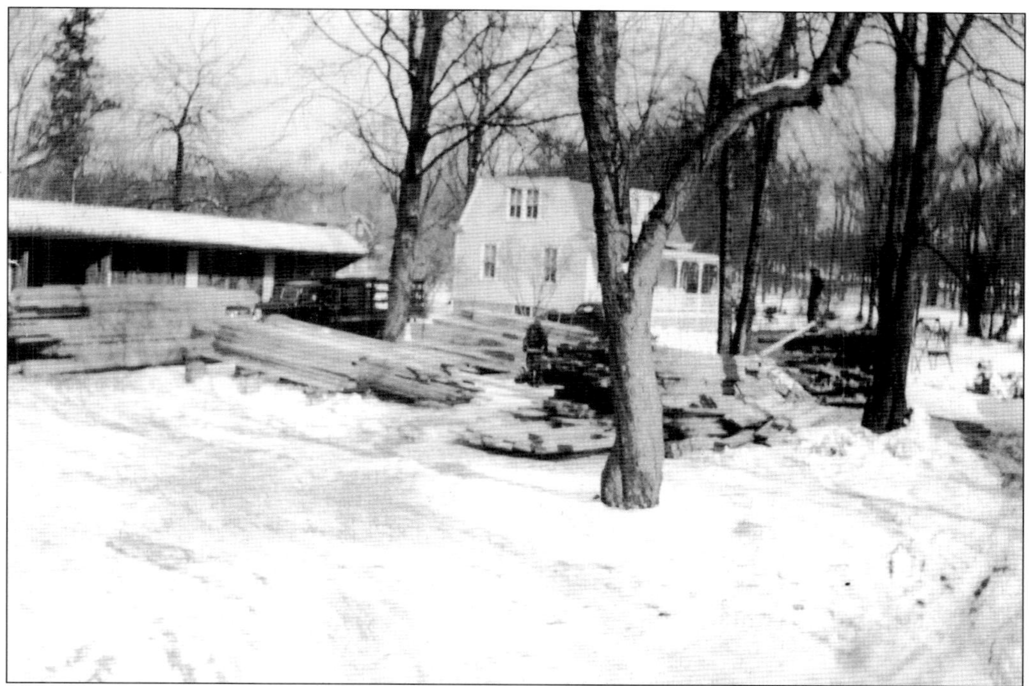

The first structure at the Quackenbush lumberyard was a simple, one-story building (above), which still stands today, across the brook facing the Park Ridge Public Library. As the business grew, a second building was erected for lumber storage.

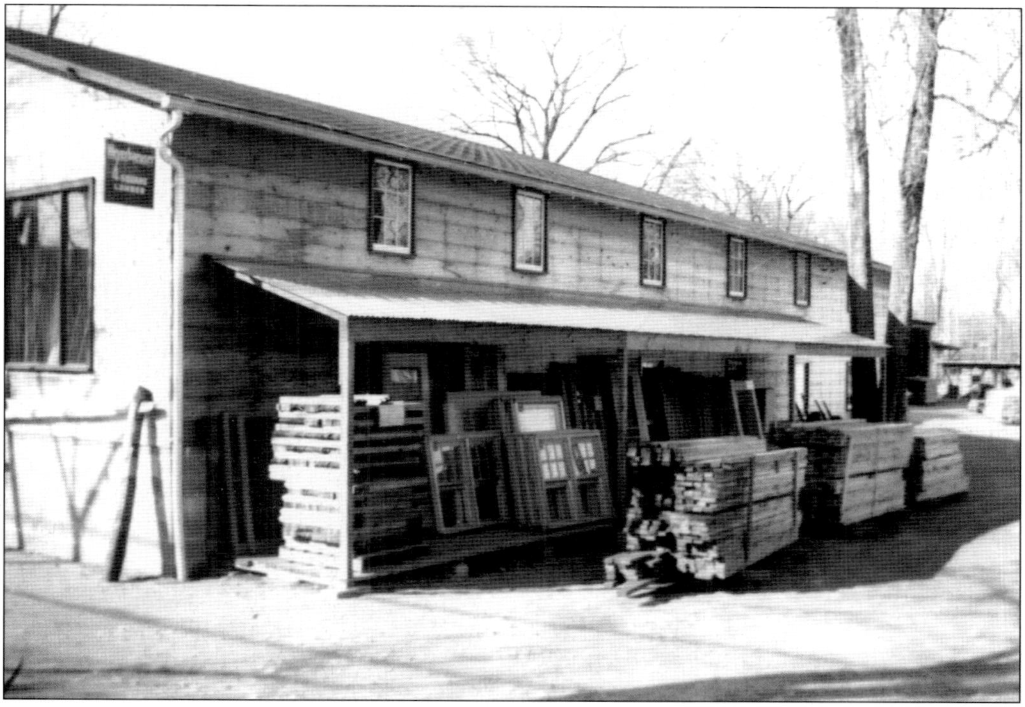

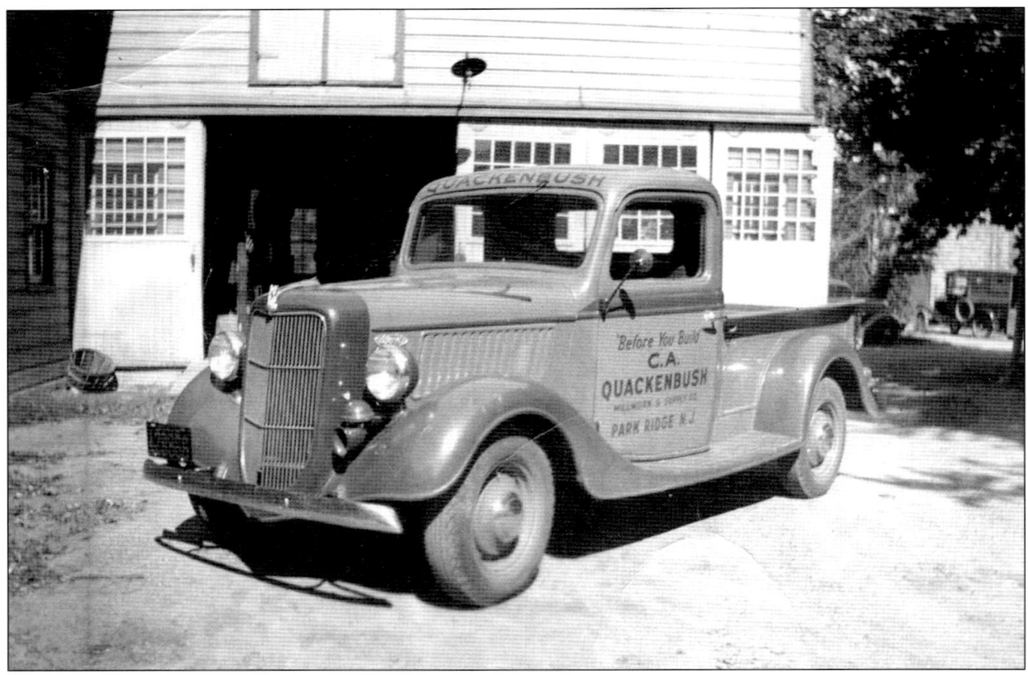


Changes at the lumberyard included a truck or two. The sign on the truck door (above) says, "Before You Build C. A. Quackenbush Millwork & Supply Co." By the time the lumberyard passed to the third generation, the business had grown to have a full fleet of vehicles for delivery of lumber. But the store and building for storage remained the same as they were when the business opened in 1896.

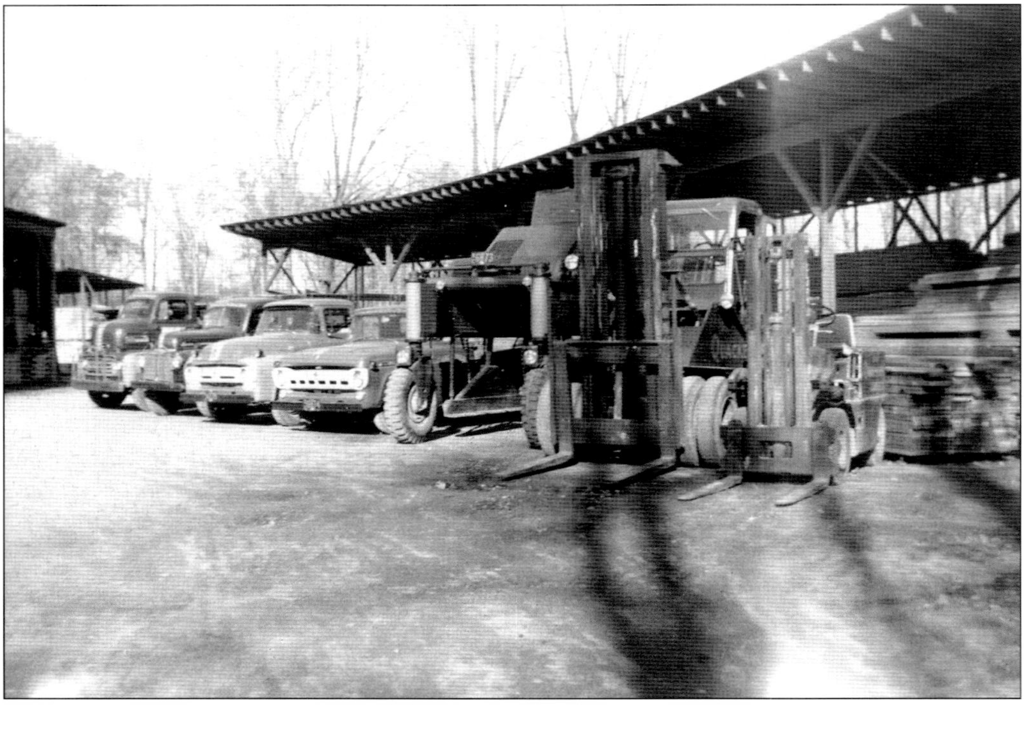

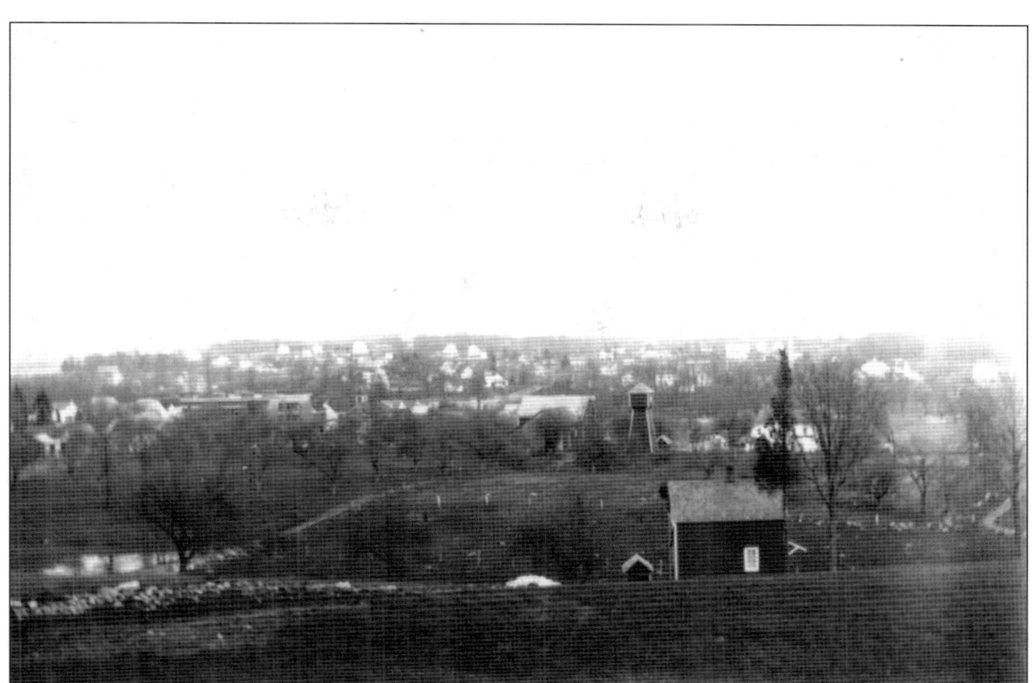

This bird's-eye view shows Park Ridge. The upper photograph was taken back in the days before many houses or buildings existed, and the gentle rolling hills still predominated. The lower photograph was taken later, looking westward.

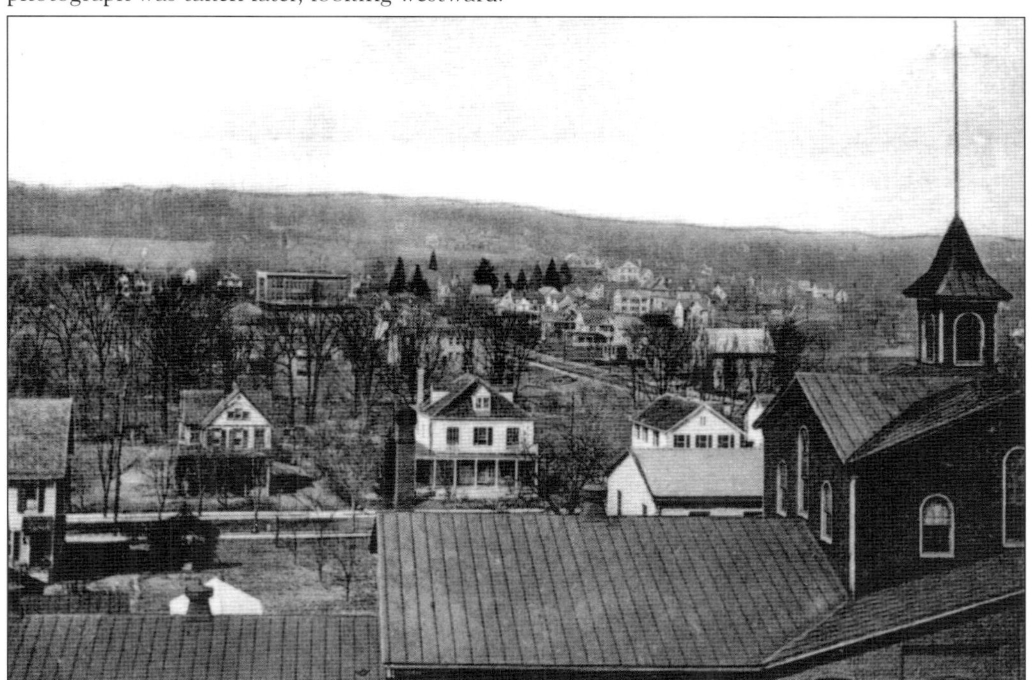

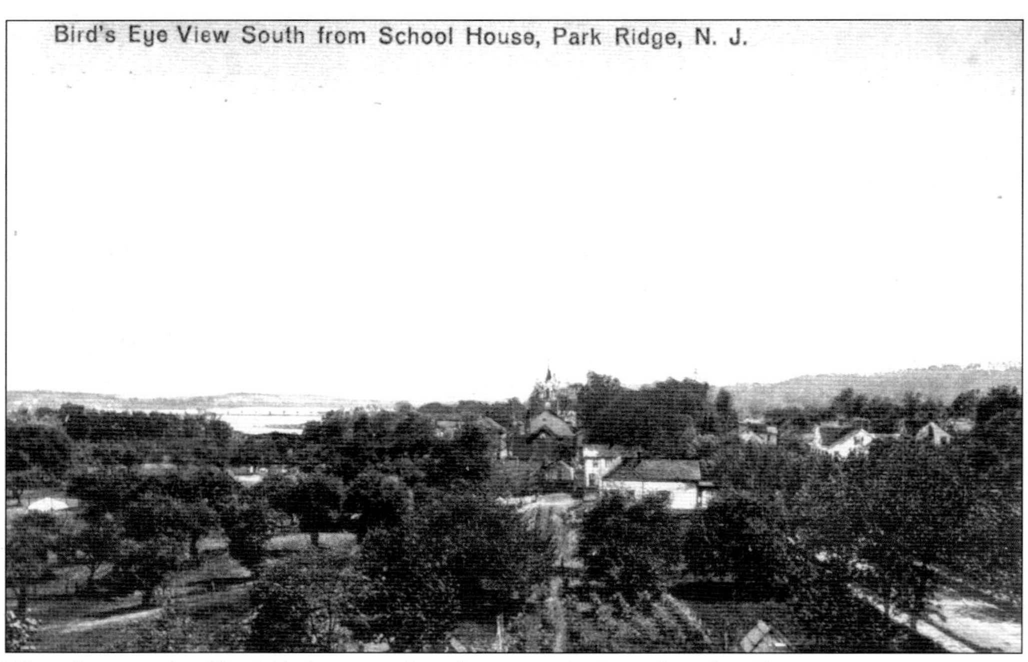


This photograph of Park Ridge was taken facing south from the schoolhouse.

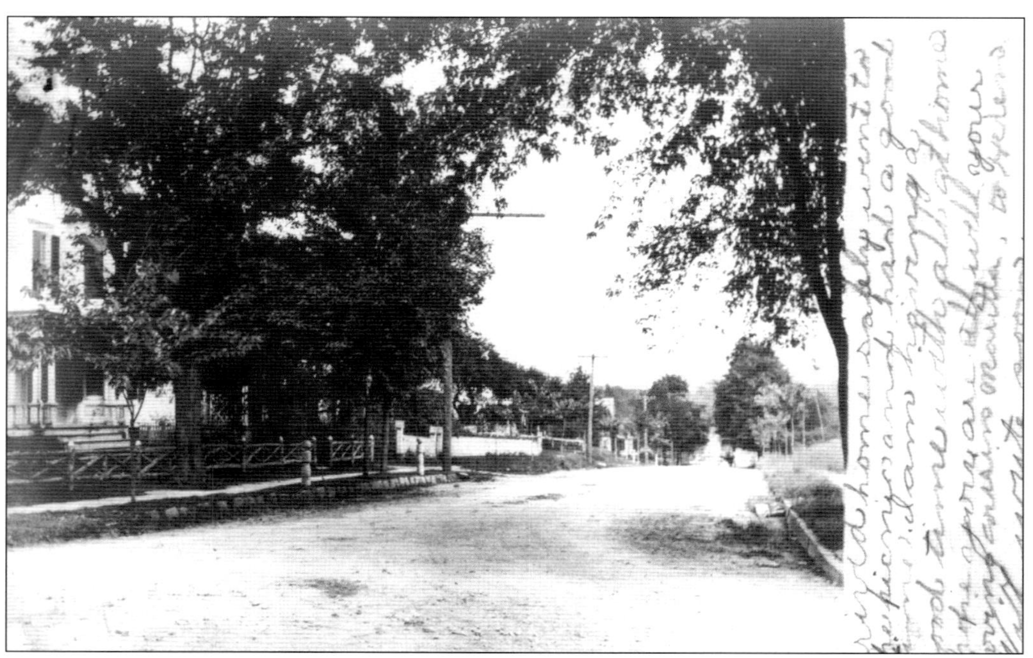

Many of the earliest houses were built in the area of Pascack Road and Park Avenue.

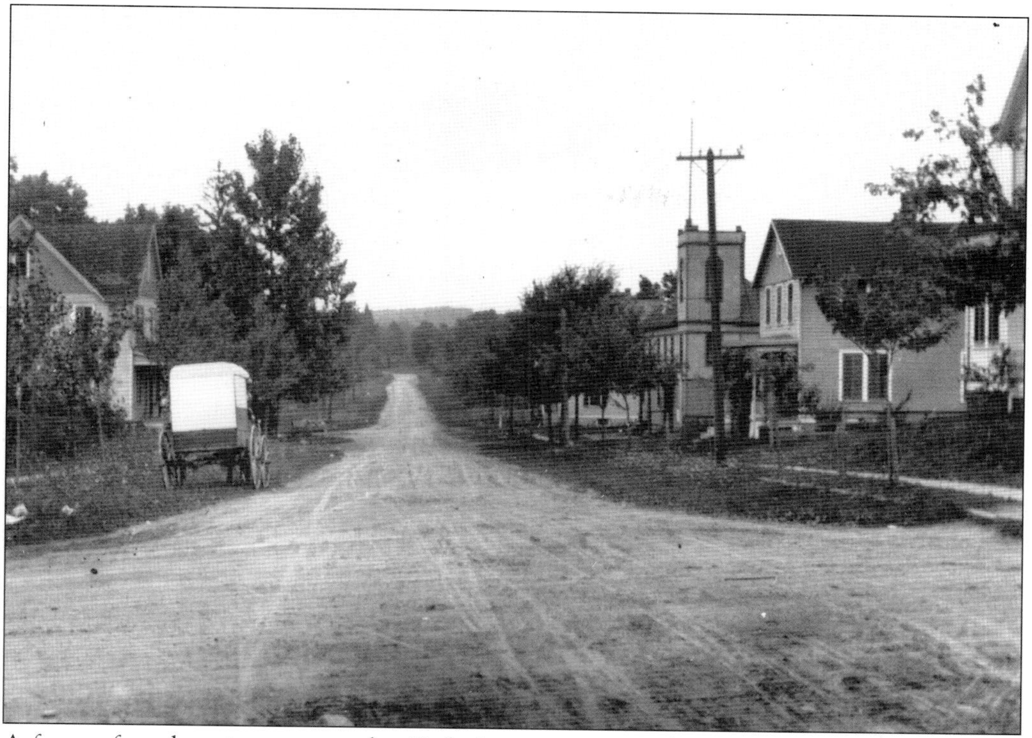

A far cry from how it appears today, Park Avenue is pictured in the late 1800s. A horse and buggy passes down the road. On the right is Forrester Hall, which was the early meeting hall.

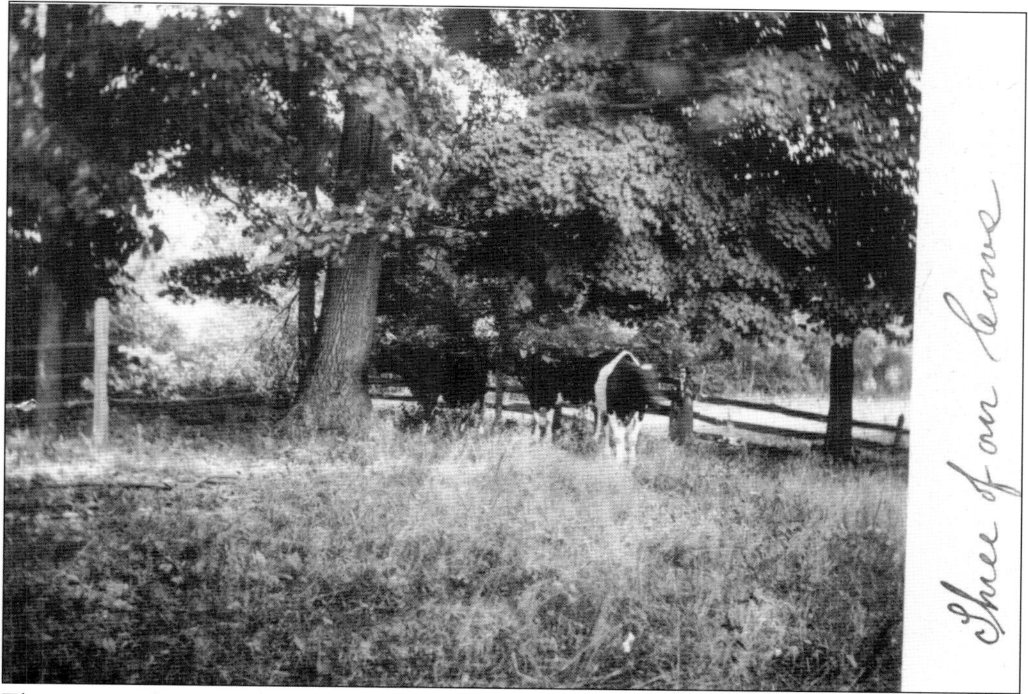


The note on this postcard from Park Ridge reads, "Three of our cows."

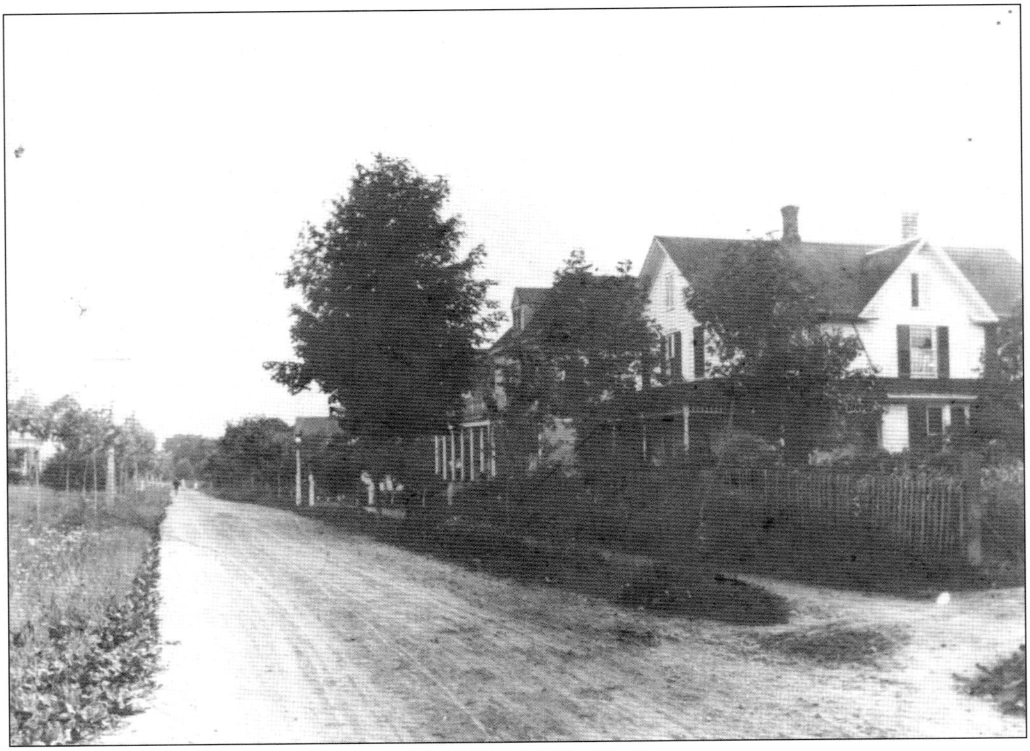

This is a view of Maple Avenue in Park Ridge.

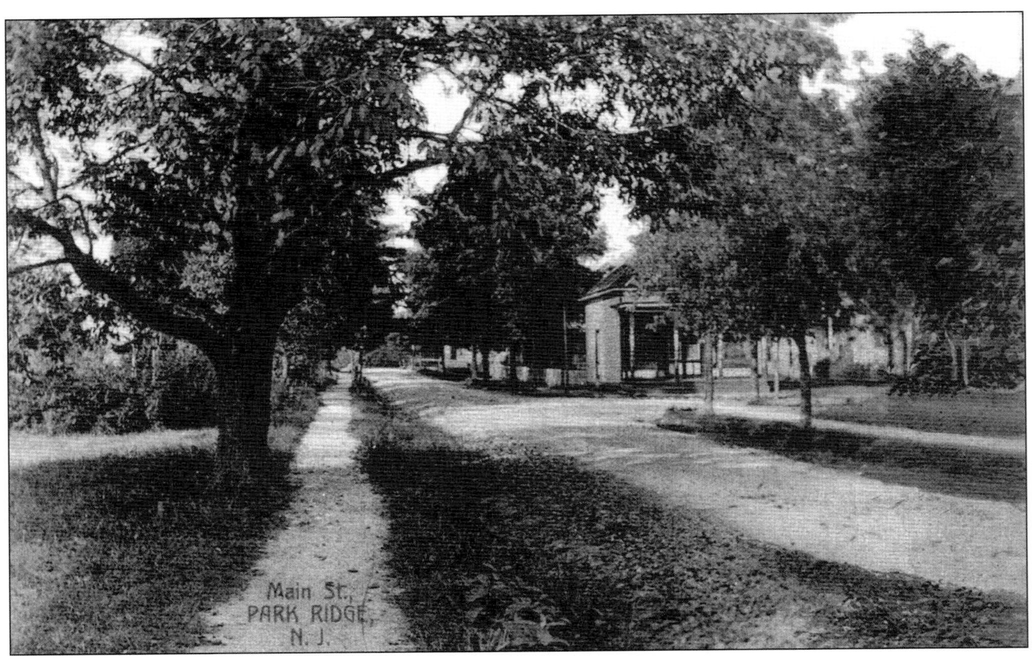


Shown is Main Street in Park Ridge.

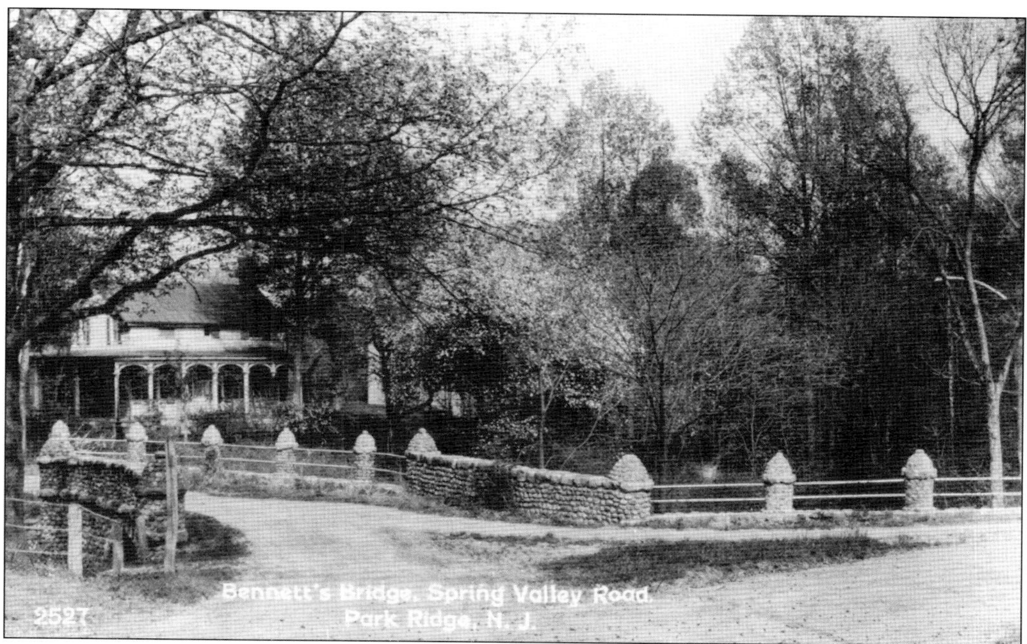


This is Bennett's Bridge on Spring Valley Road in Park Ridge.

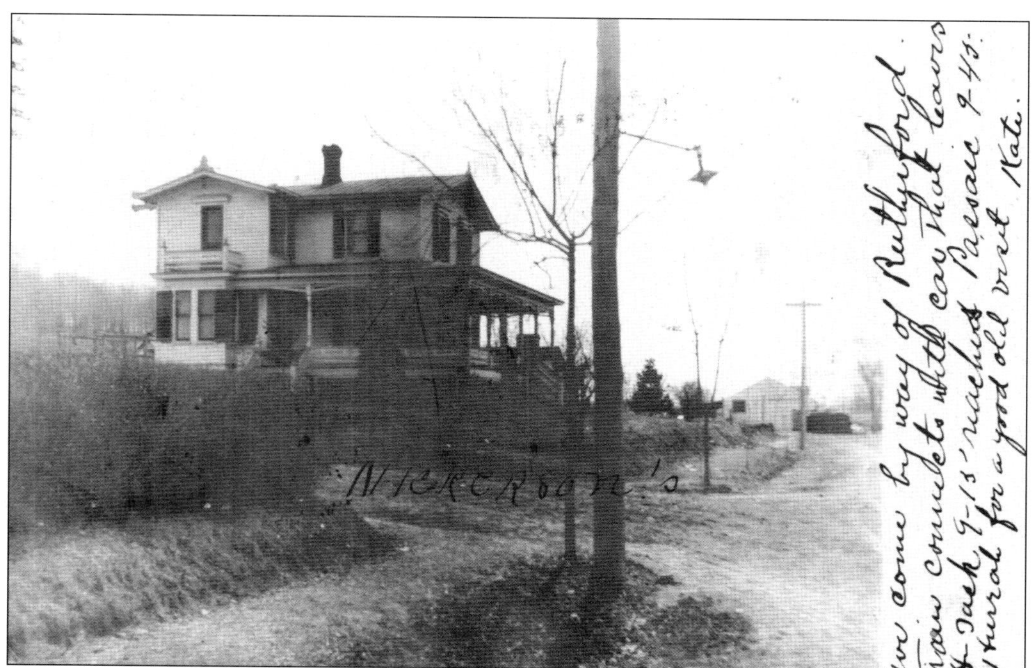


This Park Ridge property is identified as the Nickerson's.

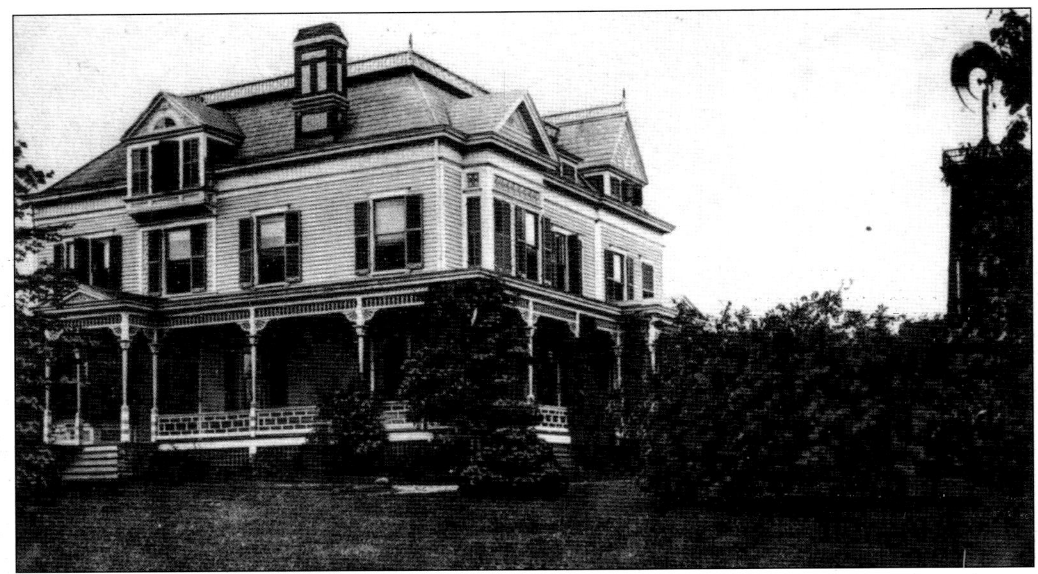

The Leach family was influential in the early days of Park Ridge. Seen here is the Leach residence, which stood on Fremont Avenue. The house was demolished later.

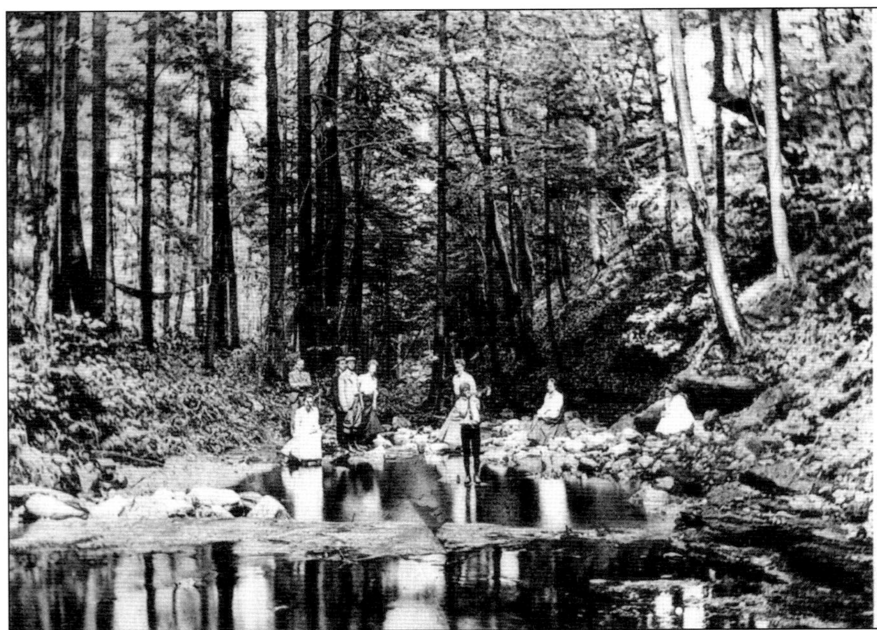


A group of young people enjoy the day at Leach's Glen.

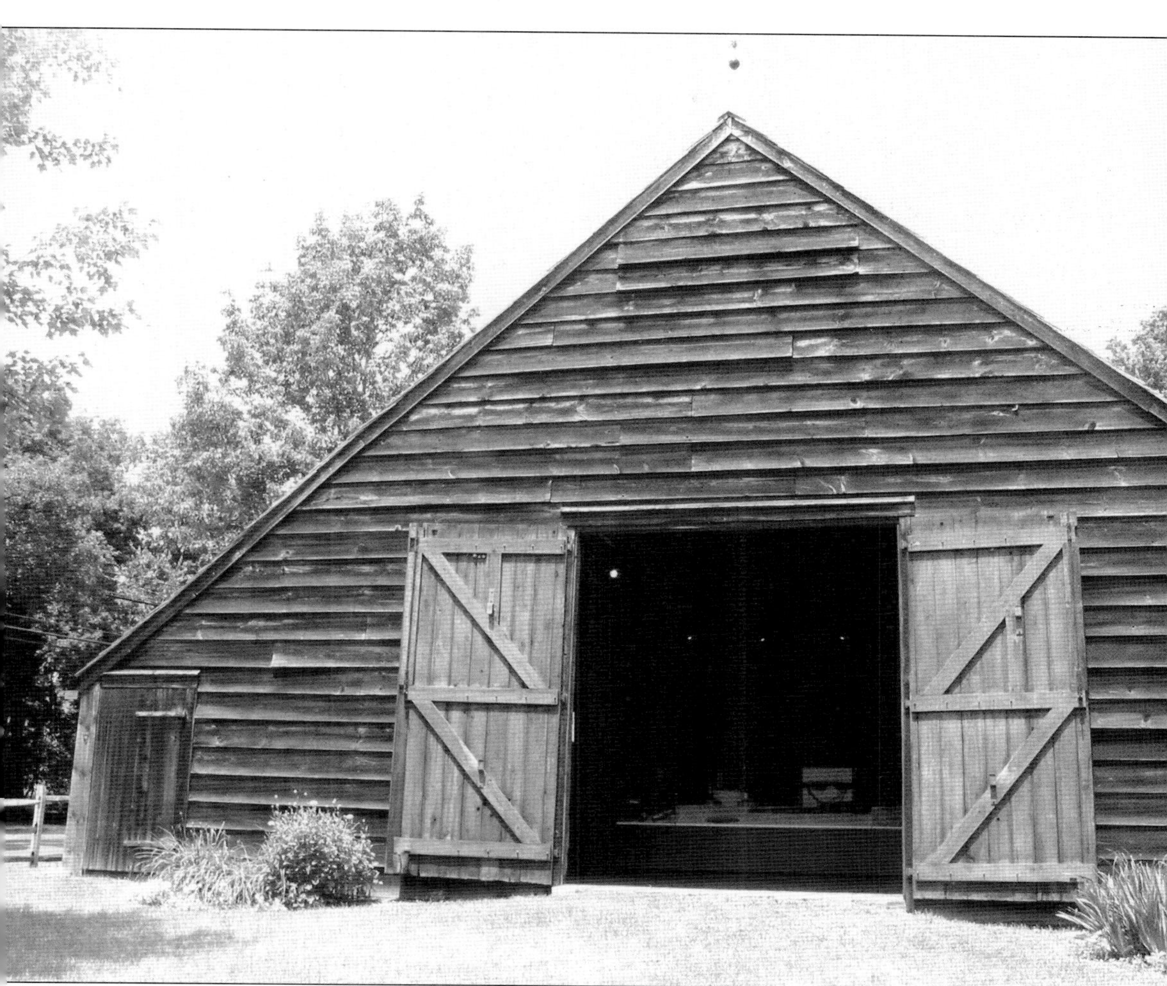

The Wortendyke Barn was built near the Bear's Nest on the 460 acres of land given to Frederick Wortendyke Jr. by his father, who lived in Harrington Park. The barn was built in one day, in typical Dutch style of the time, with long sloping rooflines and large doors. It is one of the few barns of its type still standing today. It is now a museum containing artifacts, photographs, and information about Dutch barns and the history of early settlers. Groups and individuals are welcome to browse, and tours are given. The museum is maintained by Bergen County and is listed in the State and National Registers of Historic Places.

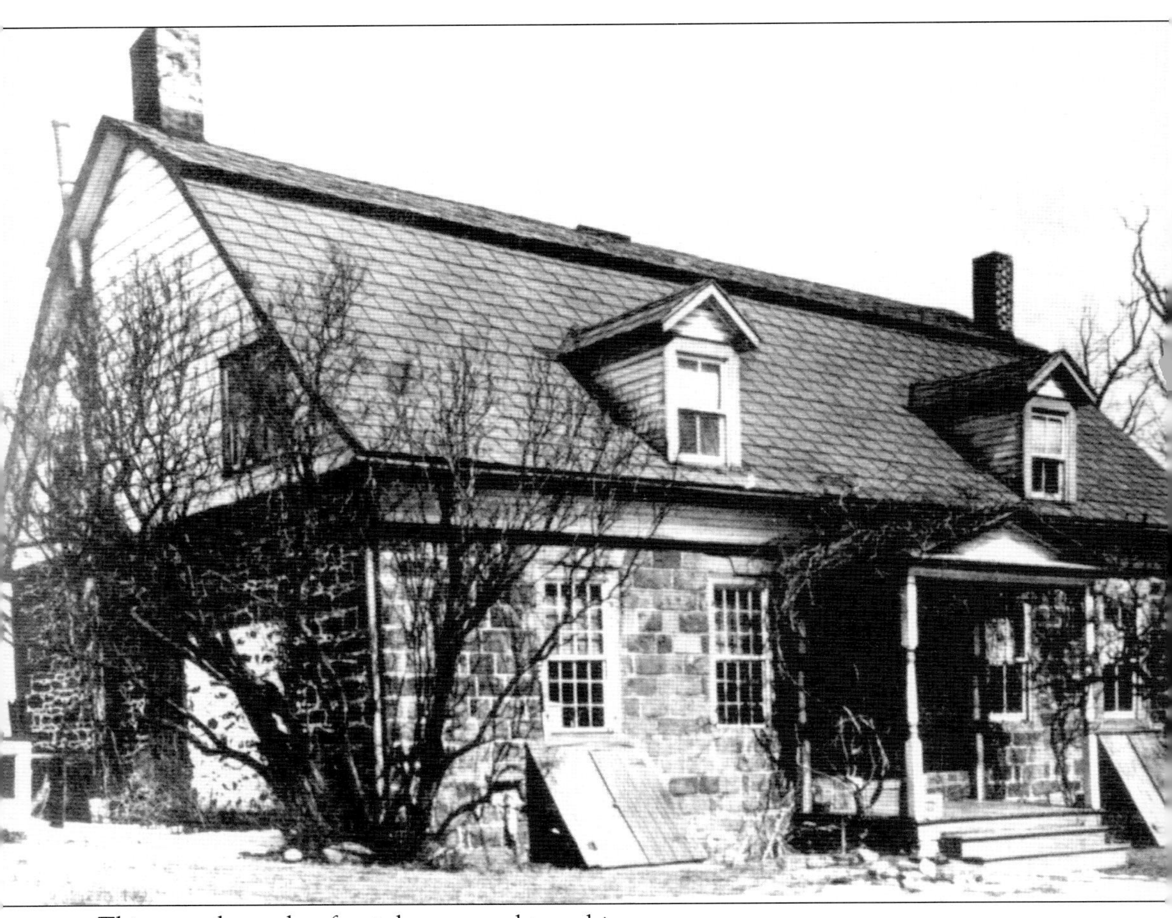

This stone house has front dormers and two chimneys.

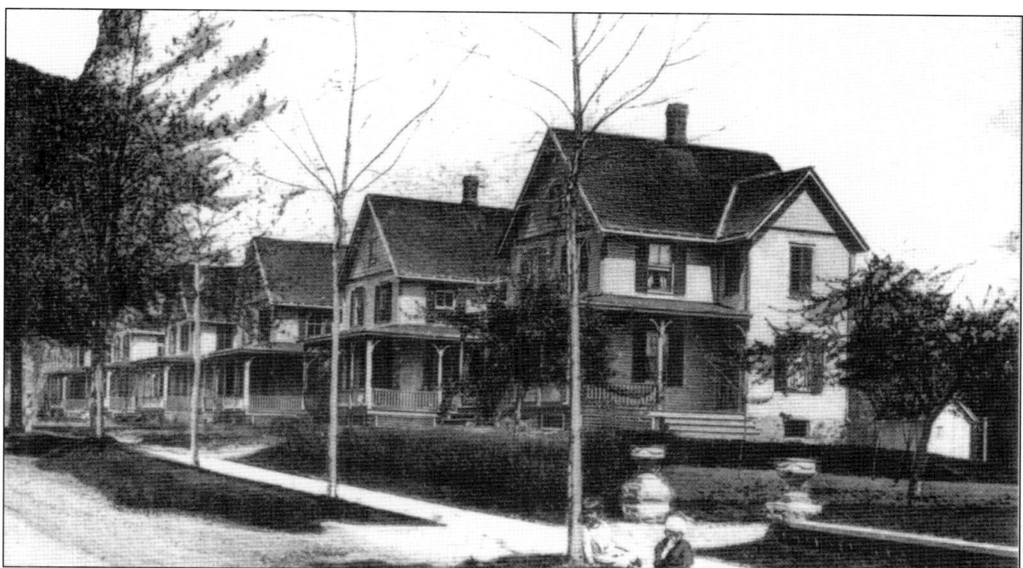

These houses are along Ridge Avenue in an area called Riley's Ridge. They were constructed by a father for his family members as they got married and had children. The houses still stand here today.

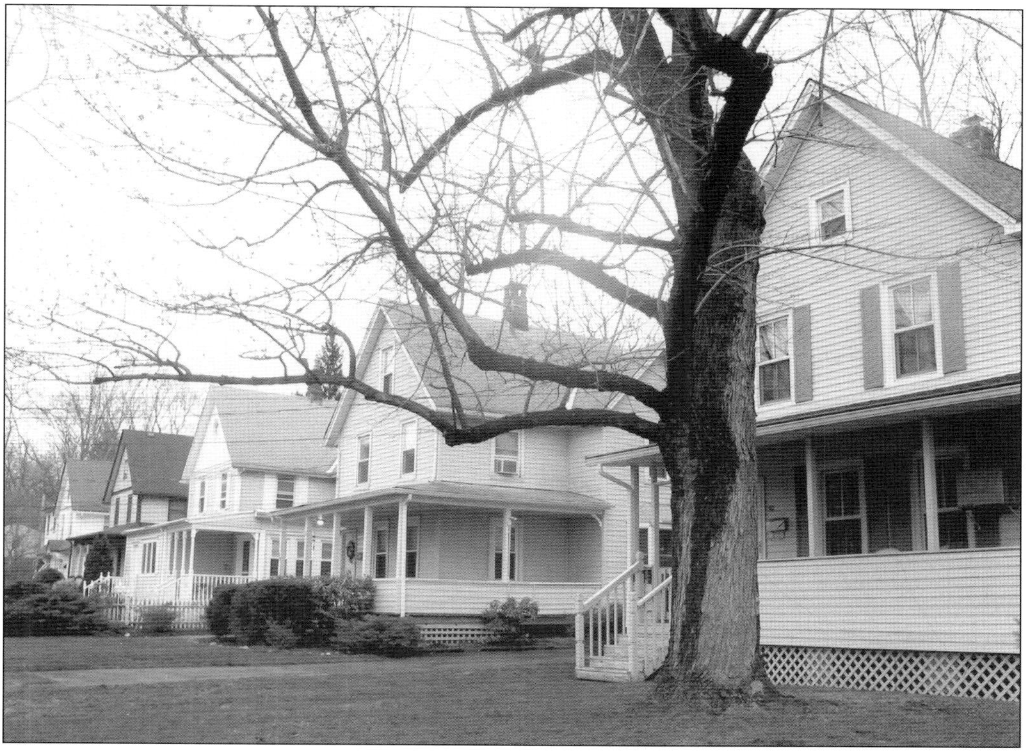

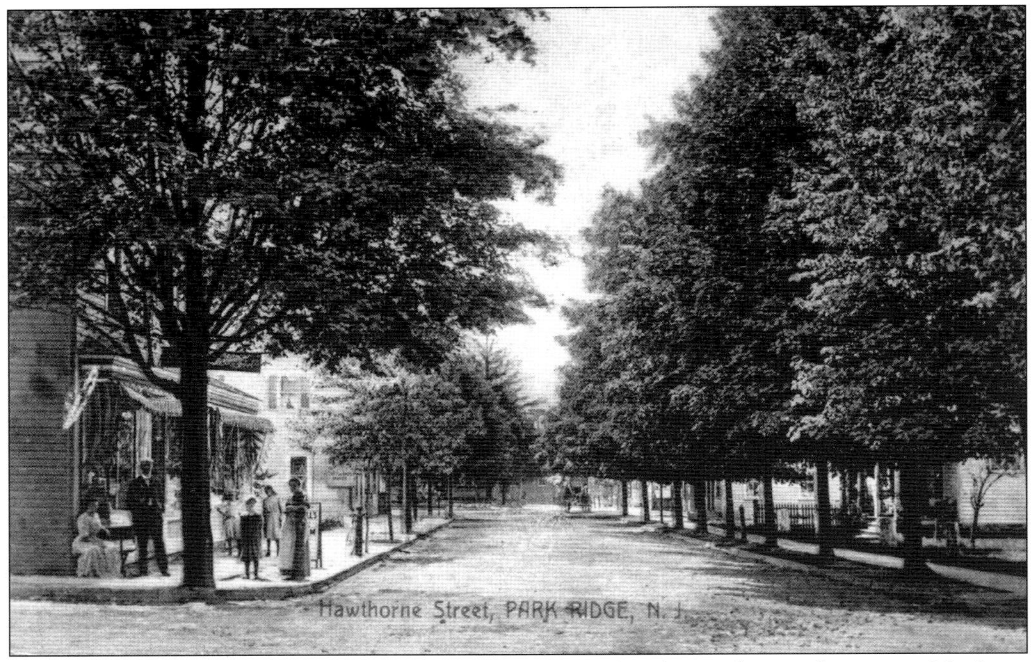


These are early views of Hawthorne Street. One shows a family standing at the corner. Hitching posts can be seen along the street. In the other, a boy stands in the street, which is still a dirt road, although there are curbs and sidewalks. The store at the left advertises Coca-Cola and has a sign that says, "Papers for sale here." A horse-drawn buggy can be seen in the distance. The scenes date from the early 1900s.

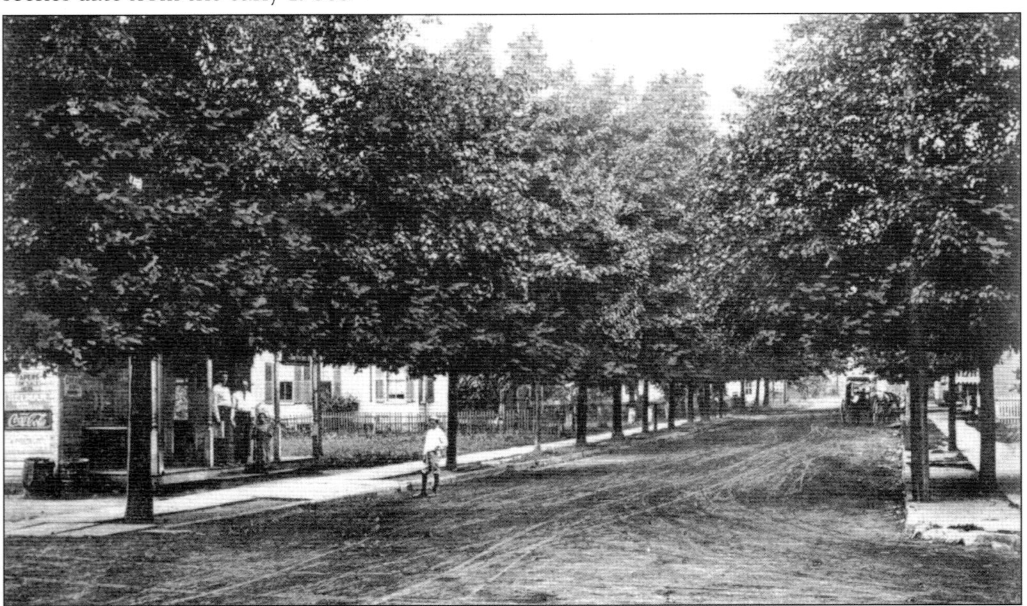

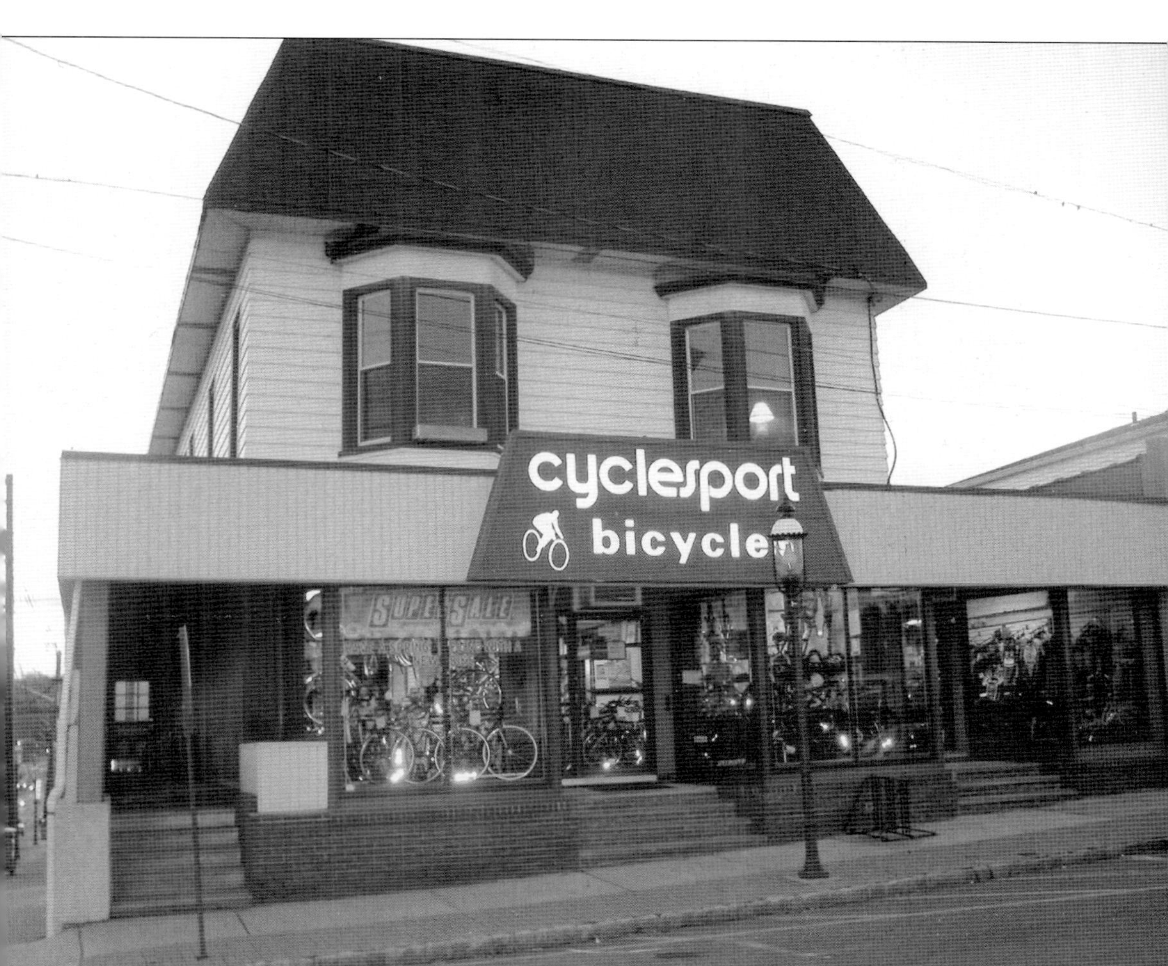


Today the former post office is the home of a bicycle shop. Cyclesport started a Park Ridge summer tradition of having cyclists come from across the country and beyond to participate in a bicycle race, known for an especially tough climb up Highland Street.

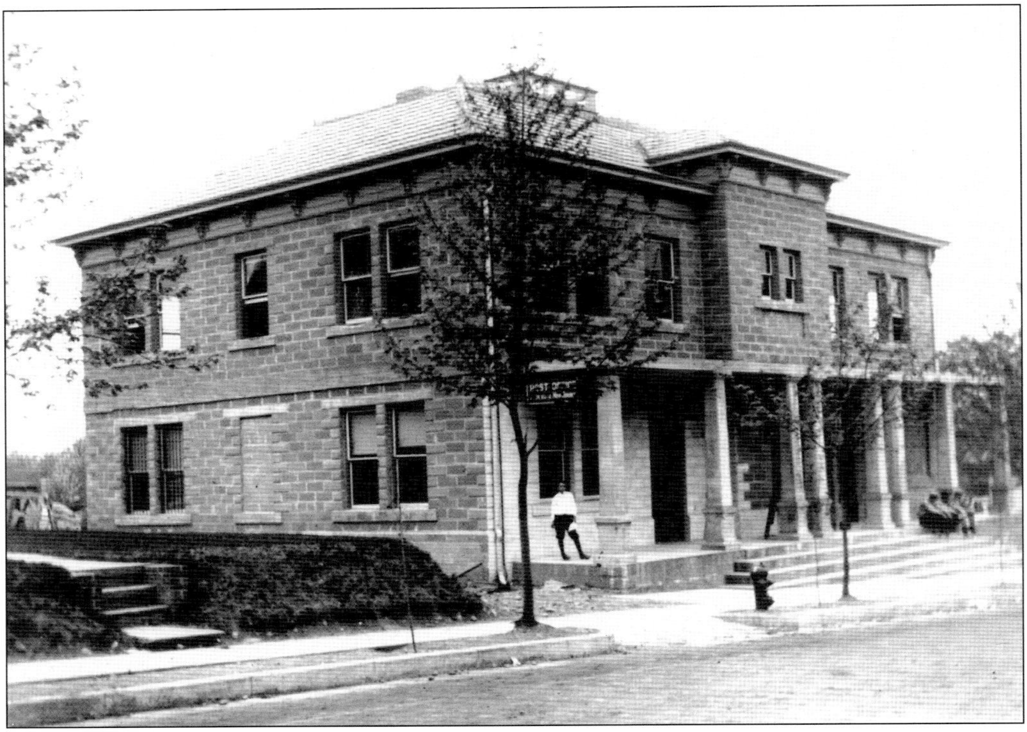

Over the years, the post office has been in several different buildings including this large stone structure on Park Avenue. On the left was the old post office, and on the right was Mitchell's Drugstore. Today it is Krell's Lighting.

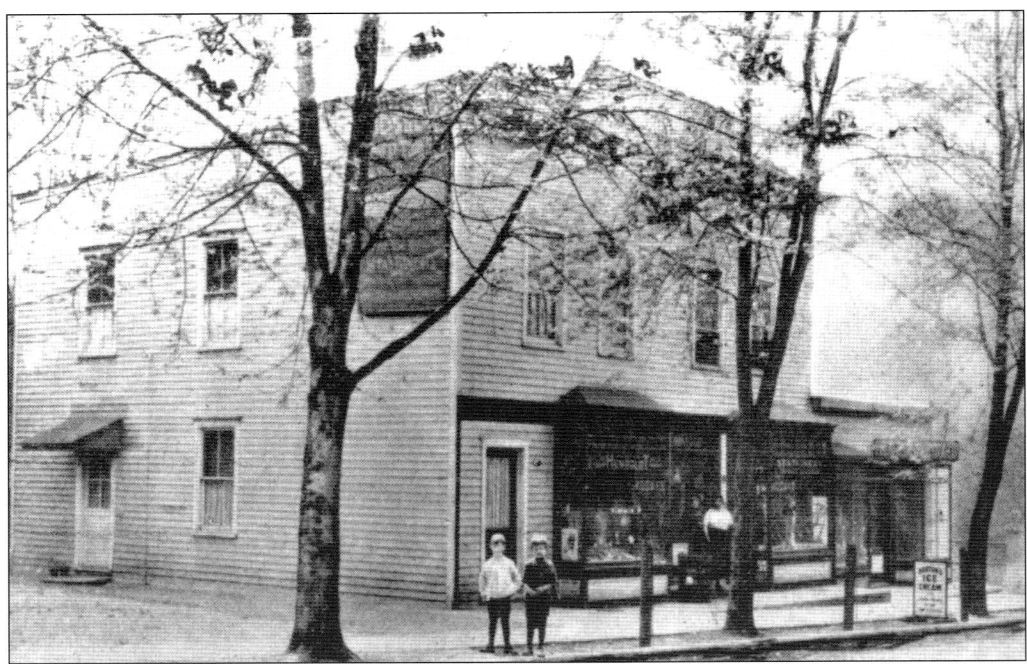


This downtown store sold cigars, stationery, and ice cream, among other items. It was later known as Julie's and is now Cash's Stationery.

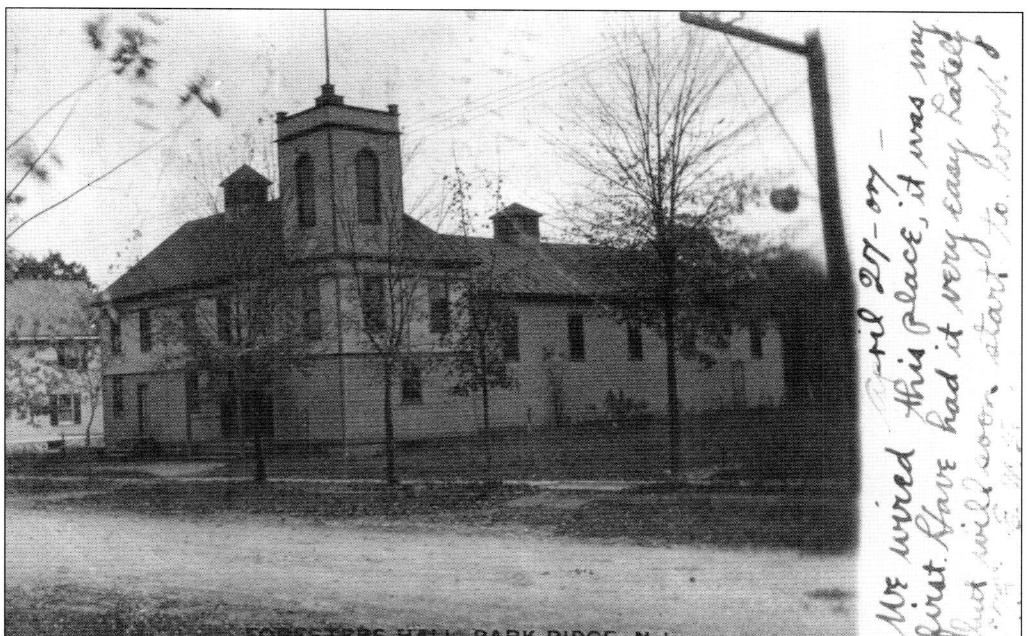


Shown is Forrester Hall on Park Avenue. Written on April 27, 1907, the postcard informs the writer's family that he "wired" the place, meaning he was one of the workers who brought electricity to the town hall.

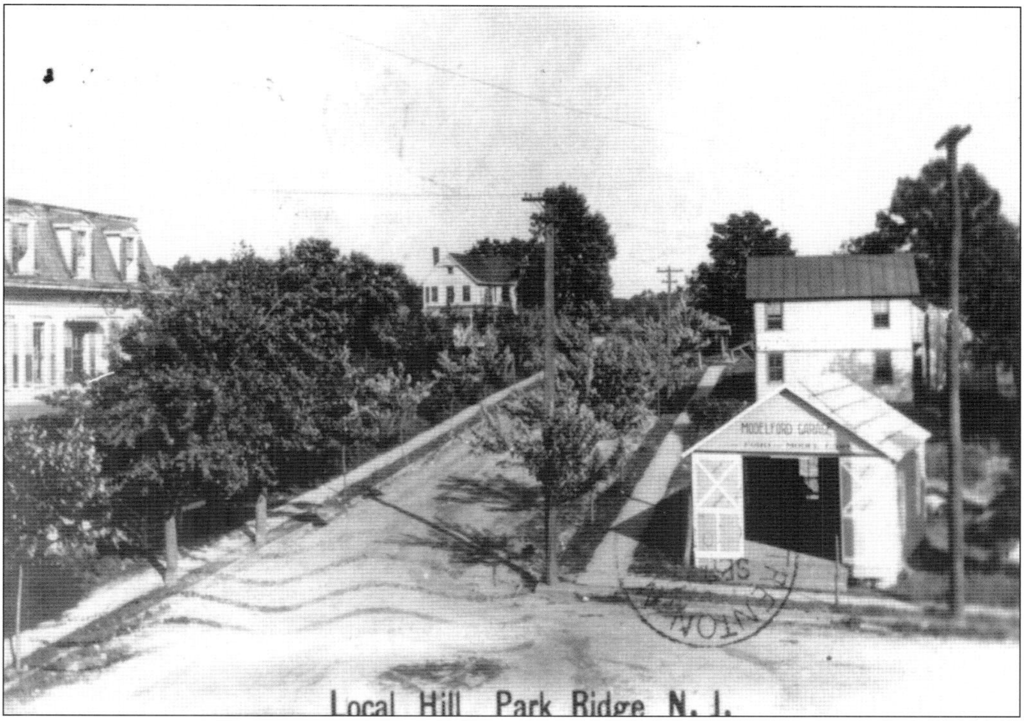

Local Hill Park Ridge N. J.

The first newspaper, the *Local*, was published in this area, which was known as Local Hill. The building on the right bears the sign "Model Ford Garage."

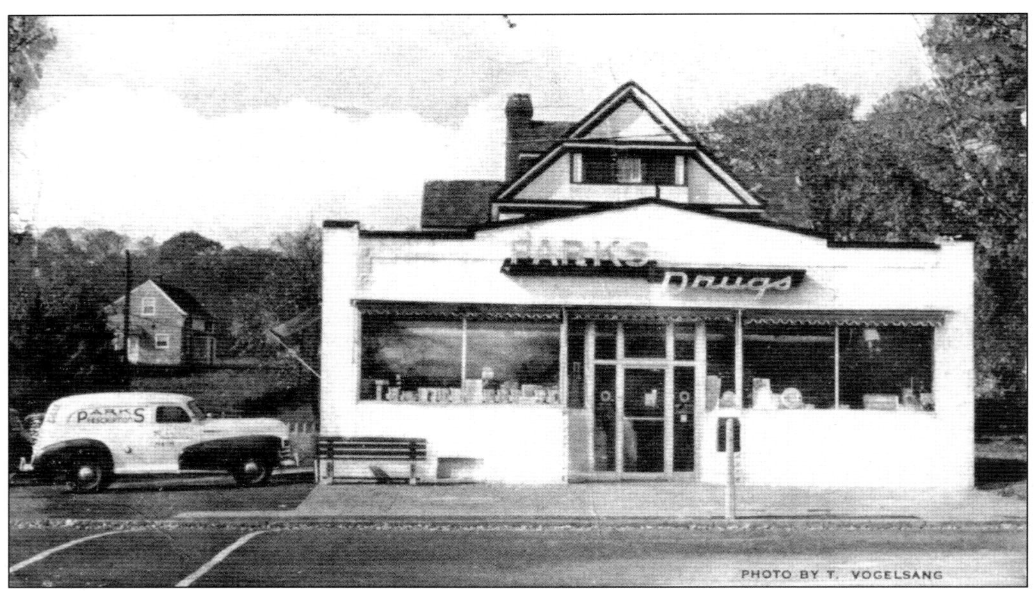


Parks Drugs was located at 102 Pascack Road, opposite the high school. The drugstore had a soda fountain and booths, a telephone number of 6-1199, and a delivery truck.

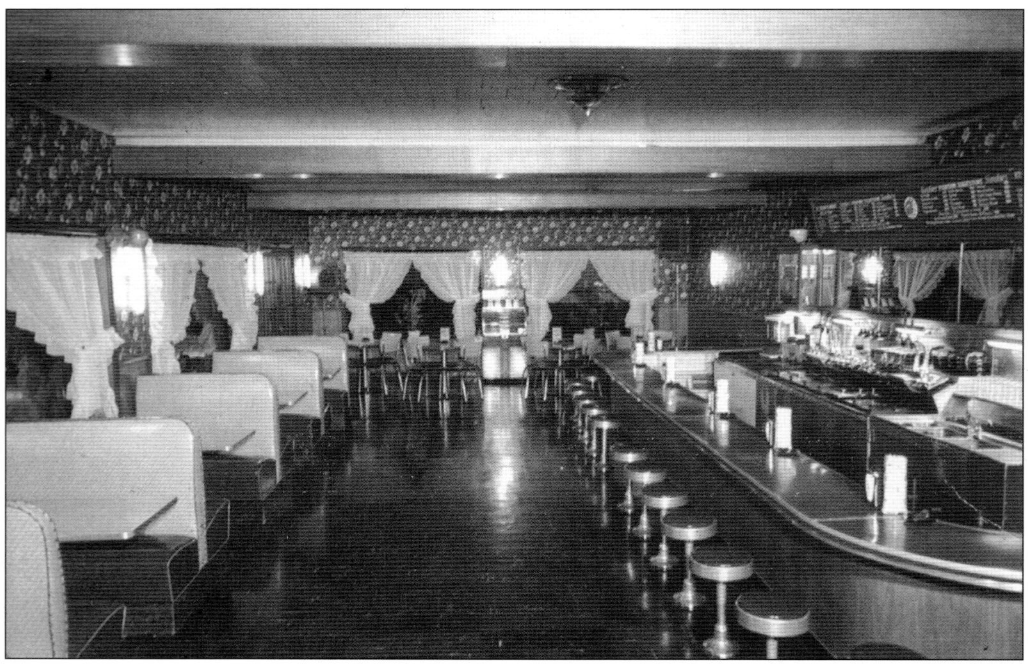

This photograph shows the interior of Huffs Ice Cream Bar, where many Park Ridge residents enjoyed ice cream or other refreshments.

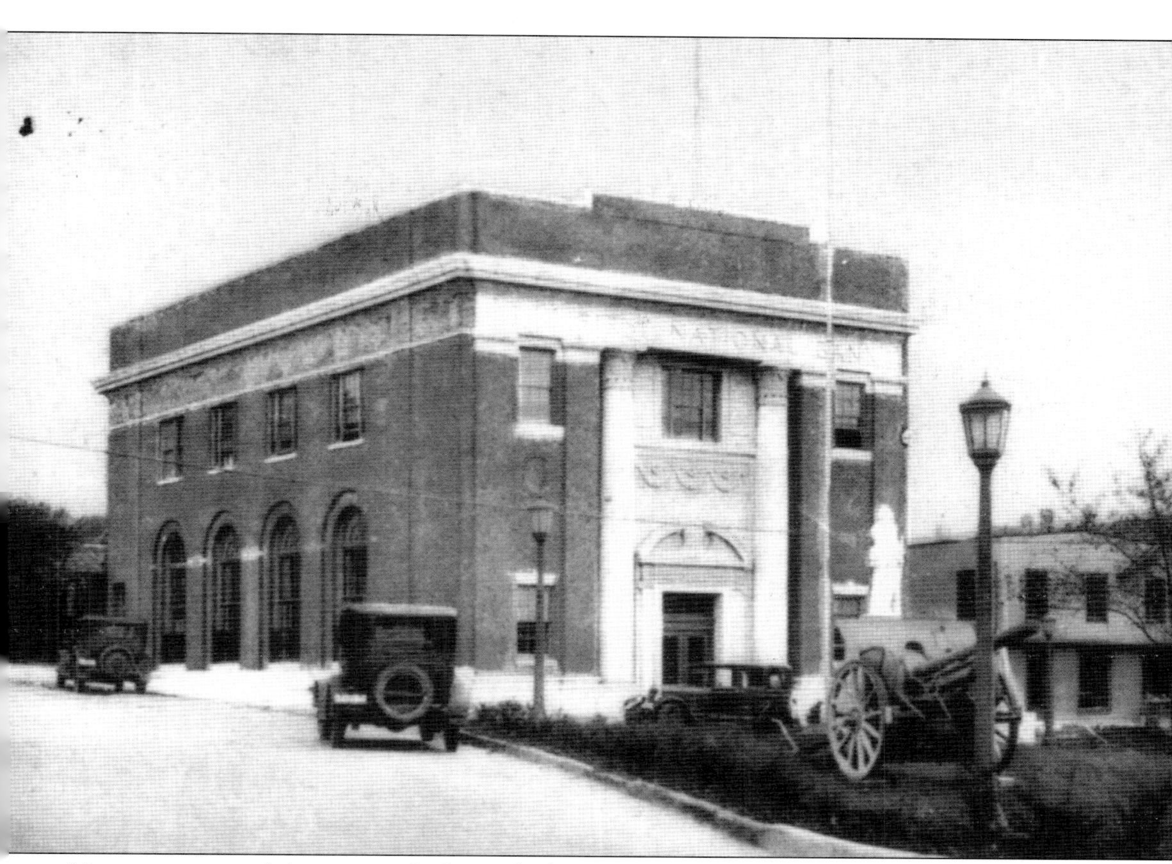


Not many automobiles were parked outside the First National Bank on this day in the 1900s.

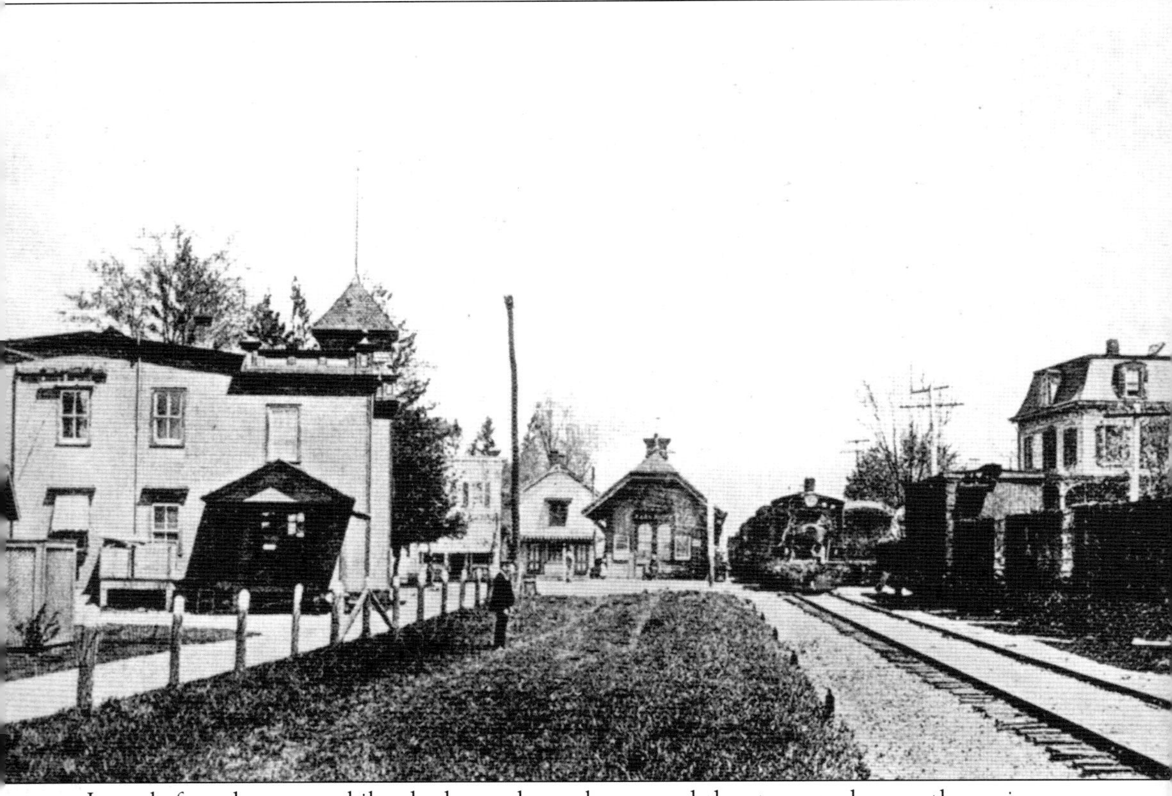

Long before the automobile, the horse-drawn buggy and the stagecoach were the main means of transportation to Park Ridge. Then, beginning in 1871, the railroad passed right through the borough—without stopping. It was not until after residents signed a petition agreeing to build a depot that the train agreed to stop in Park Ridge.

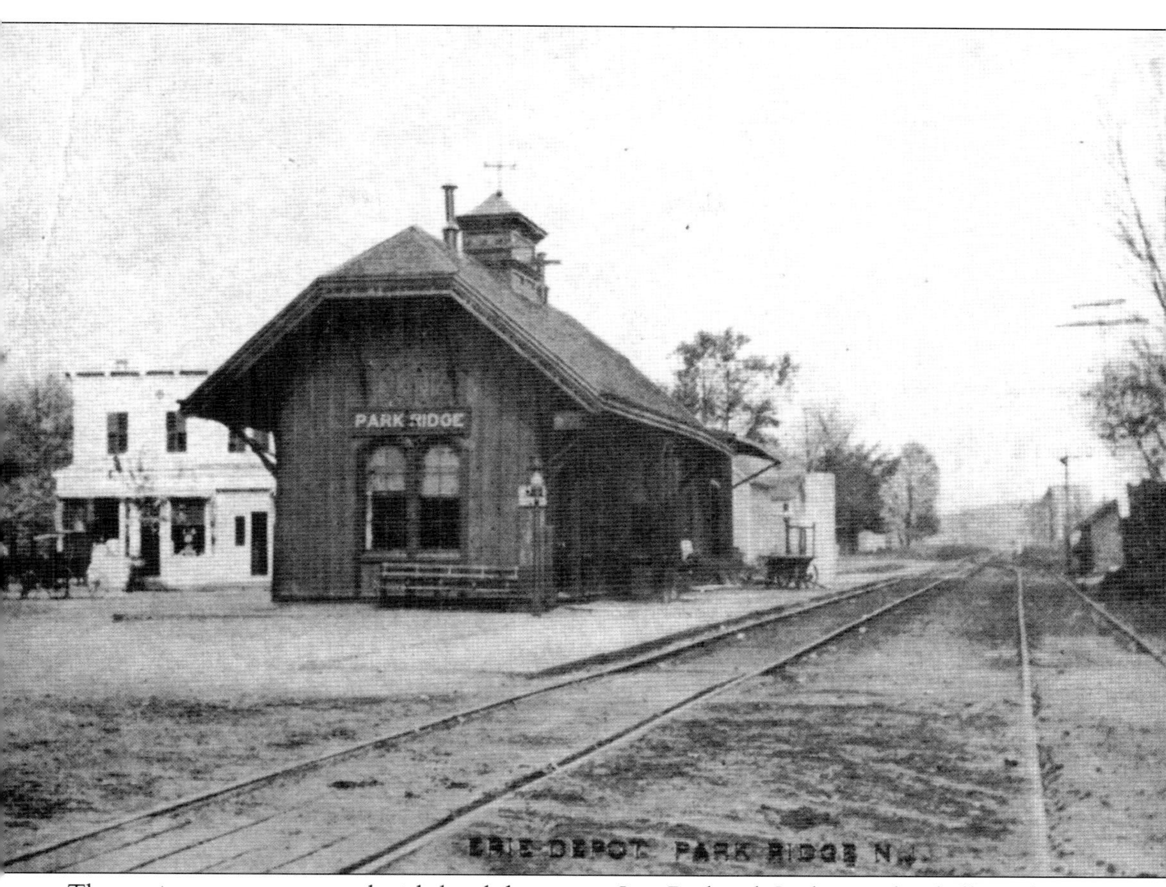


The station was constructed with local donations. It is Railroad Gothic, with a balloon frame and windows shaped in similar fashion to the line of the roof.

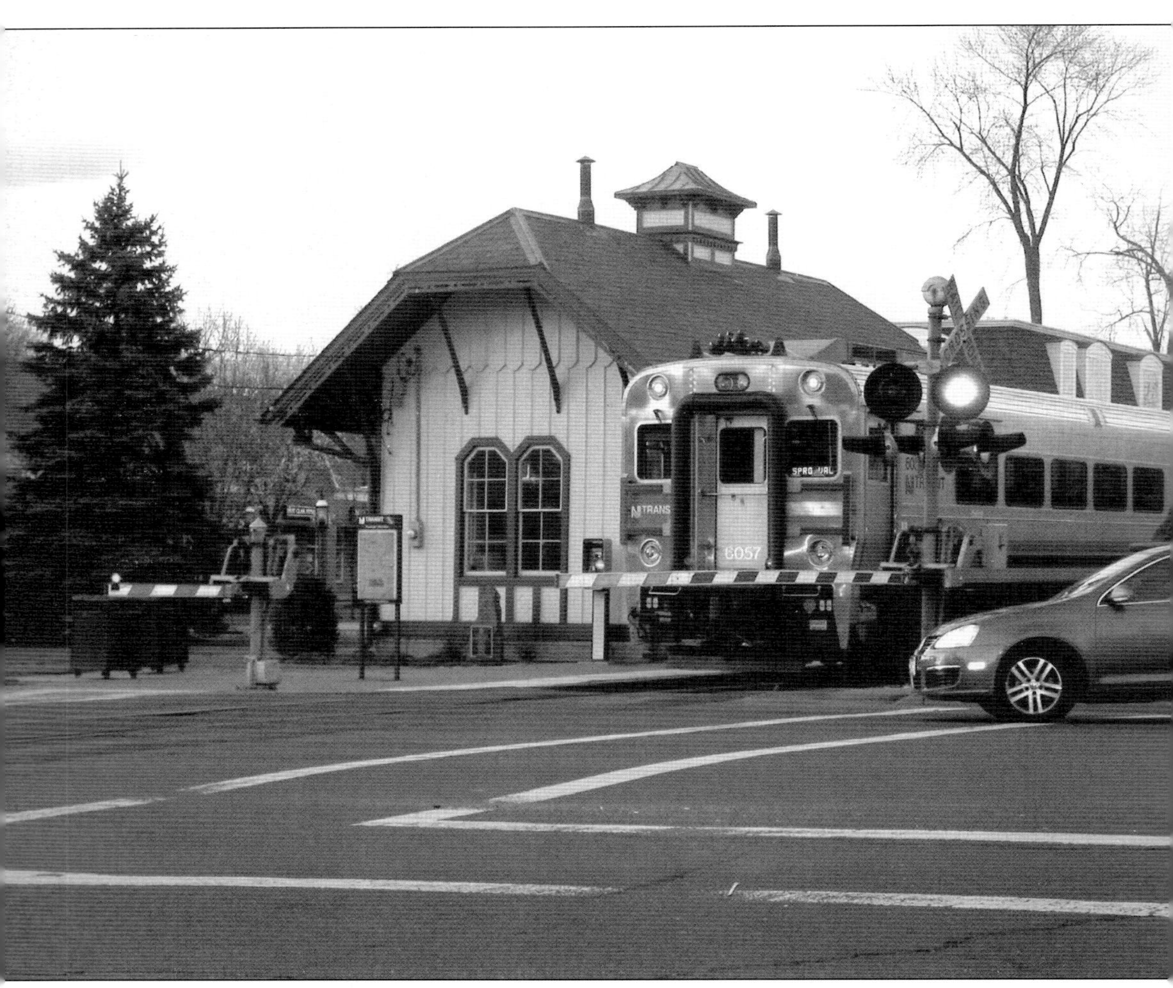


The modern-day train station area does not look much different from how it appeared 100 years ago. In a large undertaking, volunteers restored the station to its original look, keeping the same colors and same charm. Today commuters wait in front of the same station house at Depot Square, but on the track is an N Transit, No. 6057, rather than the Erie locomotives of yesterday.

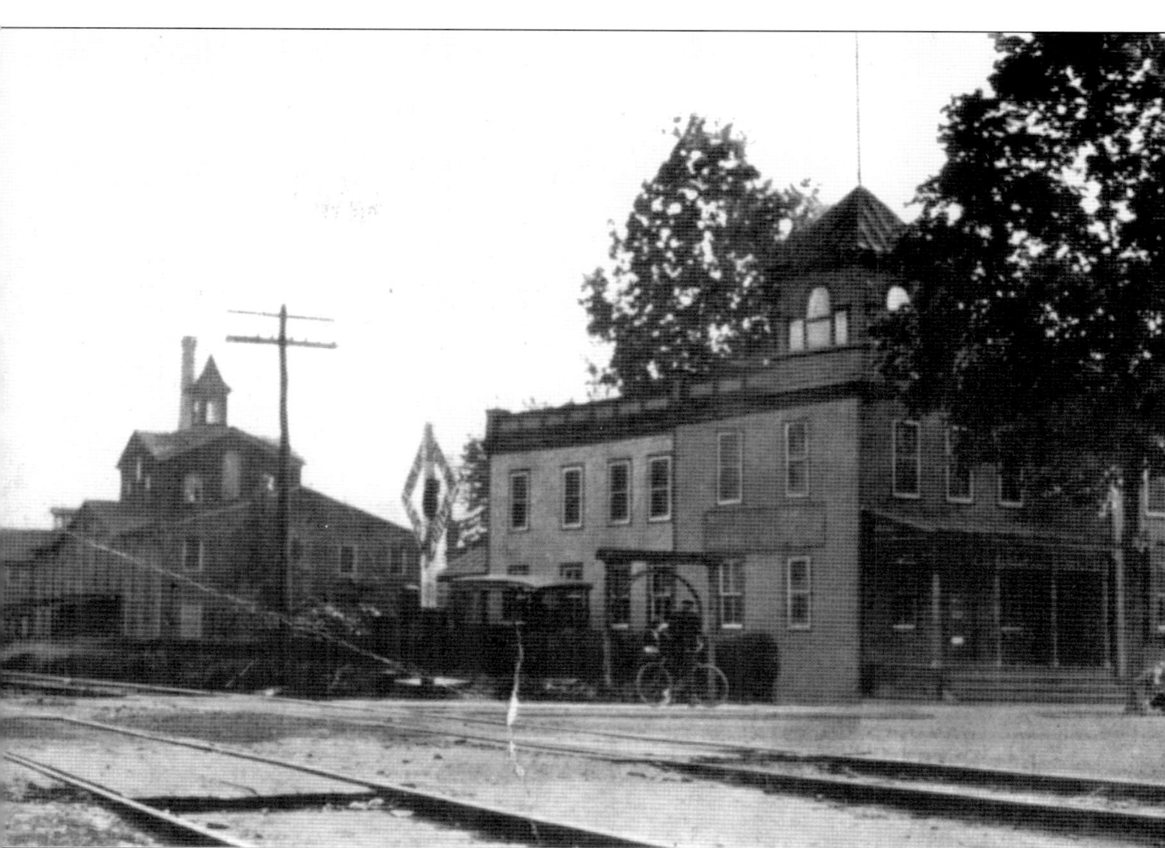

In this early scene, the sign at the railroad crossing says, "Look out for the locomotive."

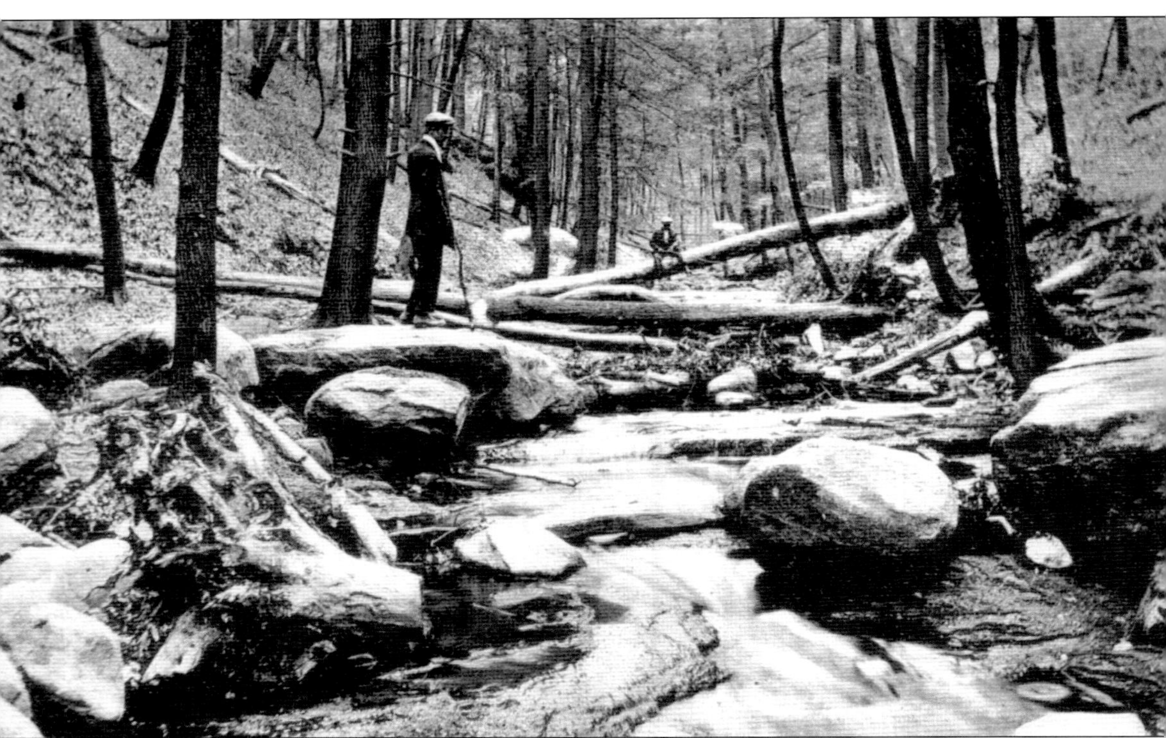

The area began to grow in population, and vacationers came, especially after the railroad arrived. Known for rest and relaxation, Park Ridge offered wooded areas like Atkin's Glen.

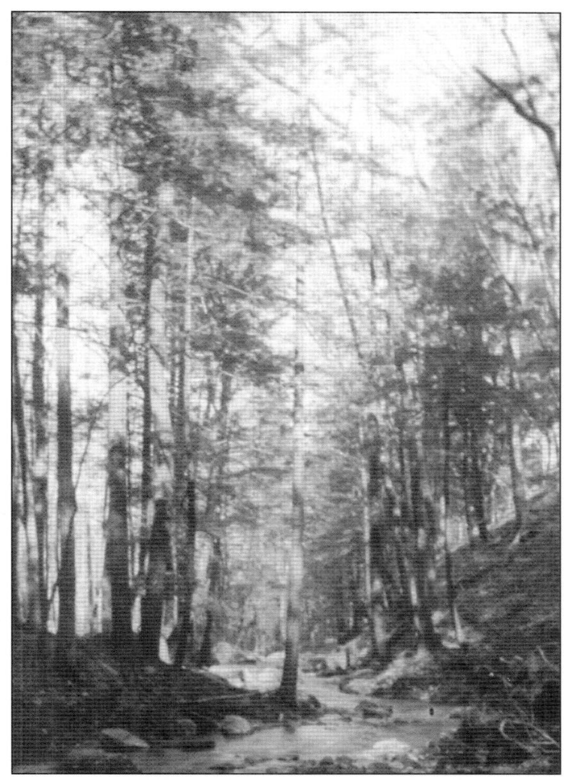

The glen was a peaceful and refreshing place to visit.

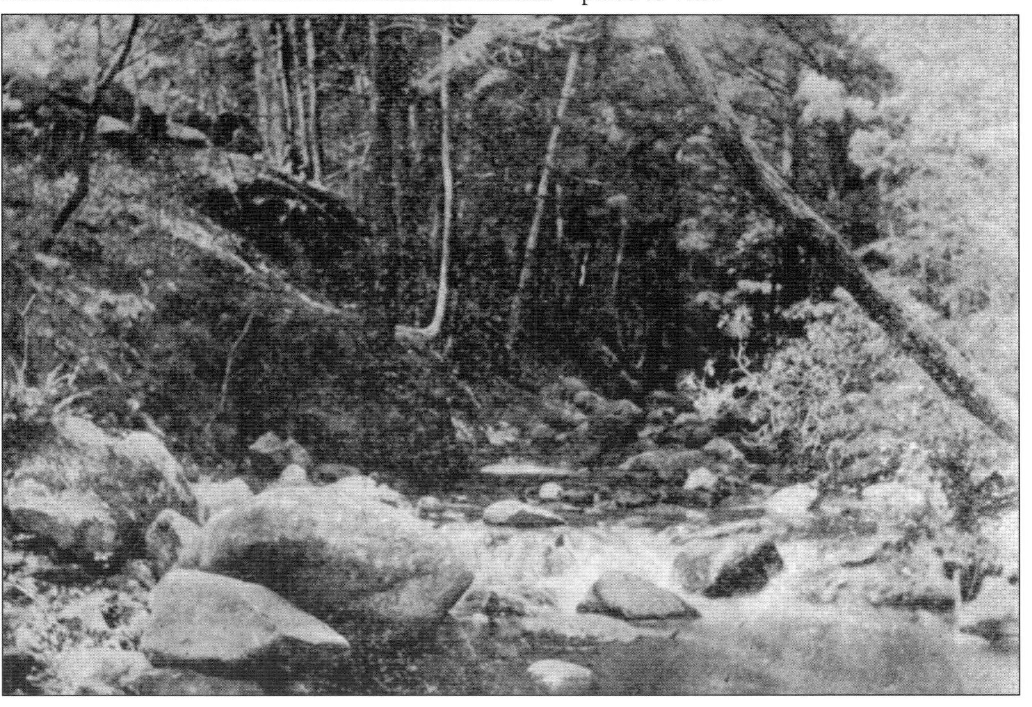

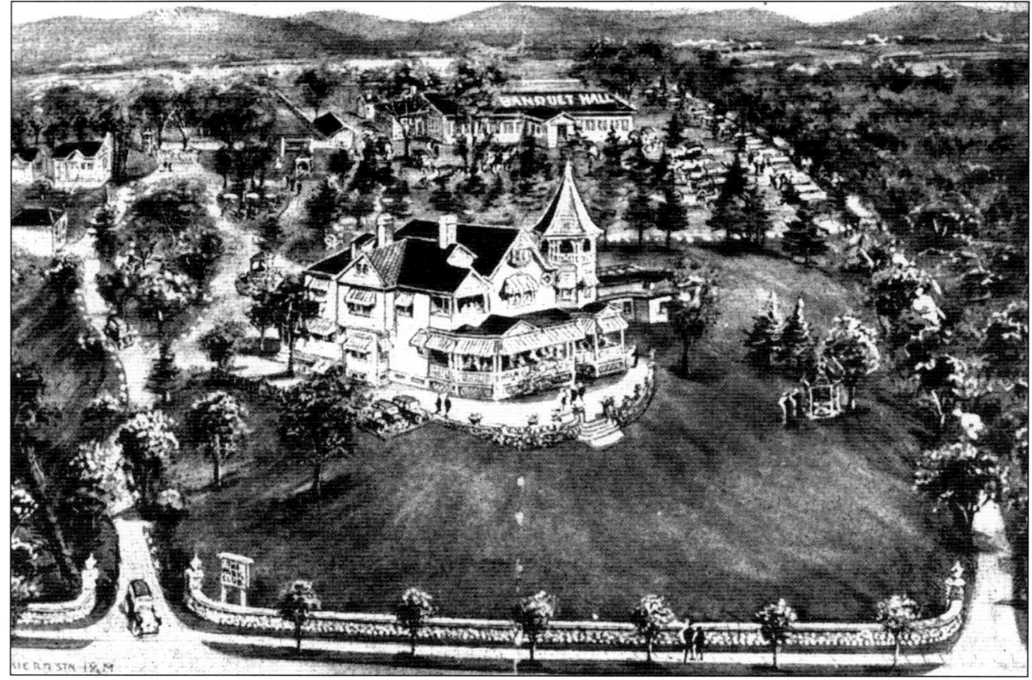


The sketch shows the house of Theodore Volger at Pascack Road and Mountain Avenue in 1899. The house was purchased by M. Steinen, who called it the Park Club. In the 1920s and 1930s, William Atkins and the Rhythm Rascals played at the Park Club. Painted on the roof of the building in the distance are the words "Banquet Hall." The Park Club was eventually destroyed by fire.

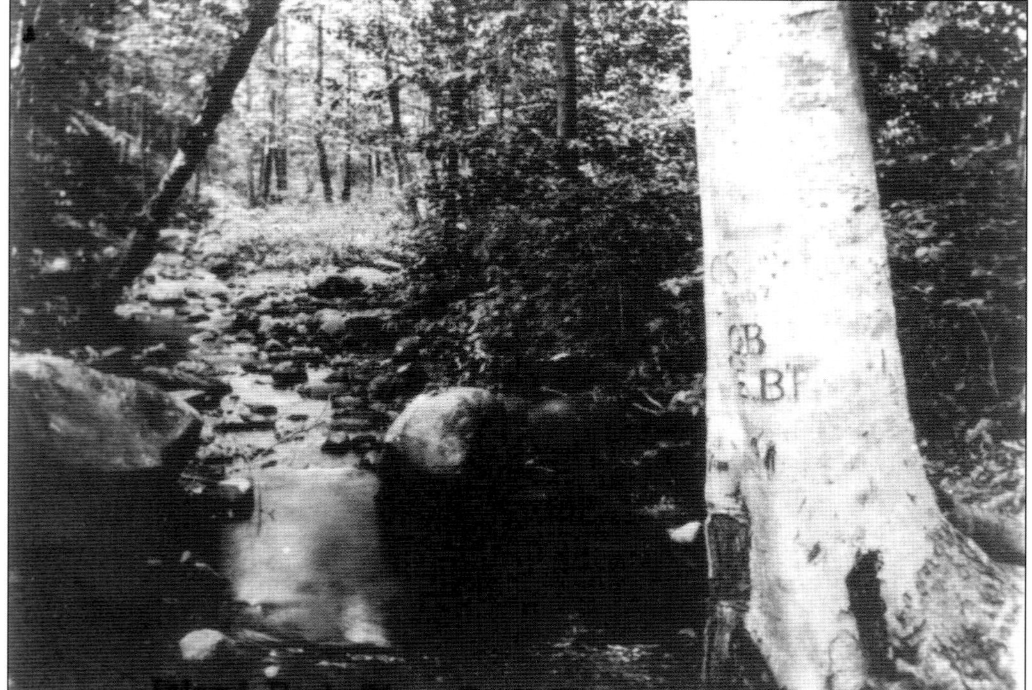

This is Island Park Glen in the late 1800s.

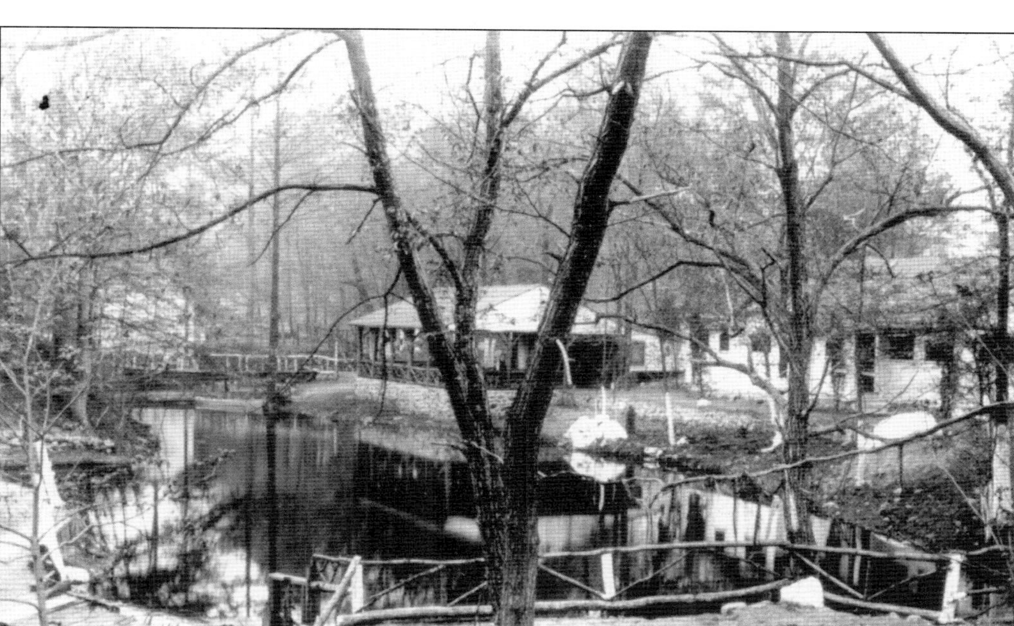

Pictured is Echo Glen Park in the late 1800s. This view shows the area to be a relaxing vacation spot for those looking to rest and to get away from the heat of the city.

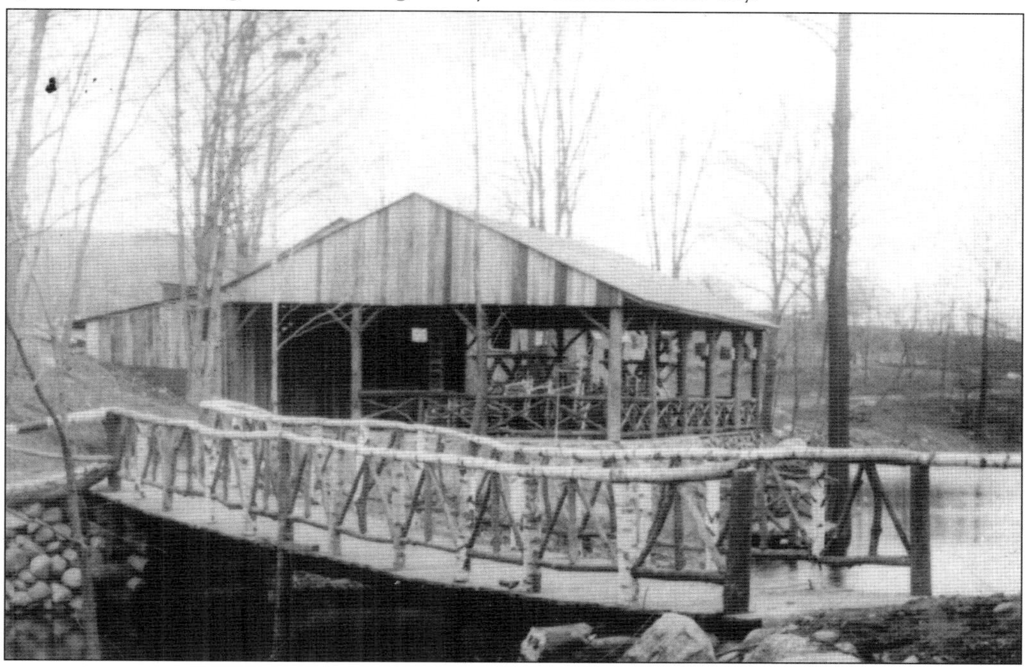

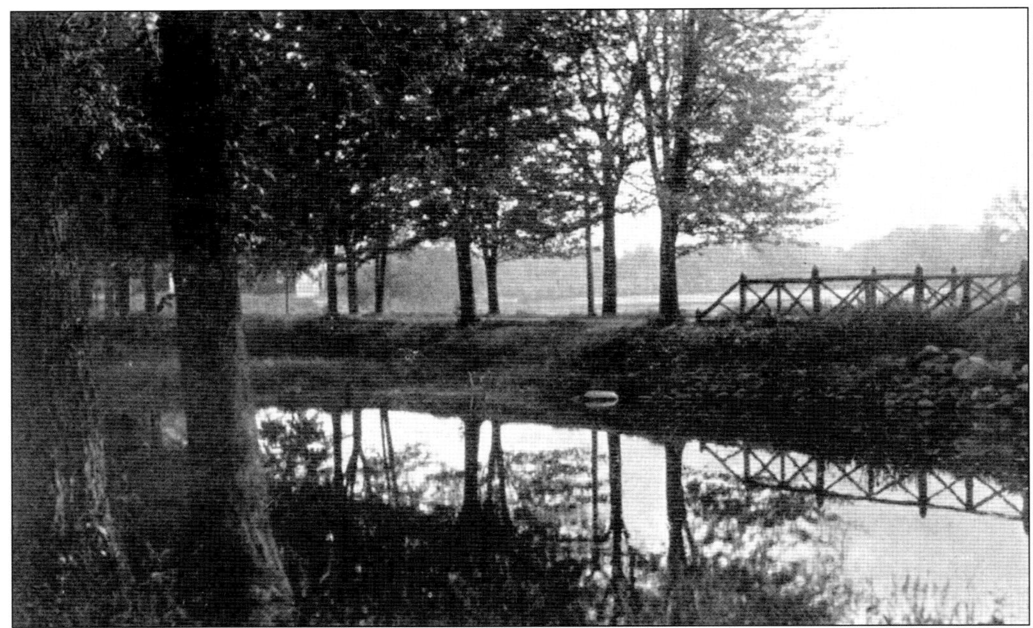

This photograph is a view of Woodcliff Lake from Park Ridge.

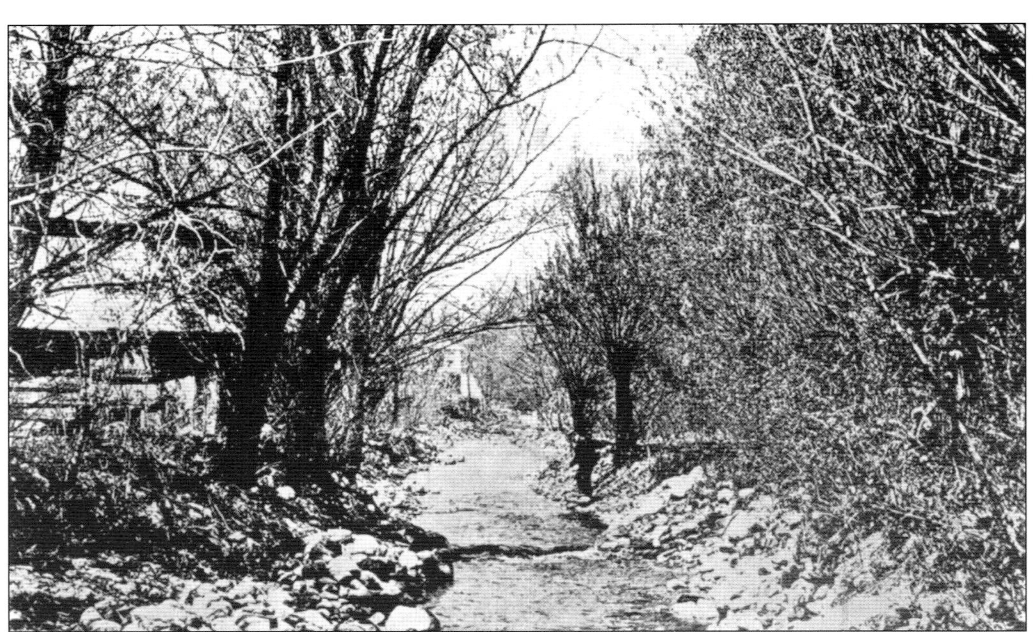

Shown is the Pascack Creek, a local trout stream. The streams of Park Ridge were filled with trout and provided recreation, as well as a chance to catch something to prepare for dinner.

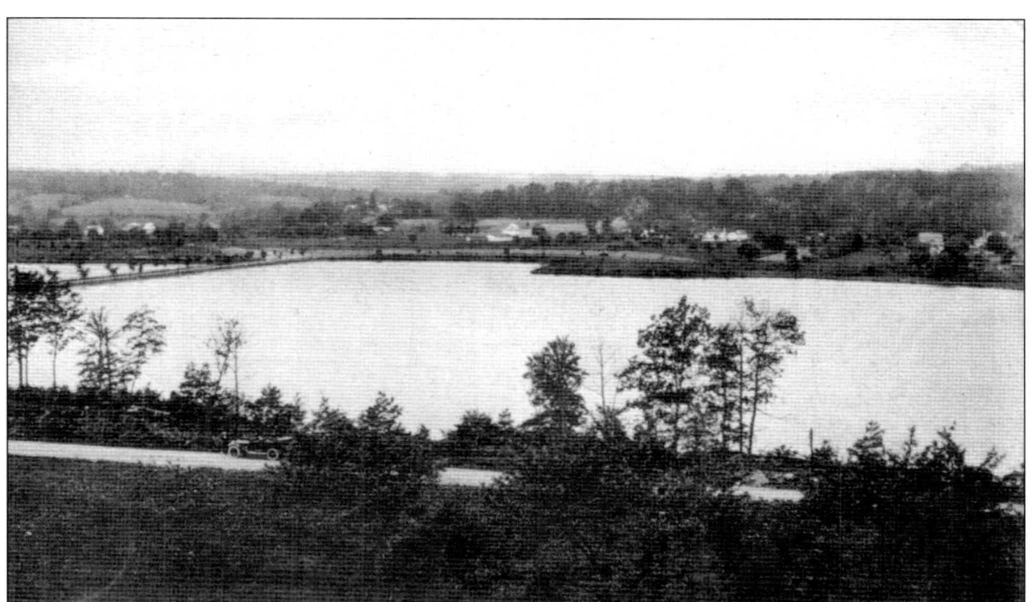

This a Park Ridge view of Woodcliff Lake. The lake is not naturally formed. It was man made at the beginning of the 20th century.

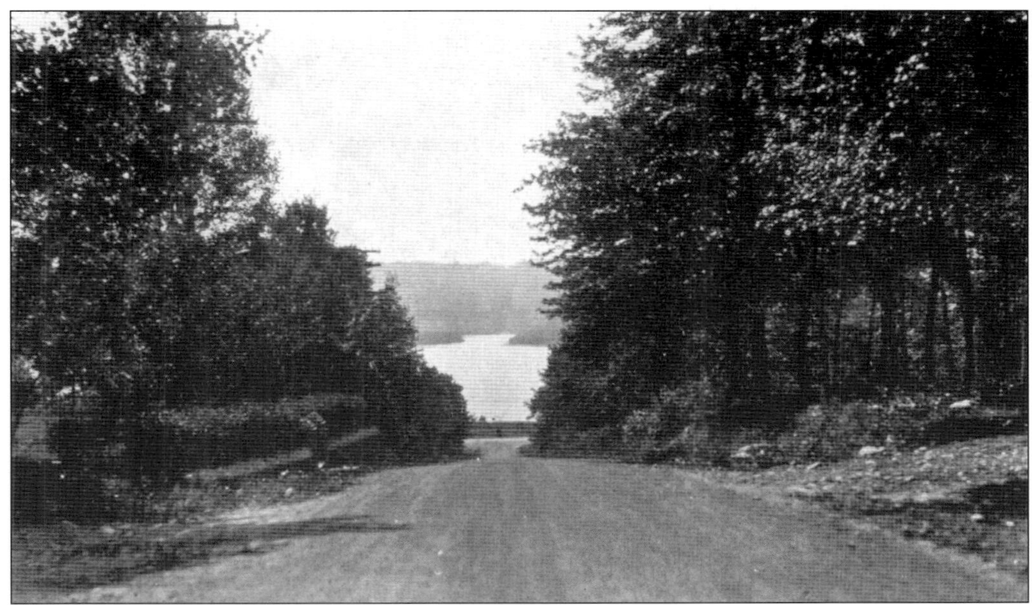

The Woodcliff Lake Causeway is pictured at the beginning of the 20th century. The current bridge had not yet been built.

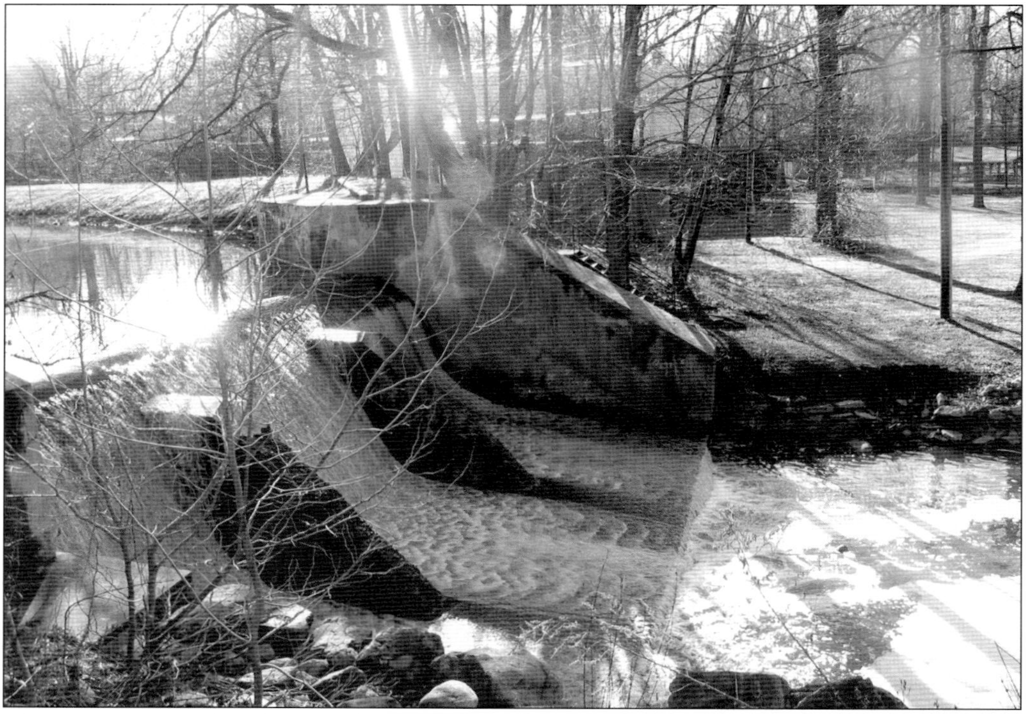

These views show the falls and Electric Lake today. Across the lake are an apartment complex and luxury senior citizen housing.

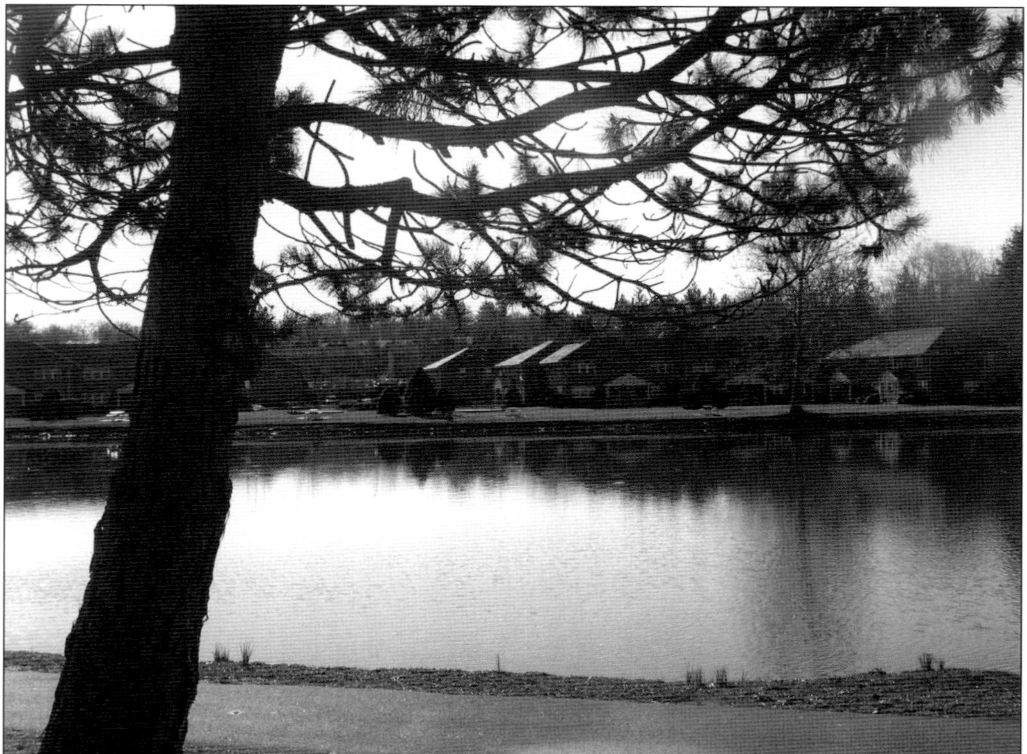

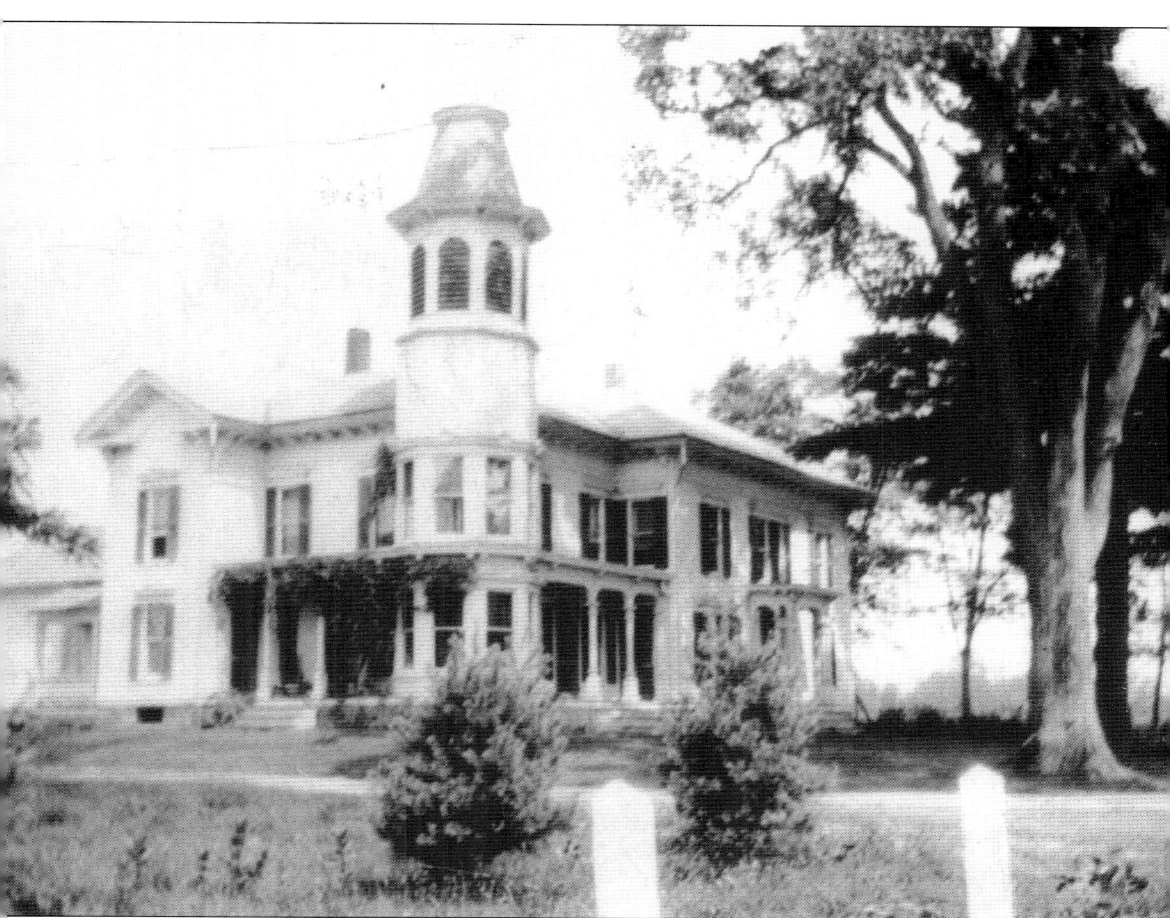

In the early 1900s, several writers and performers lived in Park Ridge. Paul Shiers, born and raised in Park Ridge, performed on Broadway in *Oklahoma* with Celeste Holmes in the 1940s. The house pictured was owned by Billy Rose, a 1930s producer. The house stood on Oak Street.

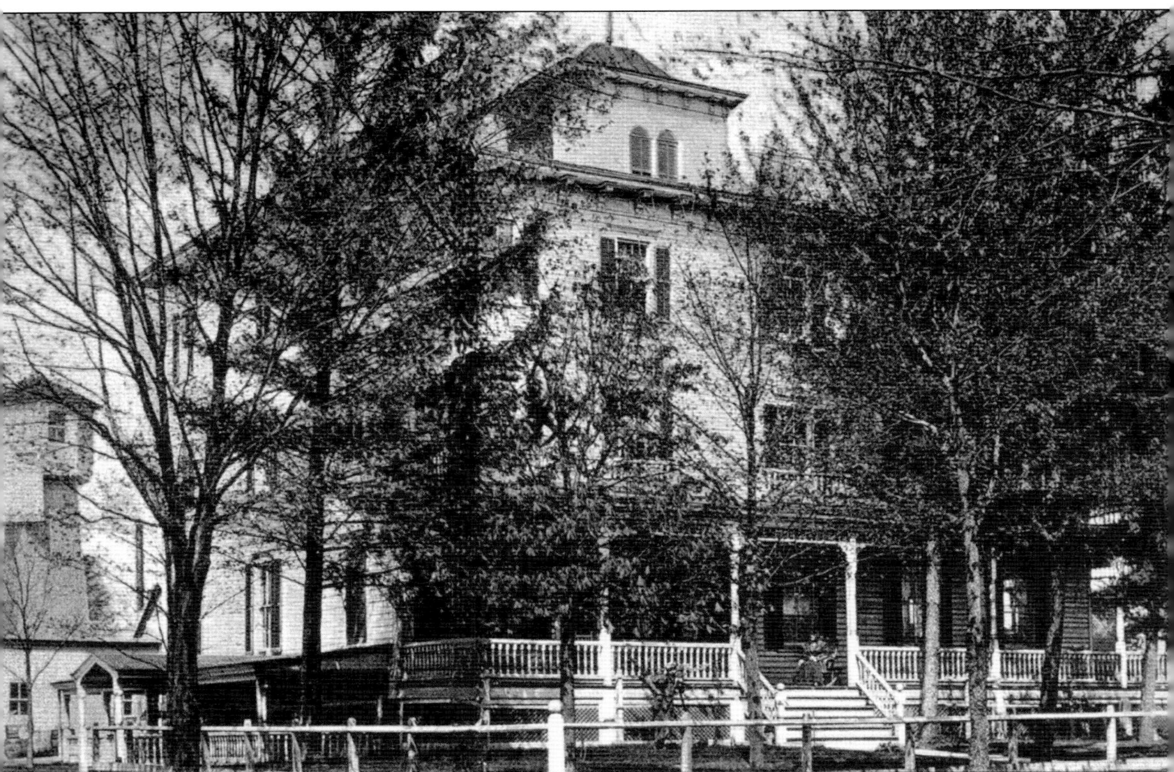

The Park Ridge Hotel was a popular vacation spot. Located on Park Avenue, the hotel changed ownership several times. Mr. Sunderland was the original owner and then Mr. Schoppa in 1876. Eventually it became the home of John J. Perry, who later became mayor. The hotel burned down in the 1940s.

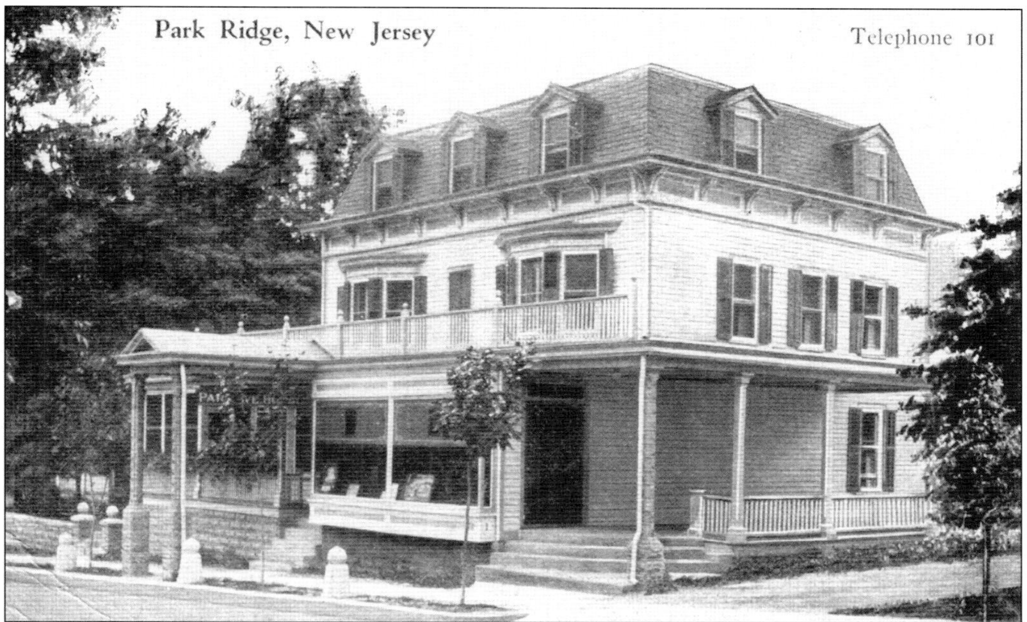


This is the Park Avenue Hotel. The proprietor was Philip Voelcker, and at the time, the telephone number was Park Ridge 101.

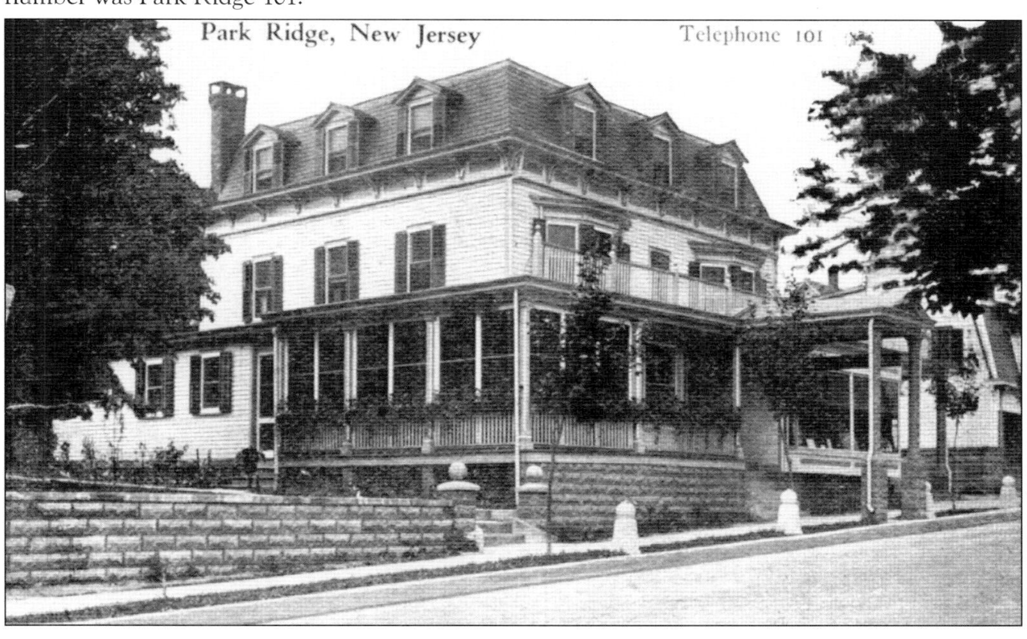

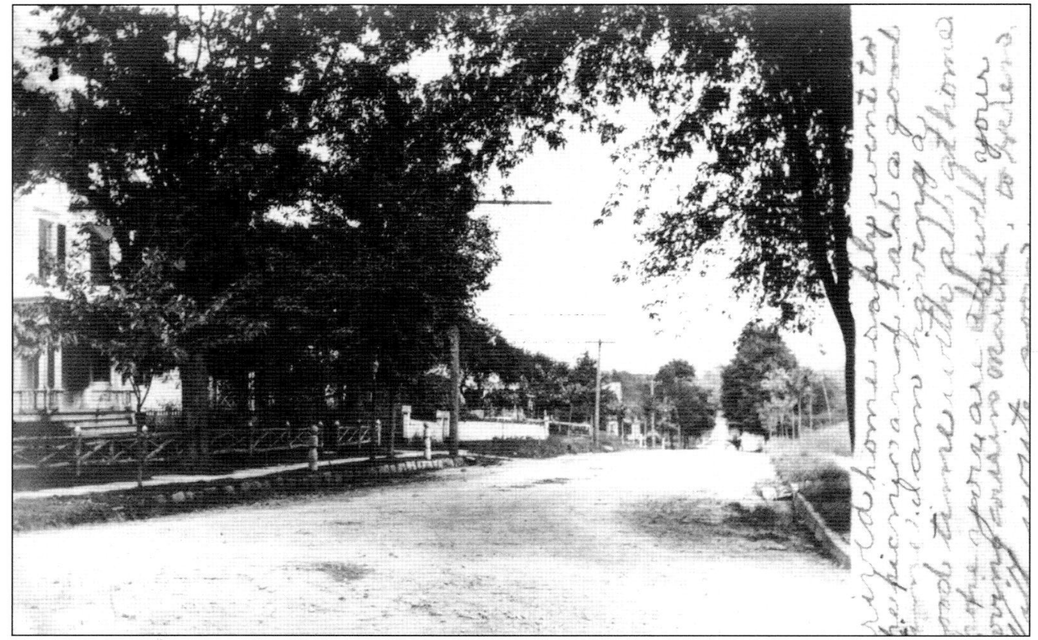

Postcards were readily available in Park Ridge, and vacationers often wrote to friends or family members who remained at home in Manhattan or in southern New Jersey. A common theme of the postcard messages was to brag about being cool while family members were inevitably suffering from the heat of the city. This postcard shows Maple Avenue around 1900.

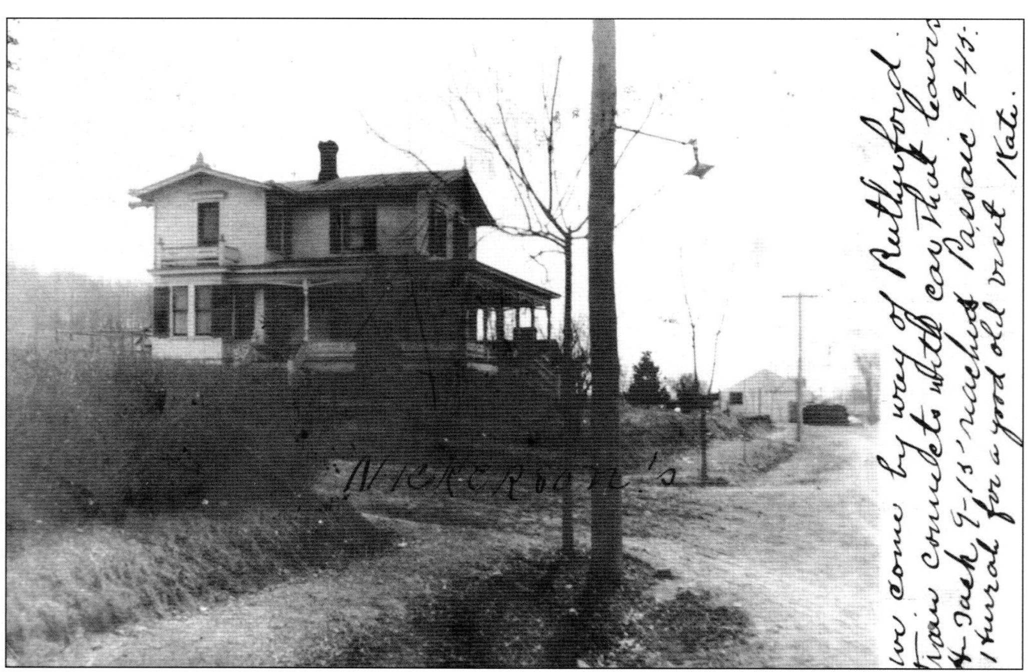

In a postcard from Kate, the train ride to Park Ridge is described. "We came by way of Rutherford. Train connects with car that leaves Hackensack 9–15 reached Passaic 9–45. Hurrah for a good old visit."

GRAND AVE. EAST OF DEPOT, MONTVALE, N.

A vacationer writes of enjoying time spent in Park Ridge but laments the choice of postcards.

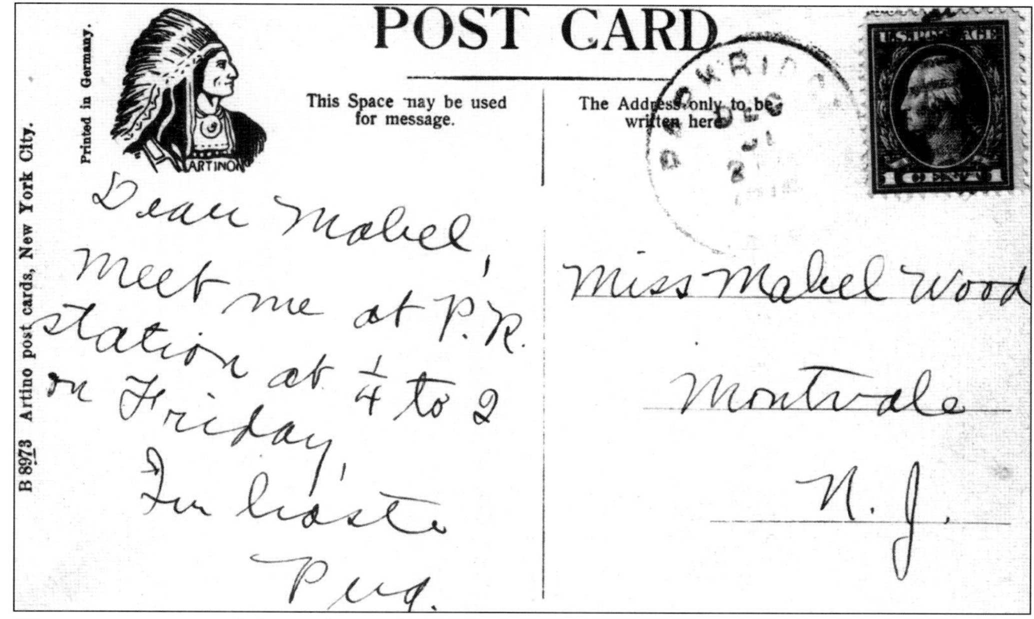


This penny postcard from the early 1900s has the typical symbol of the Pascack area: an American Indian with headdress—although that is not typical dress for the Lenni Lenape, who inhabited the area. The message says, "Dear Mabel, Meet me at P[ark] R[idge] station at 1/4 to 2 on Friday."

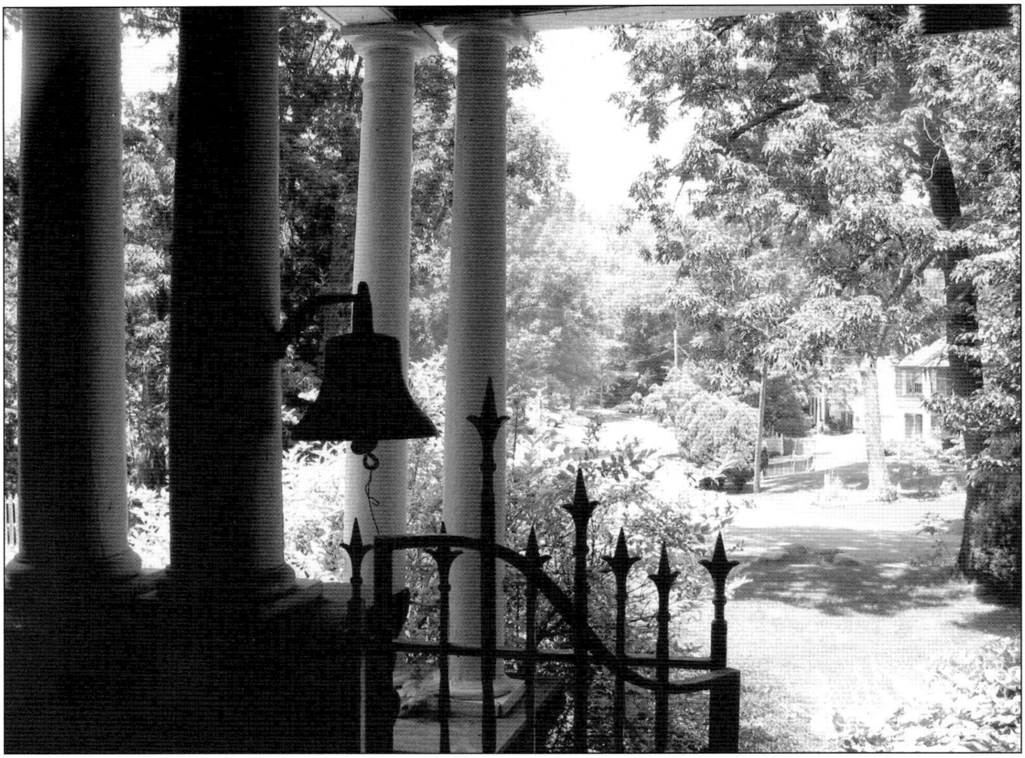

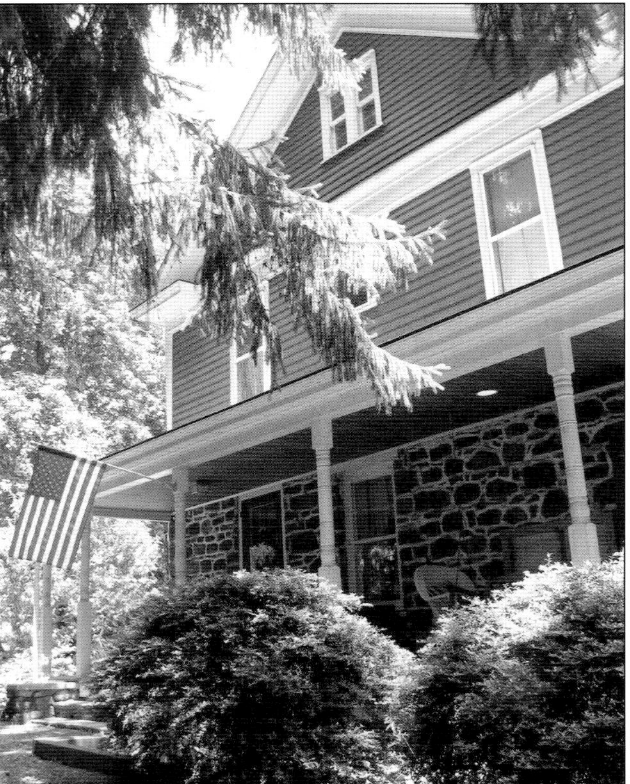

These are some of the oldest houses still standing in Park Ridge. Both were built before the Constitution was signed, and both are located on River Vale Road on what once were neighboring properties.

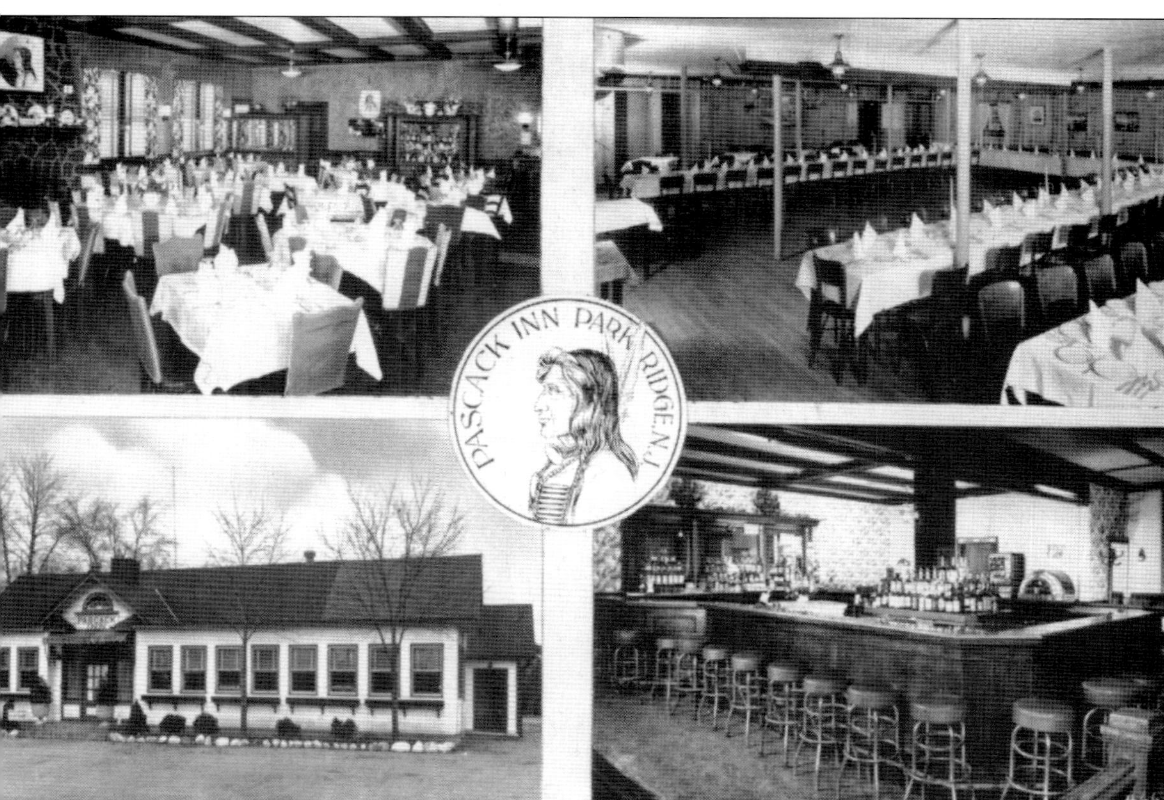


The Pascack Inn was a popular spot during World War II. This postcard shows inside and outside scenes, as well as the inn's emblem: a Pascack Indian, wearing a wampum breastplate. The inn had several previous owners and was damaged by fire several times before being destroyed in a 1957 fire.

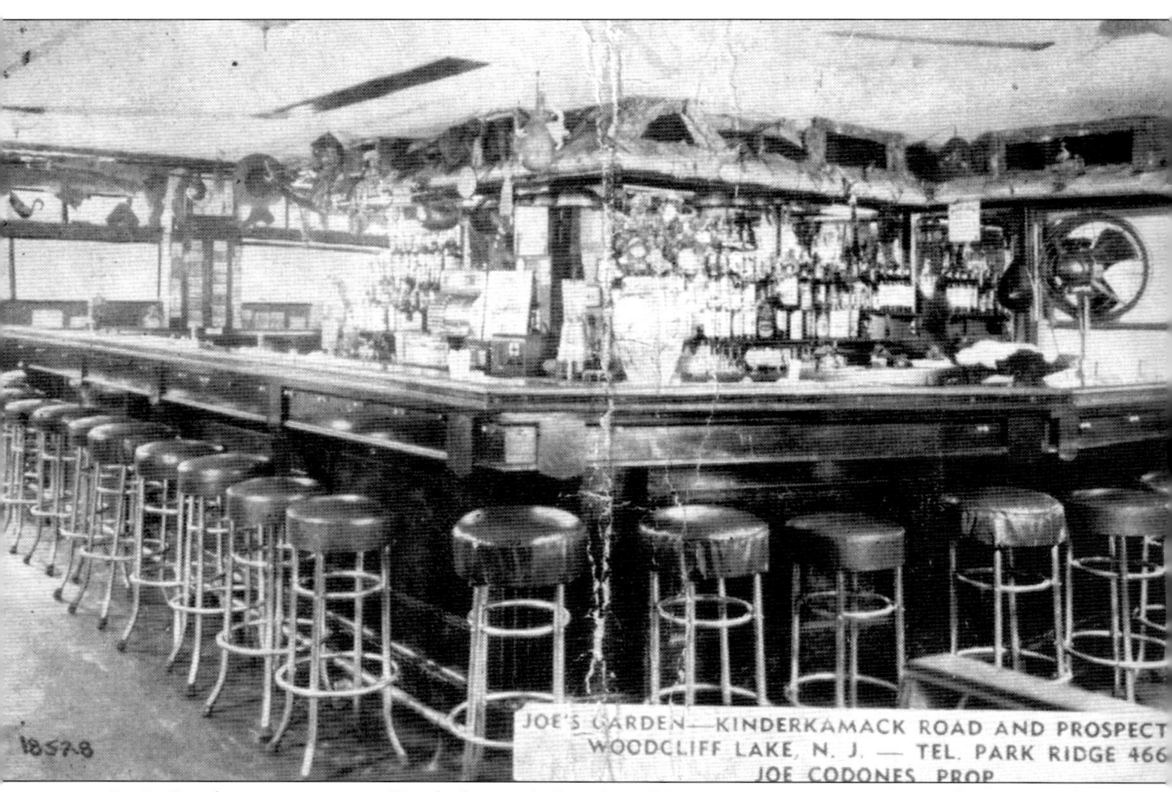


Joe's Garden, a tavern at Kinderkamack Road and Prospect Avenue, was run by Joe Codones and had the telephone number of 466. Still standing, the place is the Blue Moon Café today.

# *Five*

# Heroes and Celebration

The heroes of Park Ridge are honored in the center of town. Honor rolls for each war show which residents lost their lives in defense of their country. There is also a memorial plaque for those who died in the events of September 11, 2001.

On Memorial Day, Park Ridge honors its heroes and veterans along with surrounding towns. Park Ridge has continued the tradition of honoring its heroes and celebrating holidays with parades through town.

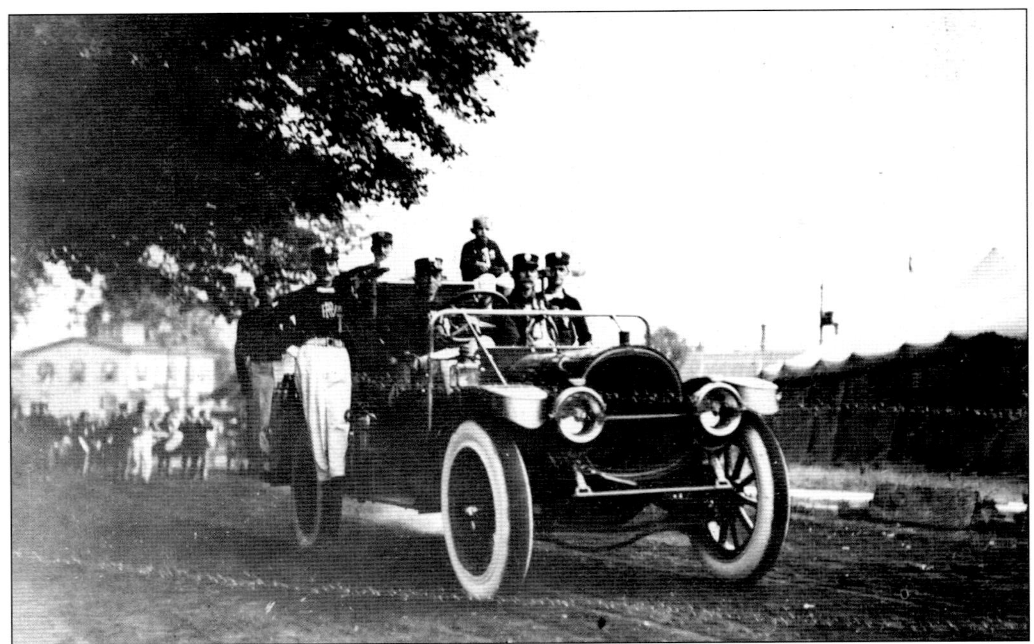

The Park Ridge Fire Department volunteers show off their new fire truck in the borough's parade. In the background one can see a tent that was possibly that of Manson, a preacher who set up in town to preach, much to the chagrin of some residents.

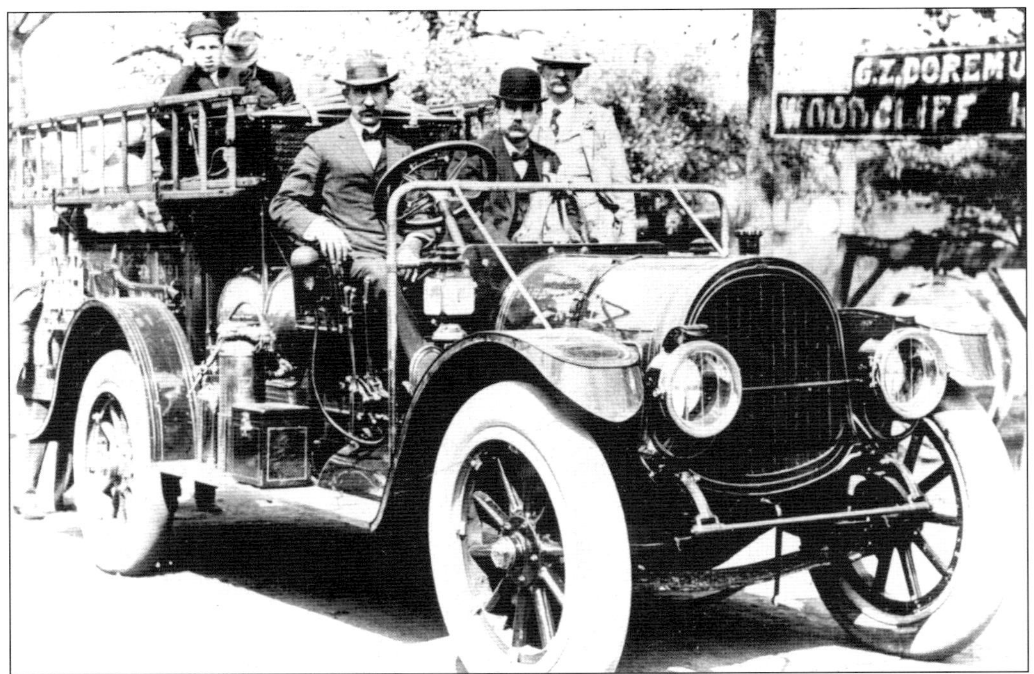


The firefighters' new fire truck was far more advanced than the earlier engines that were wagons with buckets lining the sides. The truck could make it over terrain the volunteers could not have navigated with horses. The new truck sports a ladder.

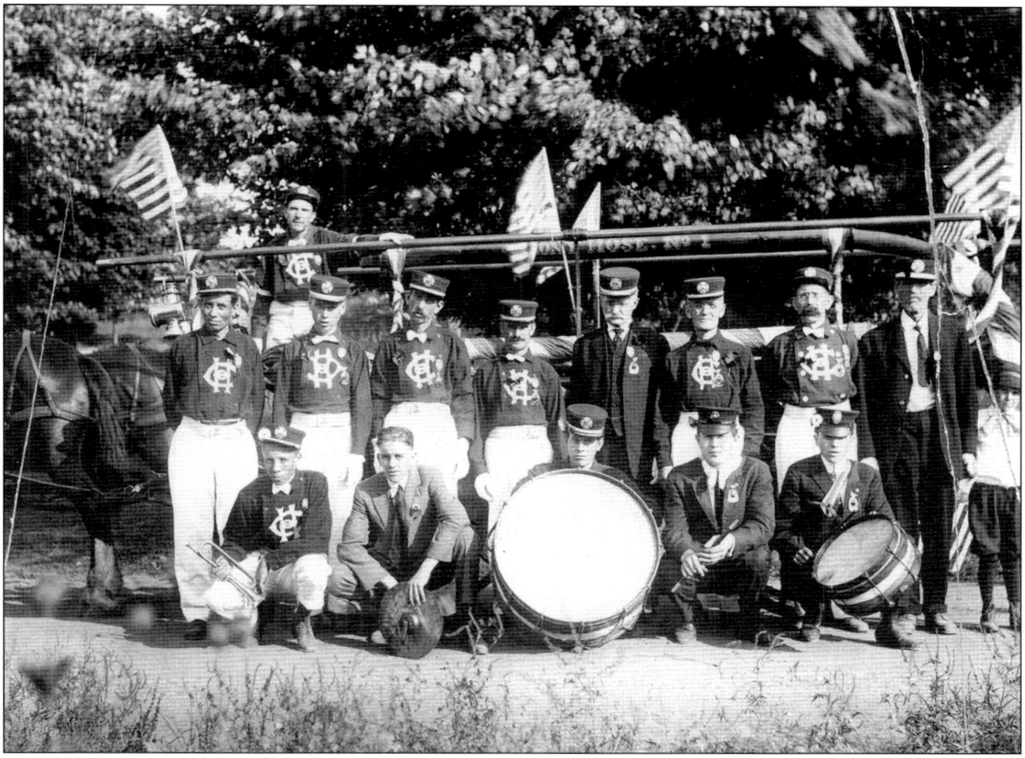

The Park Ridge Mohawk Band (above) poses for a photograph in the late 1800s. Many are under the impression that this was an official fire department band, but it was actually an independent group. About half the members were volunteer firefighters. Park Ridge has had many parades over the years. The women of the Park Ridge Fire Department's women's auxiliary (below) keep in step and in line as they march along.

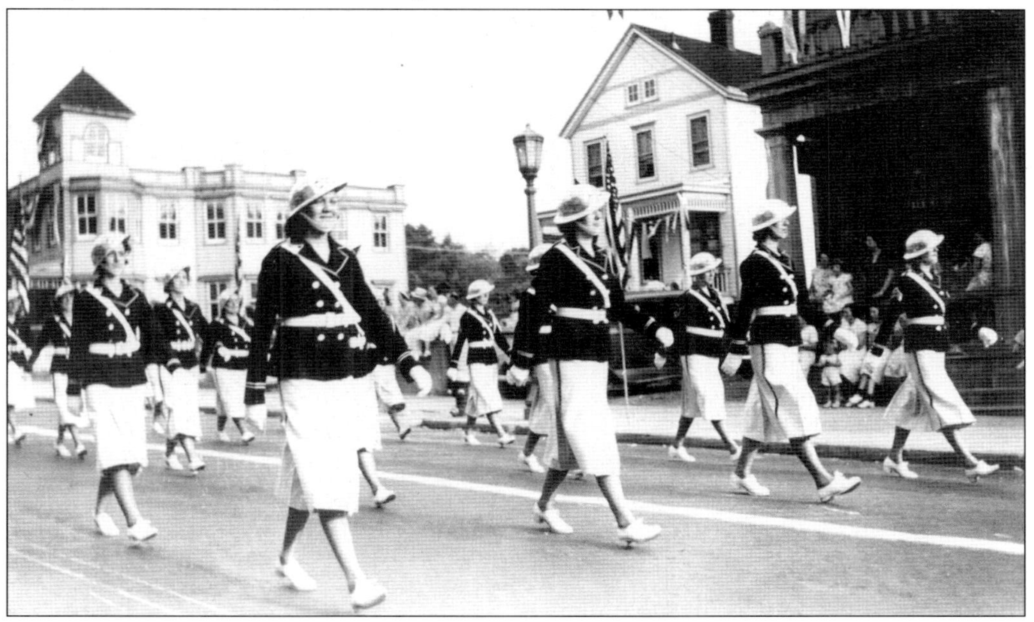

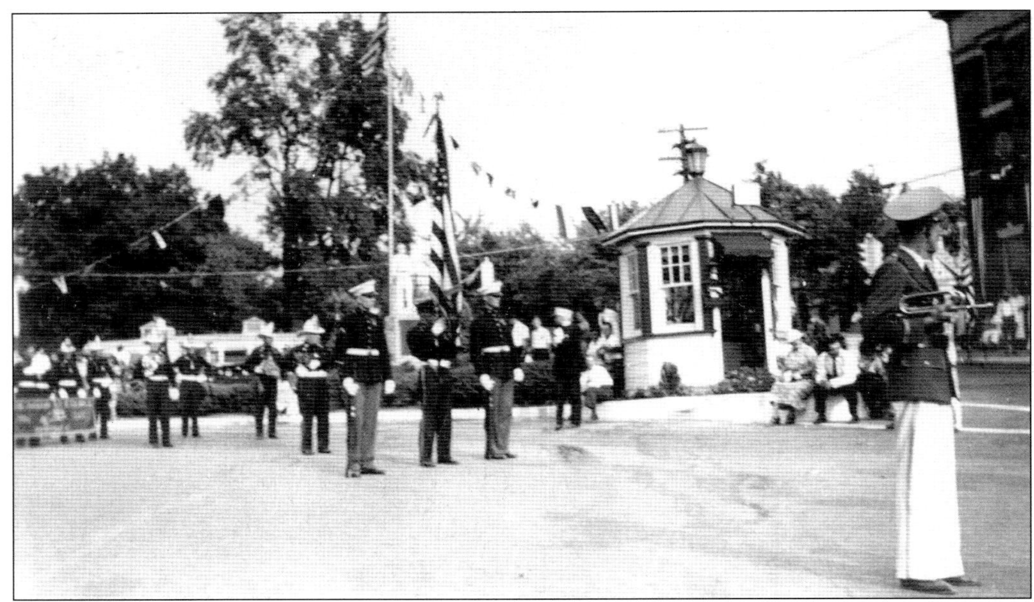

A parade passes through the center of town (above) from Kinderkamack Road on to Park Avenue, then called Triangle Park. The police booth pictured was the precursor of police headquarters. The Park Ridge Fire Department (below) marches in a parade for opening day of the borough's Little League baseball season in the early 1960s.

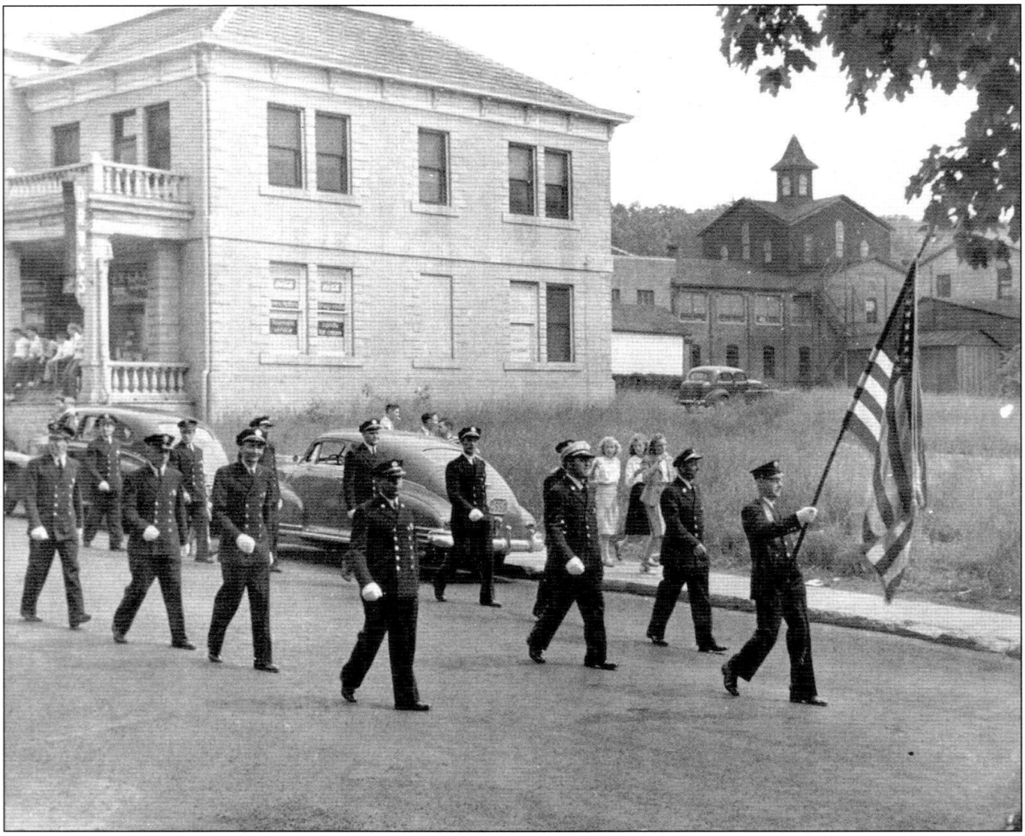

This 1917–1918 honor roll lists the names of Park Ridge residents who served in World War I. It is headed by the words "Lest we forget." It was erected by the people of Park Ridge in July 1926.

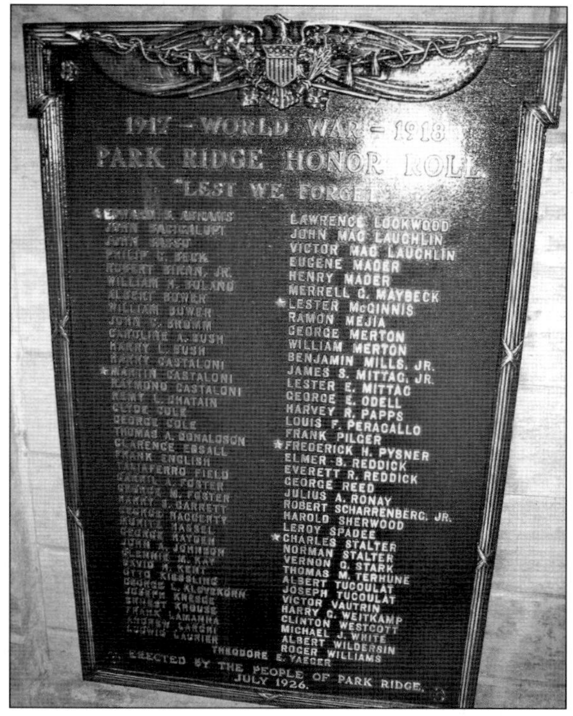

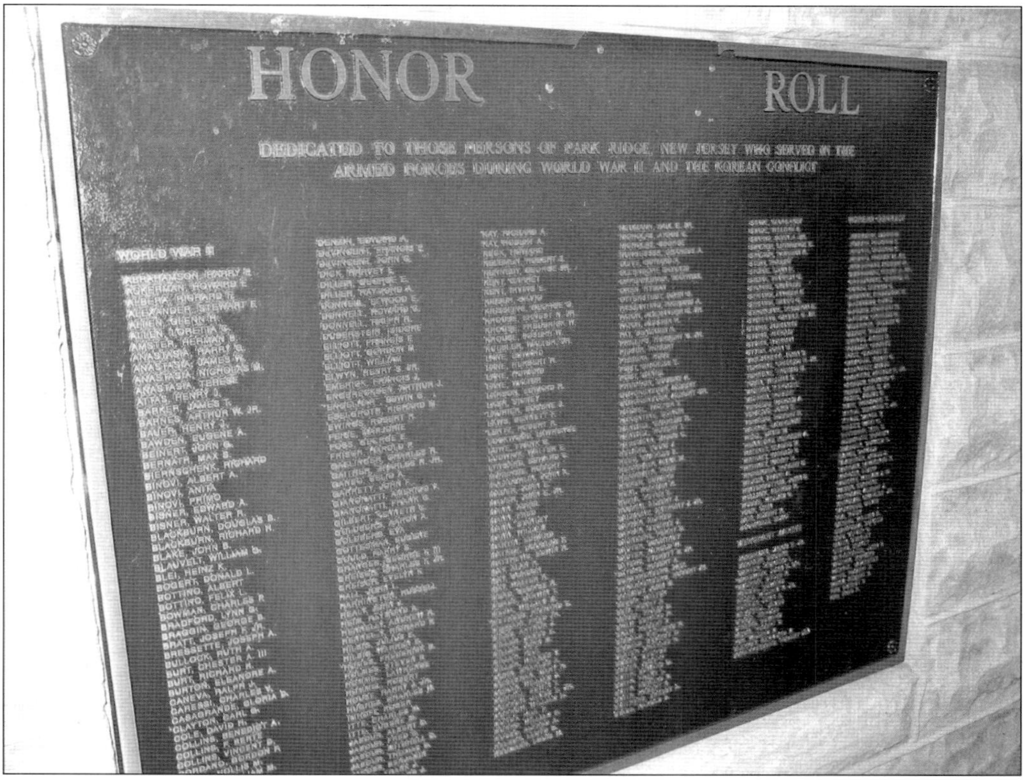

A later honor roll recognizes all the Park Ridge residents who served in World War II and the Korean Conflict.

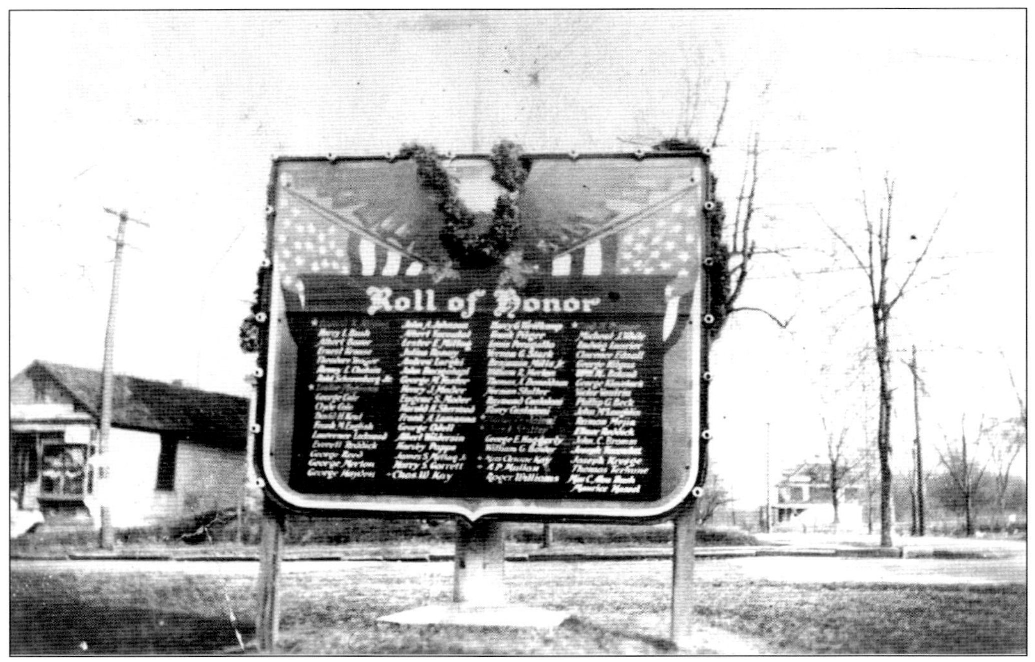


This roll of honor stood in the center of town, off Park Avenue, by Park Ridge Crossing.

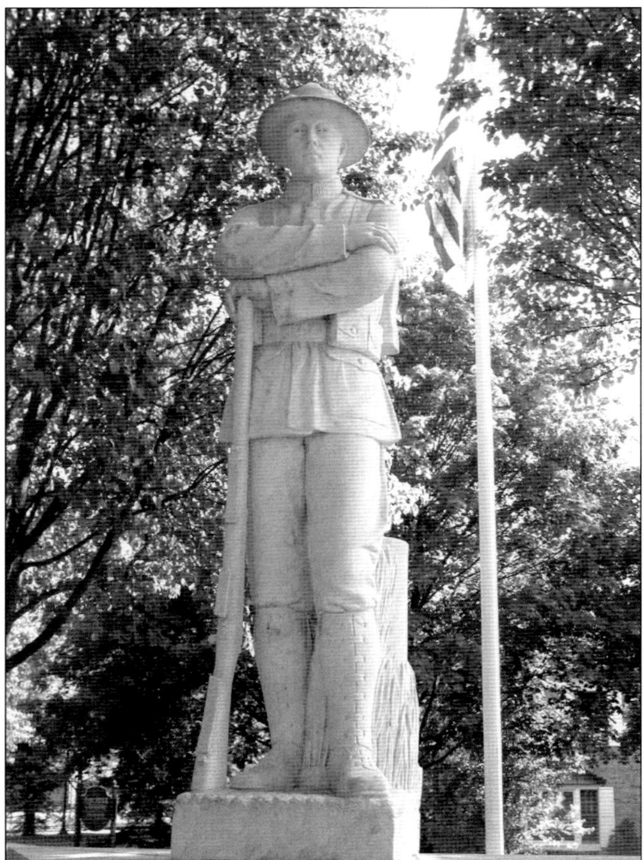

A doughboy stands at Park Ridge Crossing, where Park Ridge veterans of World War I, World War II, the Korean War, and the Vietnam War are honored. The statue previously stood in the triangle in the center of the borough, until there was a car accident, in which the original statue was destroyed. There is also a marker for Park Ridge families who lost a loved one in the events of September 11, 2001. In addition, the site has a time capsule, placed there in 1994.

# *Six*

# Sacred Places

Faith played a role in the lives of early settlers, and many of the founding fathers of Pascack, or Park Ridge, are buried in the cemetery behind the Pascack Reformed Church. The church was built in 1813 using local sandstone.

In 1890, the Park Ridge African Methodist Episcopal Zion church was built on Rivervale Road. It was also known as the black church. An earlier church had disbanded because so many of the men of the congregation served in the Civil War. In the 1880s, the congregation started up again, with Rev. G. H. Carle, who was the previous pastor, heading up the congregation. At the time, about 10 percent of Pascack's population was African American. The church still stands today, with the same stone retaining wall out front, but the house is now a private home.

In 1887, a religious revival stirred the town for a number of months. Rev. Samuel Switzer of the First Congregational Church, which was previously known as Leach's Chapel, had a disagreement with James Leach, the founder and Sunday school teacher. Switzer converted to be a Baptist and turned the academy, a vacated school building at Depot Square, into a house of worship. During this time a man named Mason T. Huntsman came to Pascack by invitation of Eliza Berry, who lived on Ridge Avenue. Huntsman declared himself a bishop and said that the Lord had instructed him to change his name to Manson. A zealous speaker who referred to anyone who left his sermons as "black devils," he drew a lot of attention to himself, setting up a tent on Ridge Avenue for service, before leaving in 1910.

St. Mary's Church was built in 1903 at a cost of $4,000. The tiny church was built on Hawthorne Avenue and was the forerunner to Our Lady of Mercy Church. St. Mary's was demolished in 1968. Pastor Lillis, monsignor of St. Mary's in 1949, when the church had some 400 families, guided members to have a new, much larger church built on Fremont Avenue, Our Lady of Mercy. The first service was held in the new church in 1961.

First Congregational Church, earlier housed at Leach's Chapel, was known to have especially stirring speakers, including the Reverend Henry Ward Beecher, brother of Harriet Beecher Stowe, author of *Uncle Tom's Cabin*. Beecher was an outstanding speaker and abolitionist who not only spoke in the North but who specialized in convincing slave owners to heed the Emancipation Proclamation. He also spoke in favor of women's suffrage and was a deeply religious man who gave sermons that supported the theory of evolution.

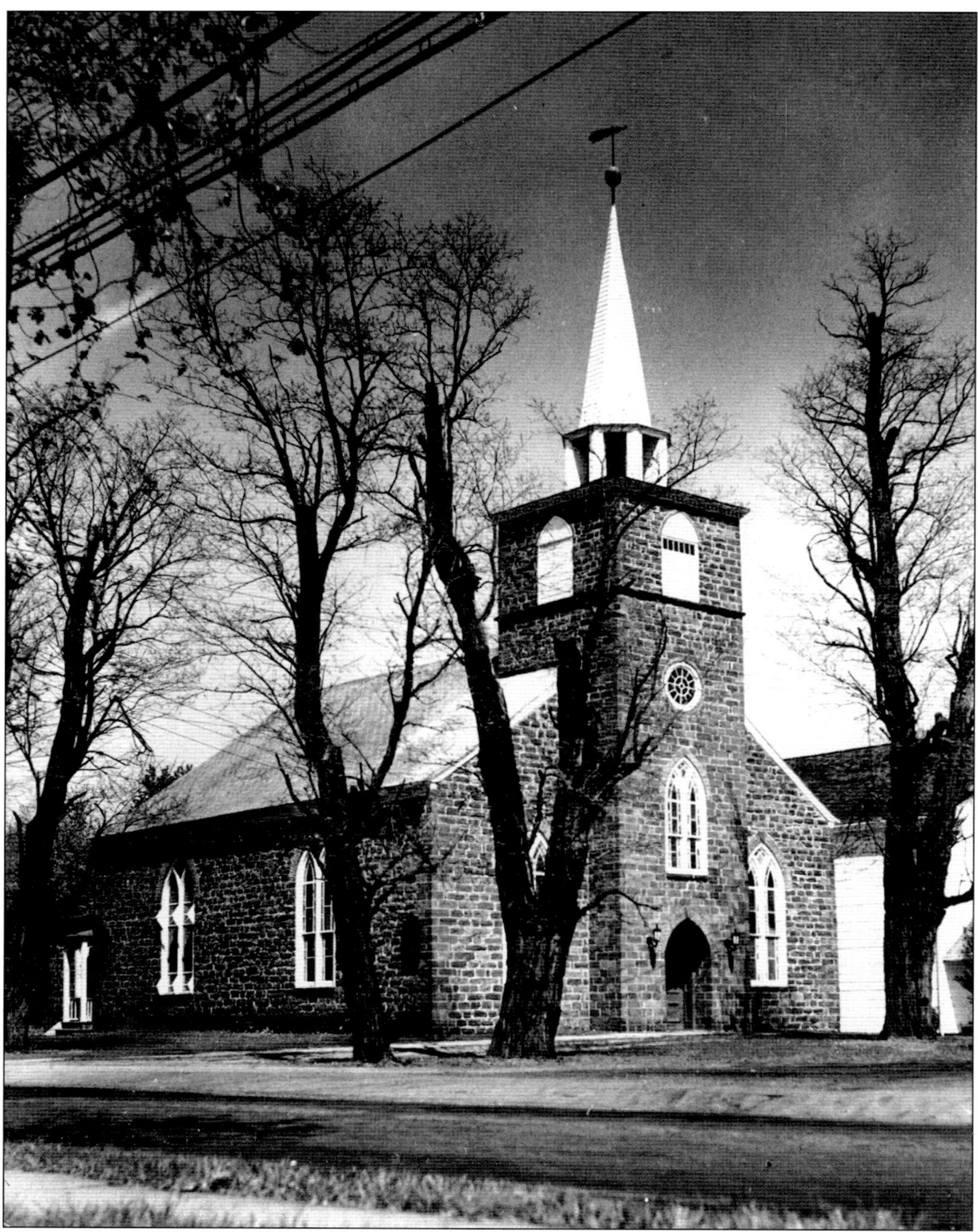

The Reformed Church has an intriguing history. In the reception area, there are artifacts from its early history, including a complete Communion gifted to the congregation by the Queen of the Netherlands. After the borough was incorporated, several of the members served as mayor. The earliest members played important roles in the community, including Dr. Neer, who served as Pascack's first doctor and who made his house calls by horse and buggy from his house, which was across the street.

Around 1873, James Leach and Jacob Hall purchased land along Ridge Avenue and erected a small chapel. Known as the Congregational Sunday School, the chapel lent books to members of the community and was the forerunner of the local library. In 1875, the chapel became the First Congregational Church. Today it is the home of the Pascack Historical Society.

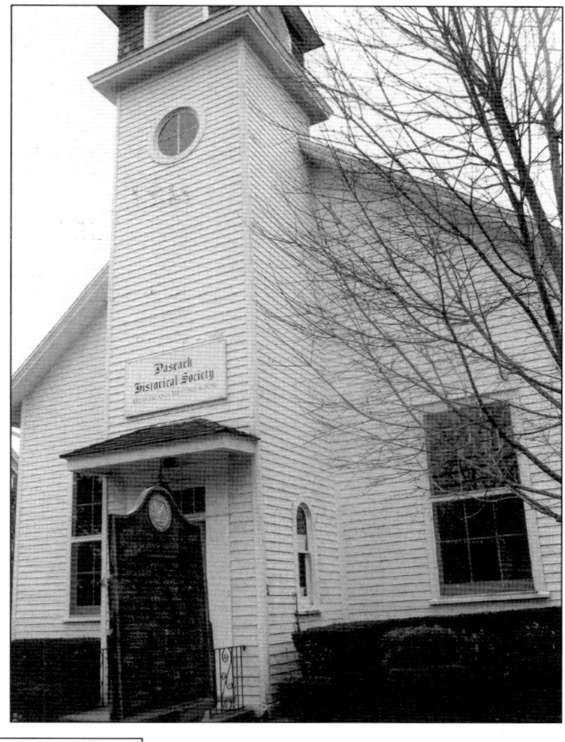


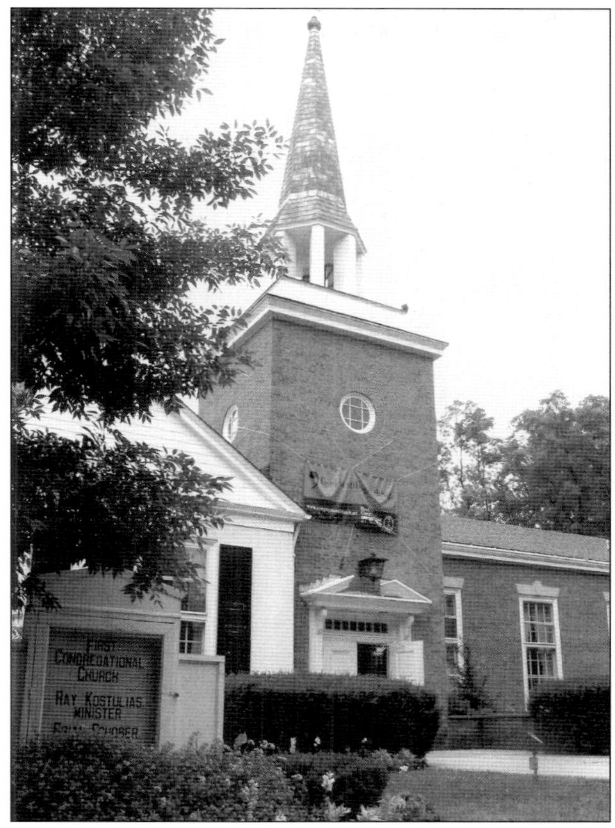


The First Congregational Church eventually needed a larger building. It moved into this new edifice on Pascack Road. Here hundreds of Congregational, Evangelical, and Reformed church members worshiped together.

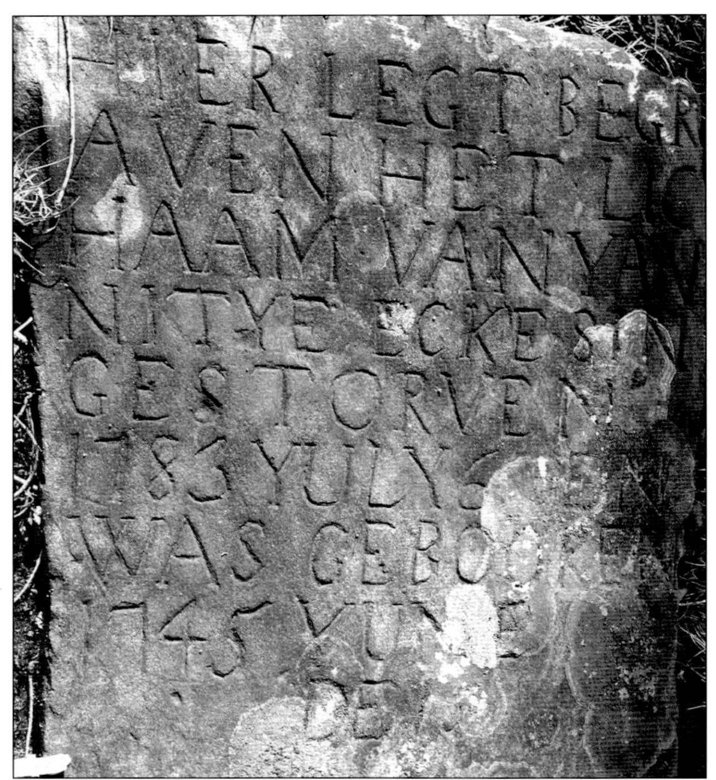


Located in the Pascack Cemetery is a gravestone that is hand-engraved in Dutch. It indicates that the person who is buried there died in the mid-1700s. The headstone of Charity Wortendyke (below) was made by a skilled engraver. The Wortendyke family lived in the house with the well-known Dutch barn, both of which still stand today near the cemetery.

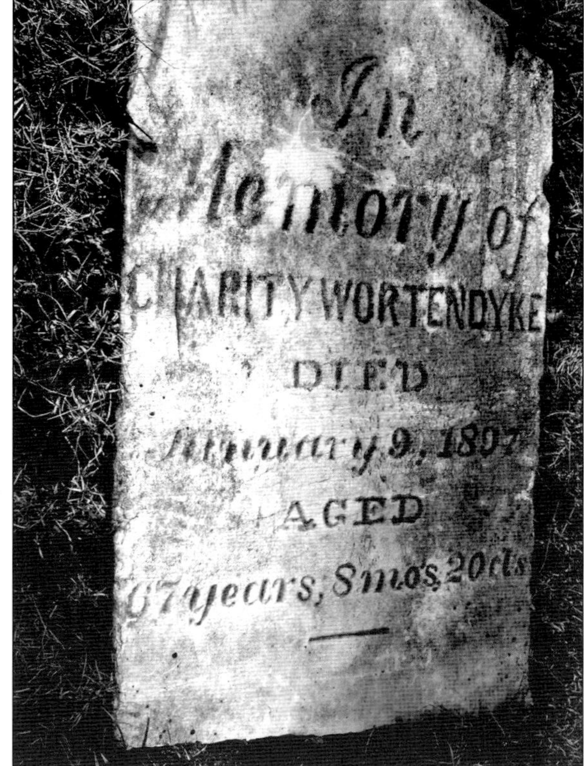

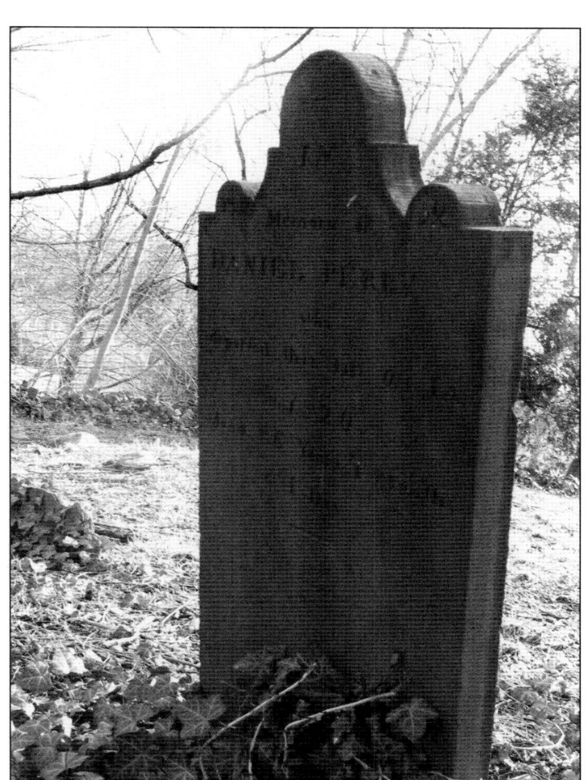

The dark gravestone is that of Daniel Perry, who died in 1820. The lighter one is the gravestone of Margaret King Foster, 1817–1885.

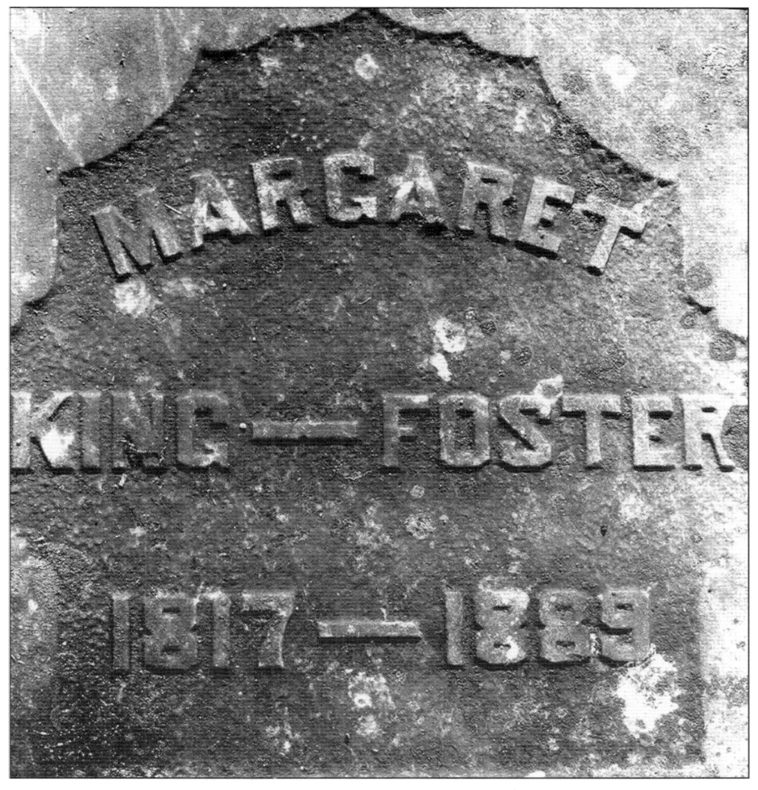

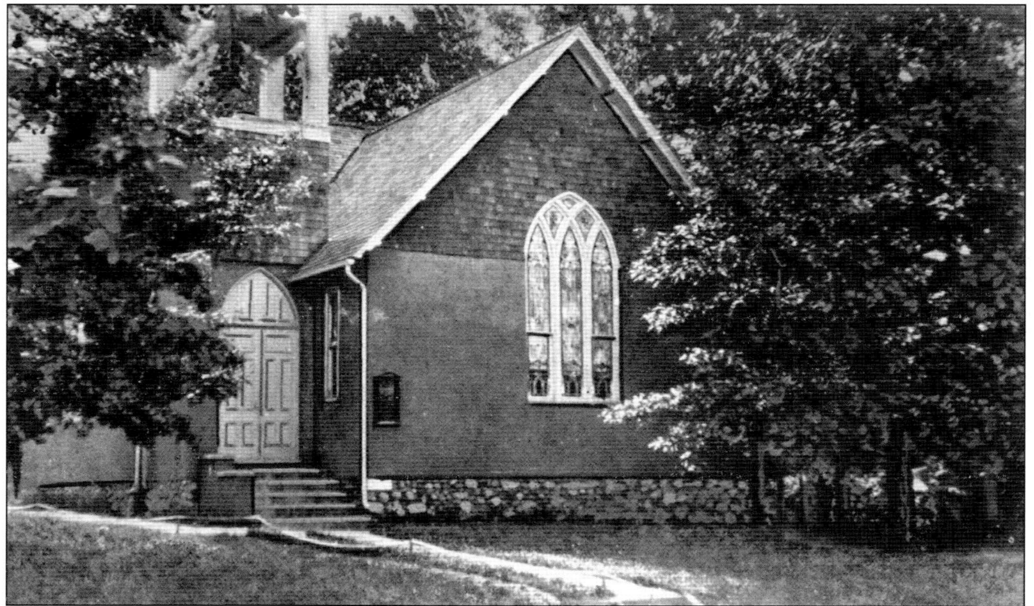

The United Methodist Church held its first service in 1909 in Leach's Chapel on Ridge Avenue and then held its meetings in several locations, including the hook and ladder company, until the present church was built at Berthoud Street and Highview Avenue in 1912. The church has a rich history and currently holds an afternoon service for those who speak Japanese.

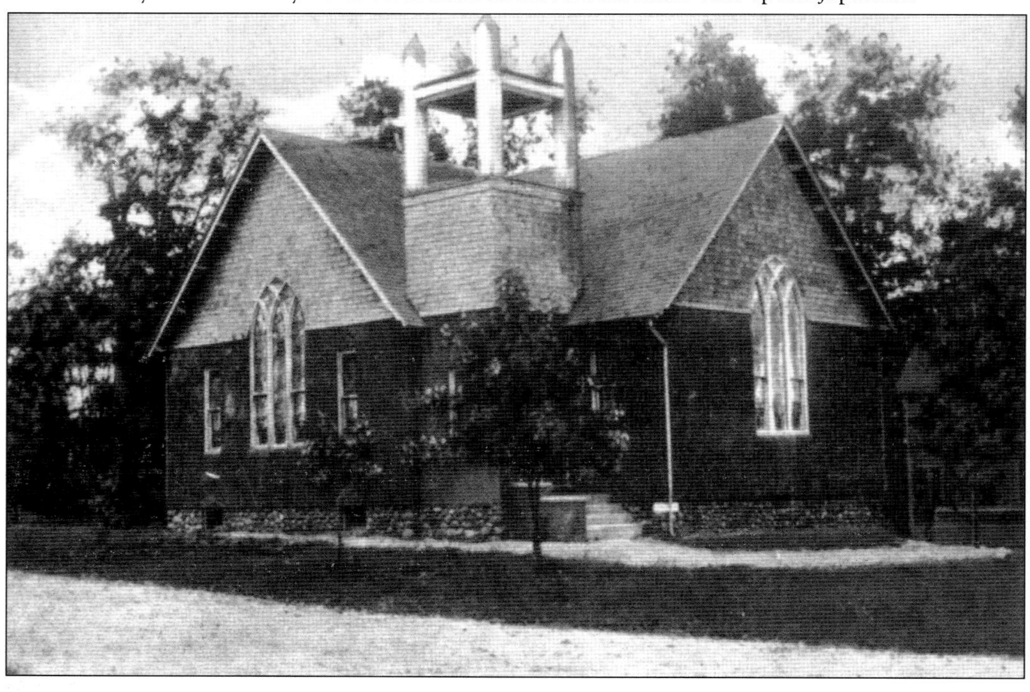

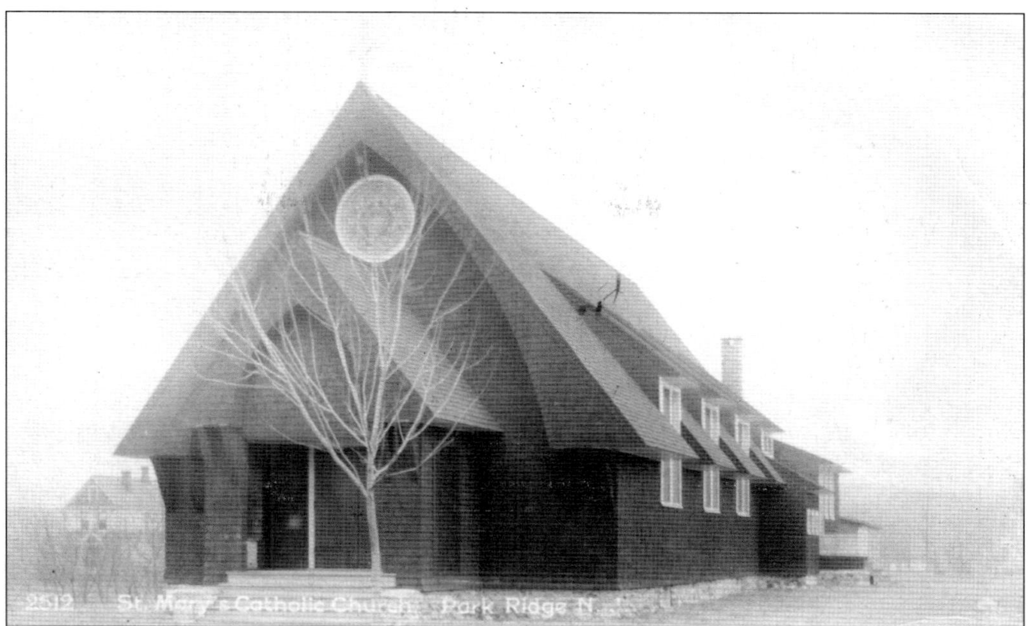


St. Mary's Roman Catholic Church was built in 1903 at a cost of $4,000. The tiny church was built on Hawthorne Avenue and was the forerunner to Our Lady of Mercy Church. St. Mary's was demolished in 1968.

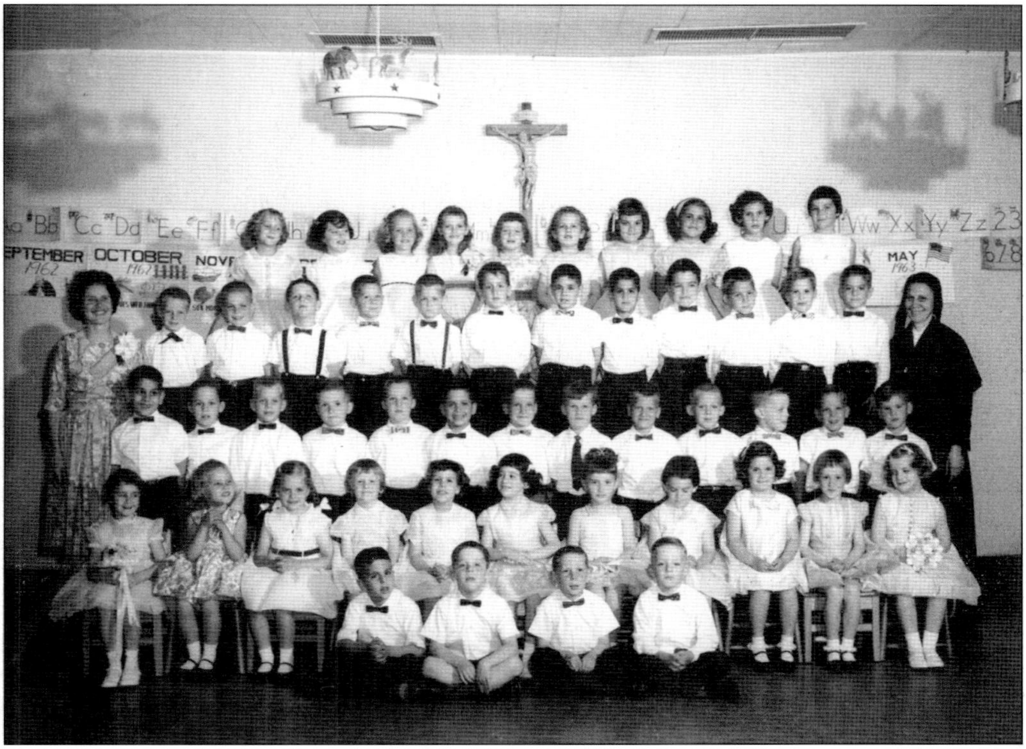

A class poses to commemorate First Holy Communion at Our Lady of Mercy Church in 1961. The girls are wearing dresses, with crinolines underneath the skirts and flowers in their hair. The boys sport bow ties. The crucifix has palm leaves tucked behind it.

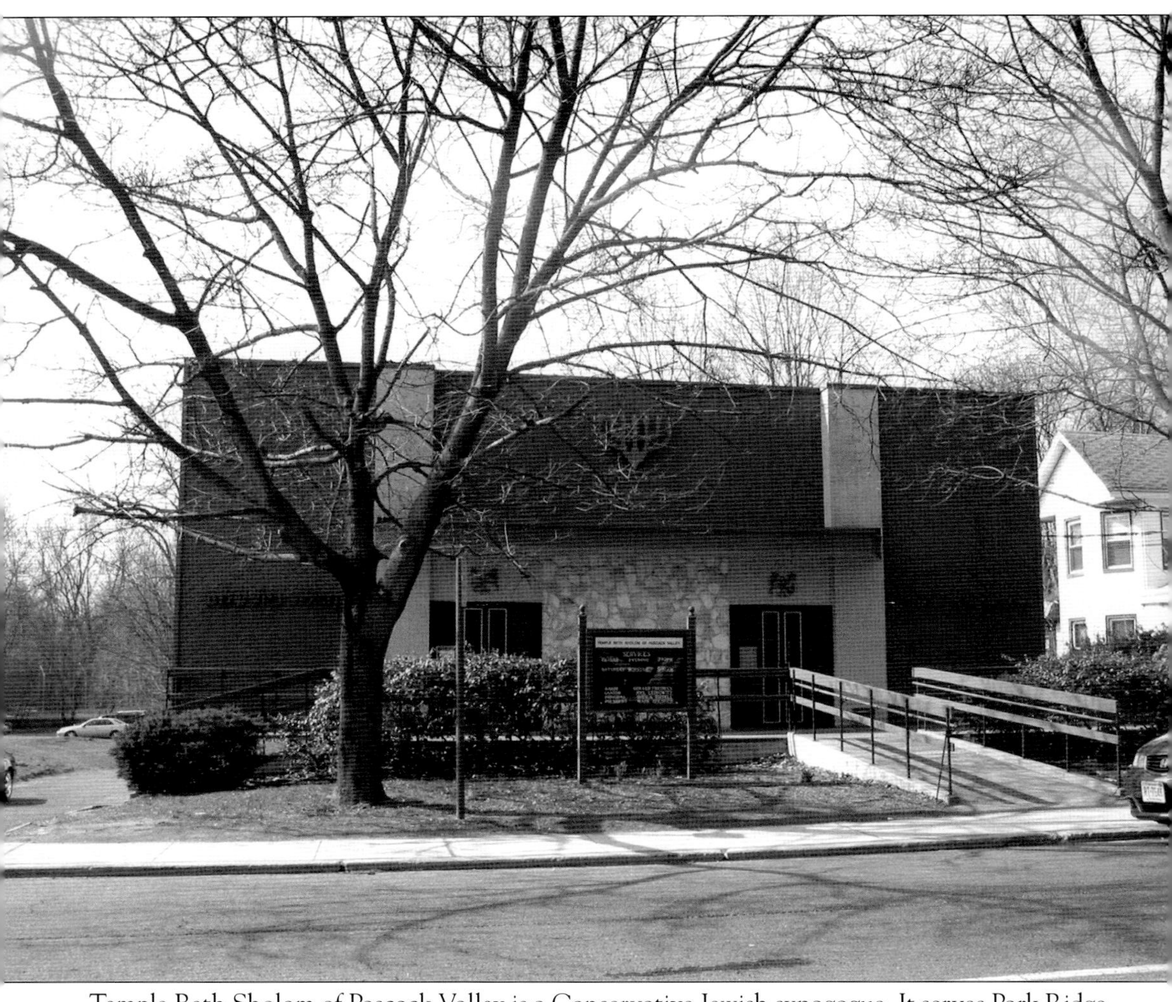

Temple Beth Sholom of Pascack Valley is a Conservative Jewish synagogue. It serves Park Ridge and several other towns, including Montvale, Hillsdale, River Vale, and Emerson.

# *Seven*

# SCHOOL DAYS

Pascack was an area that held education as highly important from its very beginnings. Much of the earliest history of the Park Ridge schools was lost in a 1920 blaze that ravaged the high school building and brought the area to mourning for lost loved ones who died in the fire.

The first school, which was one of the first schools in Bergen County, consisted of one room, built in 1808 just north of the Pascack Reformed Church. In 1856, a second building was erected, another one-room building, but with room for about 75 people. The third school building was added on in 1876.

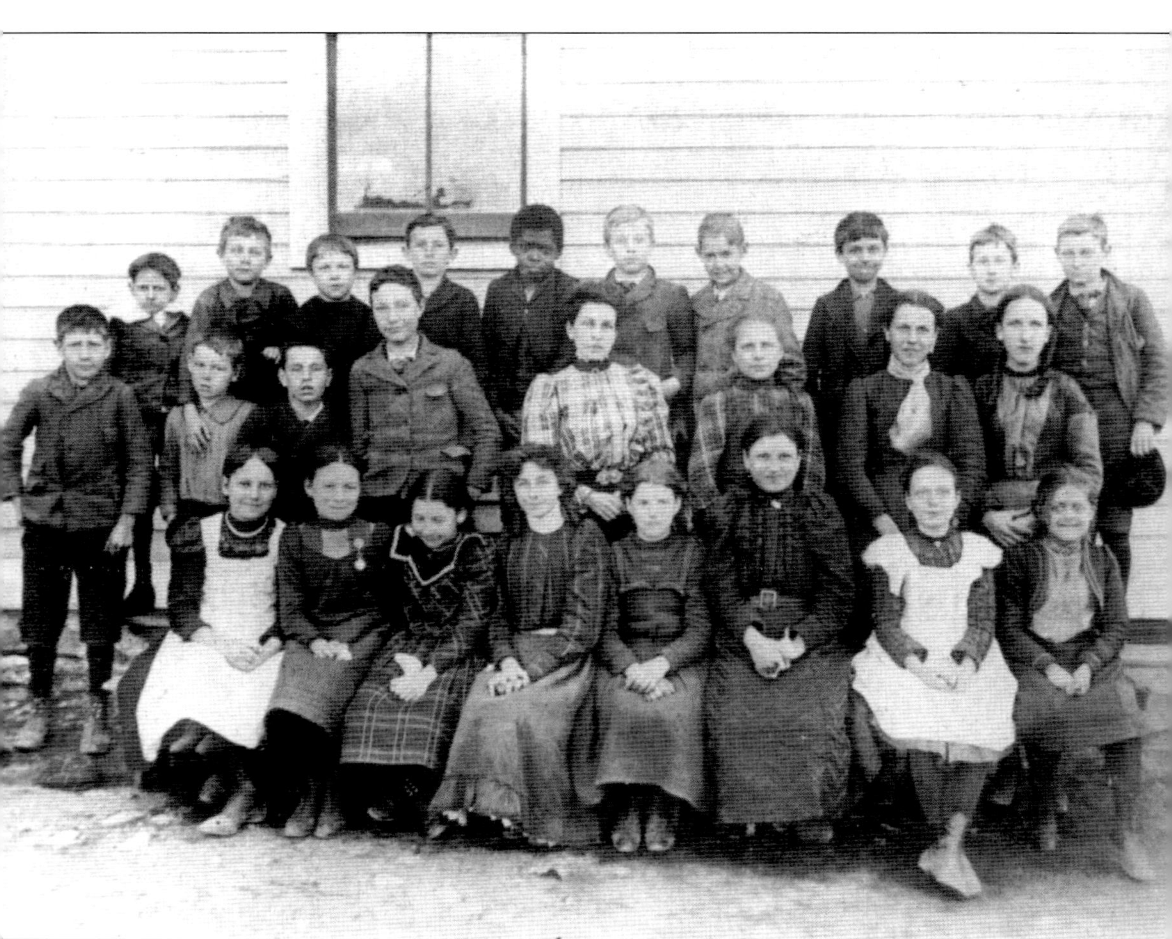

Students in all three rows smile as they have a class picture taken. The teacher may be in the center of the second row. Notice the boots the children are wearing.

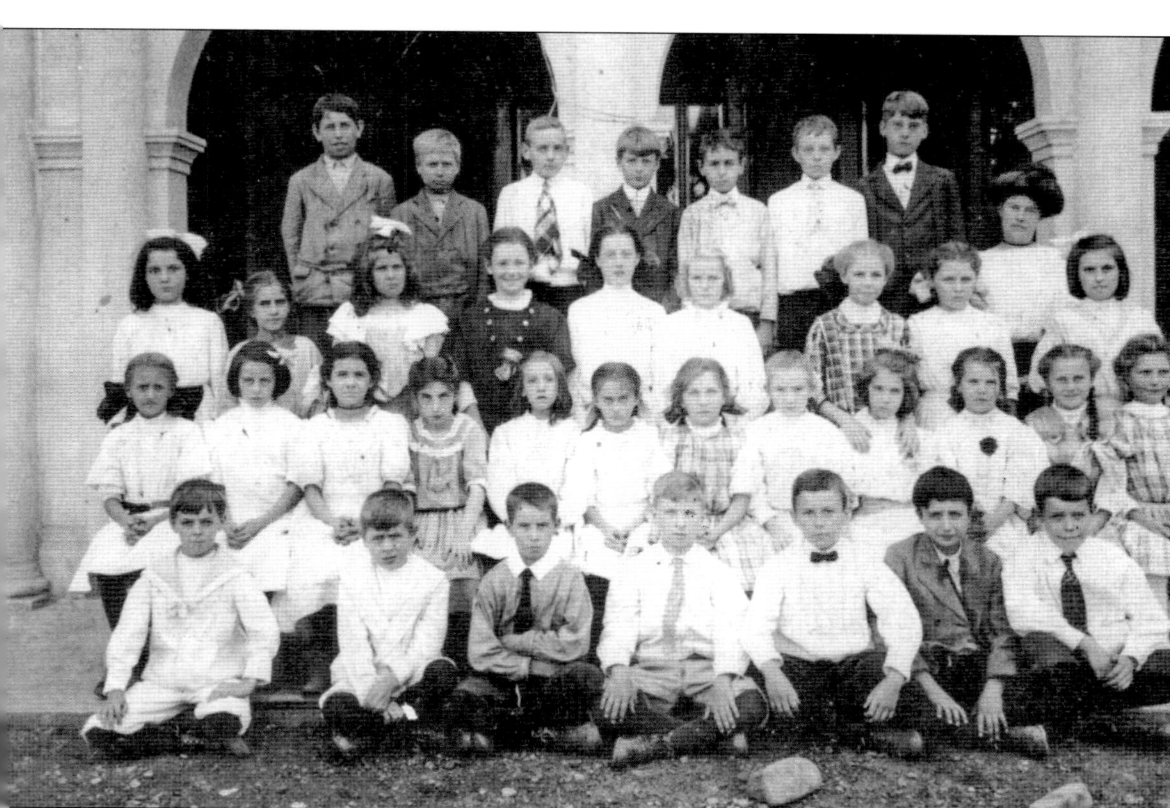

Four rows of pupils pose for a school photograph. The teacher is in the back at the far right.

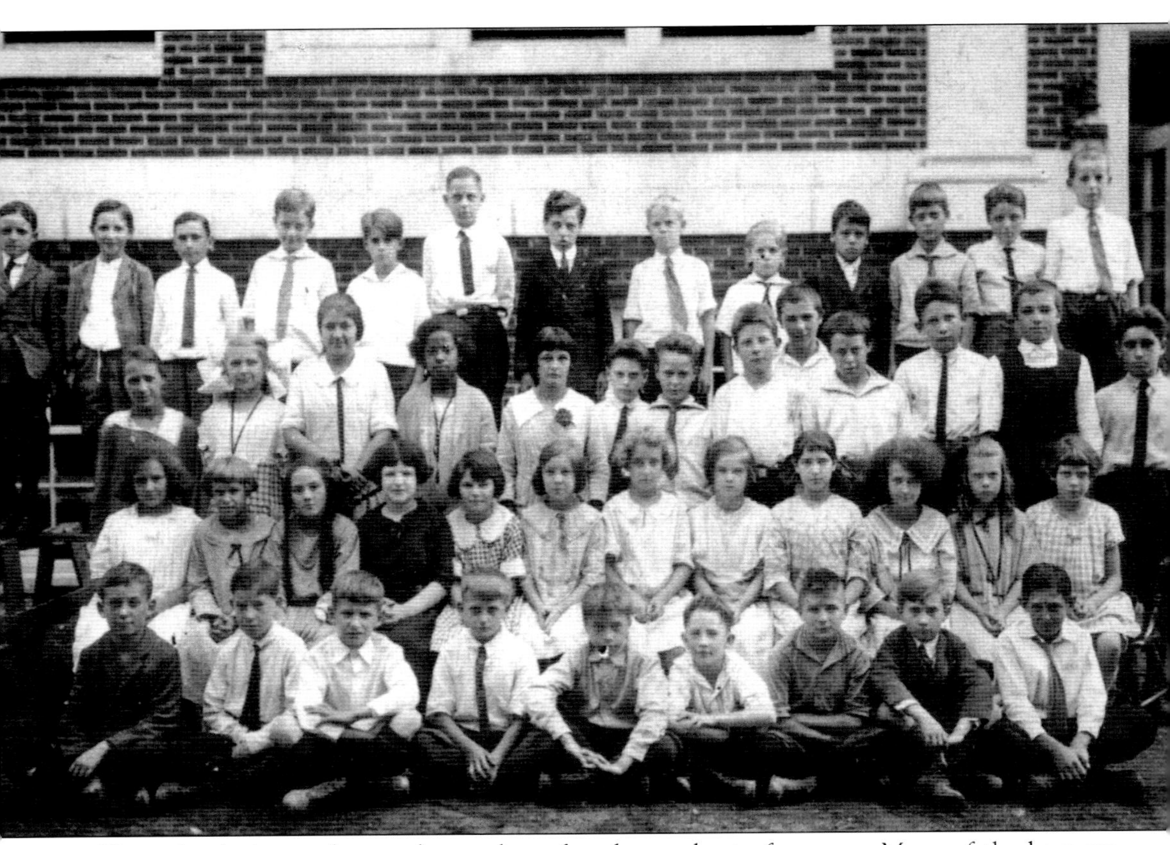

This school picture shows a larger class of students, also in four rows. Many of the boys are wearing neckties.

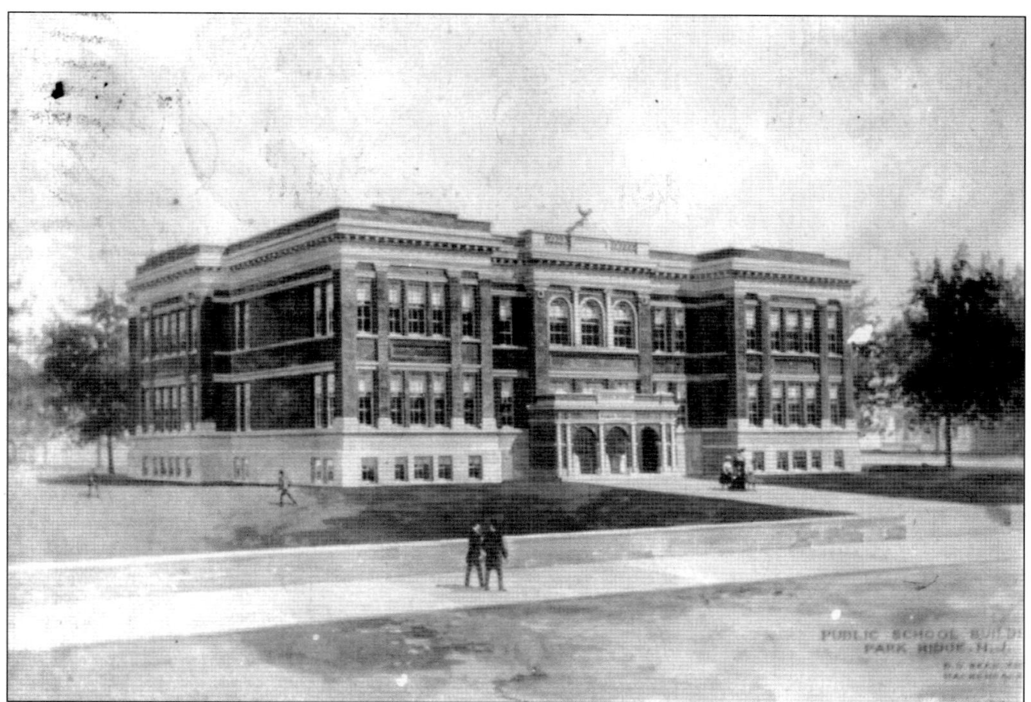


Pictured is Park Ridge Public School in the early 1900s, years before the 1920 fire. A close look shows a couple of students in front of the building.

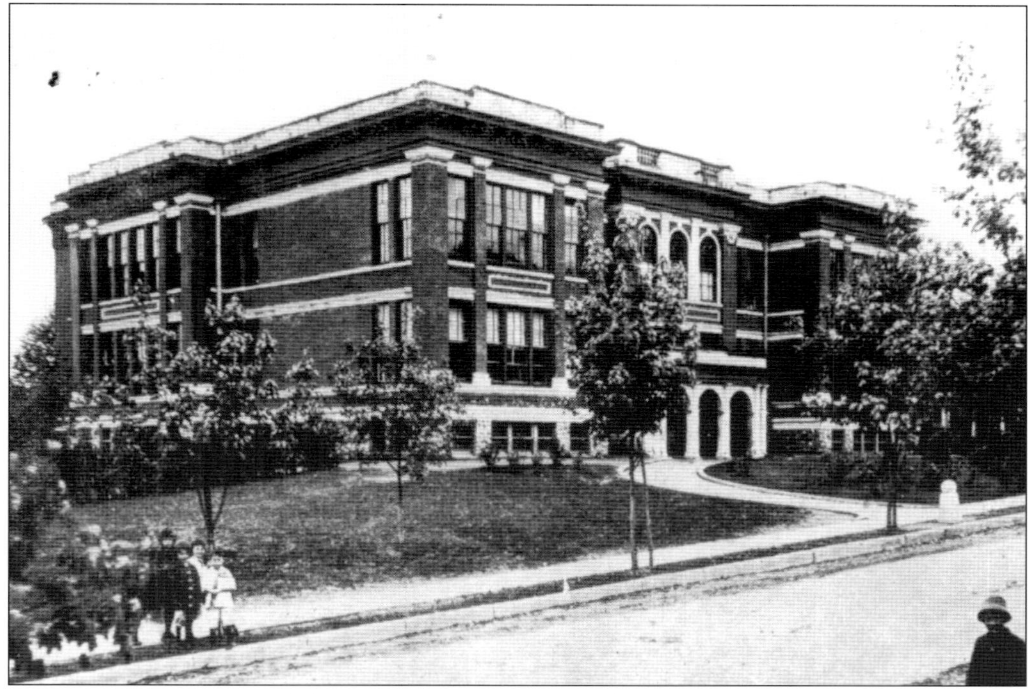

Pictured is another view of the Park Ridge Public School, prior to the big fire.

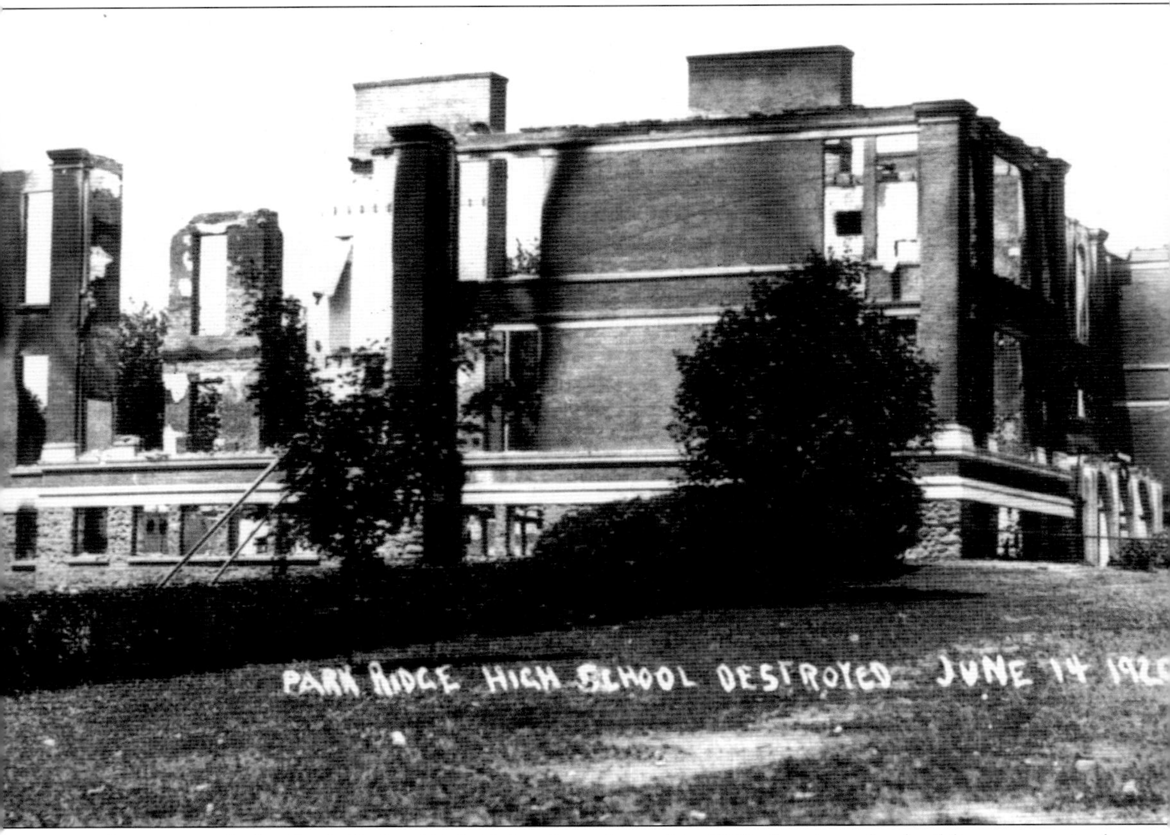


Fire ravaged the Park Ridge High School on June 14, 1920, leaving the building extensively damaged and sending residents into mourning for loved ones who died in the fire.

BACK THE JUNIOR PLAY

# THE PARK RIDGE OWL

SEE YOU AT THE HOP

Vol. XXIV, No. 1 — Park Ridge High School — Park Ridge, N. J., February 28, 1958 — Fifteen Cent

# SENIORS ELECT HALL OF FAME

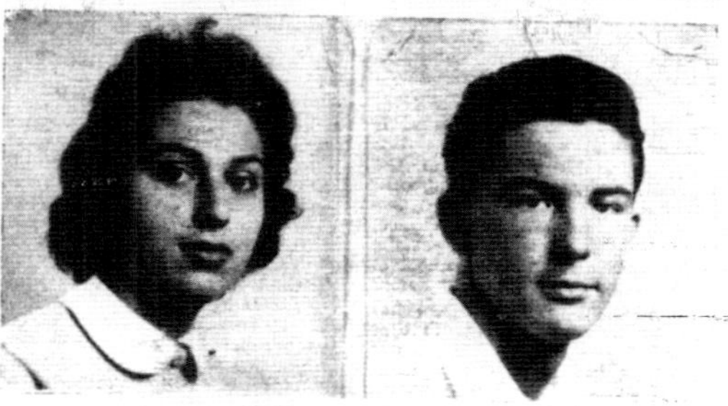

Annetta Polito and John Fegelein, who were elected Best-All-Around.

## Students Man Town Offices

Friday, February 14, was Student Council Day in Park Ridge.

This year for the first time, the student body took over the town government as well as the school administration and faculty. The purpose was to enable the students to gain a better understanding of the nature and purpose of the municipal jobs.

Michael Morrissey, chairman of the day, appointed Bill Rawson mayor of Park Ridge, assisted by Mayor Benjamin Jacobs. Bill is president of the Hi-Y and an active member of the Student Council.

Three councilmen had been appointed as the **Owl** went to press. They were Bob Ingram, Ulla Tortensen, and Bonnie Stobo. Bob is a member of the Hi-Y and plays on most of the sports teams. Ulla, an honor student, is a junior varsity cheerleader. Bonnie, also an honor student, is active in Junior Tri-Hi-Y.

Doug Stobo, appointed Chief of Police, is vice-president of the senior class, sports editor of the **Owl** and a member of the Student Council. Barbara Mortensen, who acted as Borough Clerk, is president of the senior class and the Honor Society and editor-in-chief of the **Owl**. Tax Collector Danny Kaplowitz is active in most sports. Kenneth Unger, who was in charge of Public Utilities, has also seen action in sports.

In the school, Student Council president Hugh Sanborn acted as Superintendent, taking over Mr. S. Cynamon's position. Ann Brenz took over as principal, in Dr. M. Weiner's place.

At 2:00 P. M. all the participants returned to the auditorium at the school to view a talent show put on by the students under the auspices of the Student Council.

------o------

## RIDGERS COMPETE IN SPELLING BEE

Sixth, seventh, and eighth grade students from Park Ridge and Woodcliff Lake, competed on January 4 in a spelling bee sponsored by the Pascack Grange in Grange Hall.

Top winners for the boys from Park Ridge were Arnold Rusoff, first, and James Voltmar, third. Kathy Willis and Georgia Tumioli, achieved second and third places respectively for the girls.

On January 18 the first three winners in both divisions are going to compete in another contest in Wayne Township. State finals will take place in Trenton on January 29. Watch for the results in the

## Juniors Choose War Drama

"Letters to Lucerne," this year's junior play, will be held in the school auditorium on March 7.

This play is the first serious drama given as a class play in many years. Previous productions have been comedies. Dealing with a girls' school in Poland during World War II, the play tells of the attempt to keep the true facts of the war away from the girls.

Playing the girls are Lillian Casey, Eileen Cooper, Carol Peterson, Sonja Vander Kaden, Karen Easterly, Judi Reimers, Marilyn McCarthy, Beatrice Harvey, and Carolyn Cole. Fred Krell, Leonard Sussman, Bill Pysner, and Henry Maddalone take the male parts.

Mr. Abe Steingart, class adviser, is directing the play. Fred Krell is acting as student director.

Admission for the play will be one dollar.

------o------

## SOPHOMORES CHOOSE "MAGIC MOMENTS"

Sophomores will hold the annual Soph Hop on March 14 in the school gymnasium.

"Magic Moments" is the theme, according to president Steve Larson. Mary Ingram, chairman of decorations, will carry out this theme with modernistic forms. There will be an arbor effect, with the band in the alcove.

Music will be provided by "Frank Kay and his Quintet" along with a female vocalist, entertainment chairman Steve Schnee announced. Refreshments will include sandwiches, cookies and punch, according to Adele Rocheleau, chairman. The entire class will help with this.

Susan Hatch, ticket chairman, has announced that tickets will be one dollar and seventy-five cents per

## *Schaefer Leads Over Senior Girls*

Jean Schaefer is the Betty Crocker Homemaker of Tomorrow in PRHS.

She received the highest score in a written examination on homemaking skills administered to senior girls on December 3. Her examination paper will be entered in competition to name this state's candidate for the title of All-American Homemaker of Tomorrow, and will also be considered for the runner-up award in the state. For her achievement, she will receive an award pin designed by Trifari of New York.

The national winner in the fourth annual Betty Crocker Search will be named April 17 at a banquet at the Waldorf-Astoria in New York City.

General Mills is the sponsor of the program designed to help schools in education for home and family living. Student participation in this contest over the past four years has passed the million mark. A total of one hundred six thousand dollars in scholarships will be awarded this year.

Each state Betty Crocker Homemaker of Tomorrow will receive a one thousand five hundred dollar scholarship and an educational trip with her school adviser to Washington, D. C., Williamsburg, Virginia, and New York City. A five hundred dollar scholarship will be awarded the second ranking girl of each state. The school of the state winner will receive a set of the Encyclopedia Britannica.

The scholarship of the girl named All-American Homemaker of Tomorrow will be increased to five thousand dollars. Girls who rank second, third, and fourth in the nation will receive four thousand dollars, three thousand dollars and

This year's Hall of Fame has been announced by the members of the senior class.

Selected as best all around were Annetta Polito and John Fegelein. Annetta is president of the Tri-Y and a member of the Bridge Club. She is active in sports and school affairs. Johnny, co-captain of the football team, is president of the Lettermen's Club.

Gloria Anzalone and Bob Rafferty were chosen as the seniors with personality plus. Gloria, a member of the Tri-Y, appeared in both the senior and junior plays. Bob, a member of the Hot Rod Club, also played football.

Elected as having done most for the class were Nancy Hatch and David Mecheski. Nancy, a member of the Honor Society, Tri-Y, and president of the Art Club, has had charge of decorations for the Mistletoe Dance for the past two years and was chairman of decorations for the junior prom. She is also art editor of the yearbook and second page editor of the **Owl**. Dave, a member of the Stagecraft Club, has had charge of the lighting for the plays. He has been active in all class affairs.

Voted most likely to succeed were Barbara Mortensen and Hugh Sanborn. Barb, president of the senior class and the Honor Society, is a member of the Tri-Y and editor-in-chief of the **Owl**. Hugh, president of the Student Council, plays basketball and baseball.

### Wit, Athletics Form Categories

Wittiest of the seniors are Marie Iafrate and Phil DiBella. Marie is a member of the Tri-Y and the Bridge Club. Phil, a member of the Psychology Club, is active in all sports.

Most athletic are Trudy Werner and Bob Murphy. Trudy, drum majorette, is a member of the Tri-Y and the Band. She is treasurer of the class and business editor of the **Hoot**. Bob has played varsity football and basketball.

Best dressed are Debby Schilling and Doug Stobo. Debby, president of the Library Council, is a member of the Tri-Y and the Bridge Club. Doug, sports editor of the **Owl**, plays in most sports and participates in the Student Council. He is vice-president of the class.

Selected as best looking were Cynthia Trossello and Bob Ingram. Cynthia, member of the Tri-Y and Bridge Club, is feature editor of the **Owl**. Bob plays in most sports. He is a member of the Lettermen's Club.

### COMING EVENTS

| | |
|---|---|
| Junior Play | March 7 |
| Soph Hop | March 14 |
| Sadie Hawkins Dance | March 21 |

This edition of the *Owl*, the Park Ridge High School newspaper, was printed on February 28, 1958. It was Volume XXIV, No. 1, and it cost 15¢. Included with the news were reminders of upcoming events: the junior class play on March 7, the Sophomore Hop on March 14, and the Sadie Hawkins Dance on March 21.

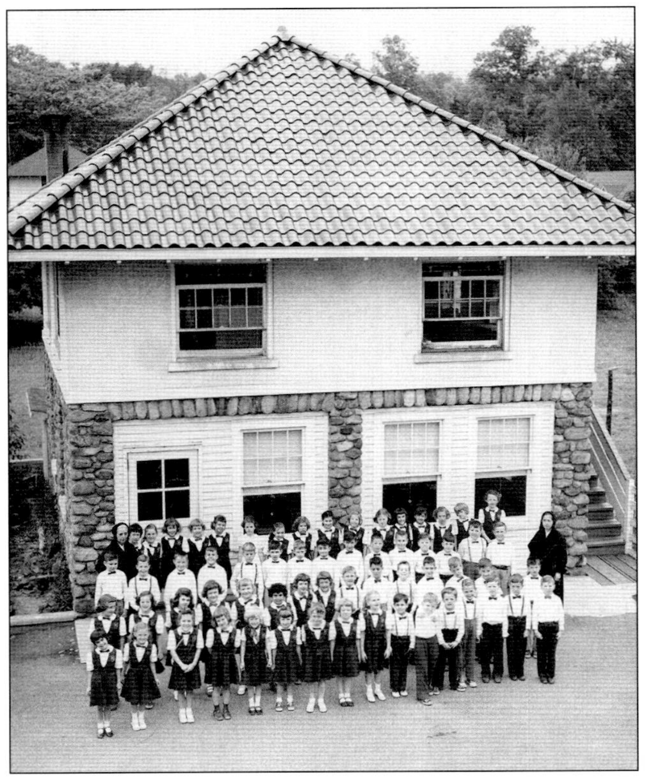

Pictured is the first class at Our Lady of Mercy, standing in front of the Catholic school's first building, a garage behind the convent. That building was later connected to the convent, originally the elegant home of a private citizen.

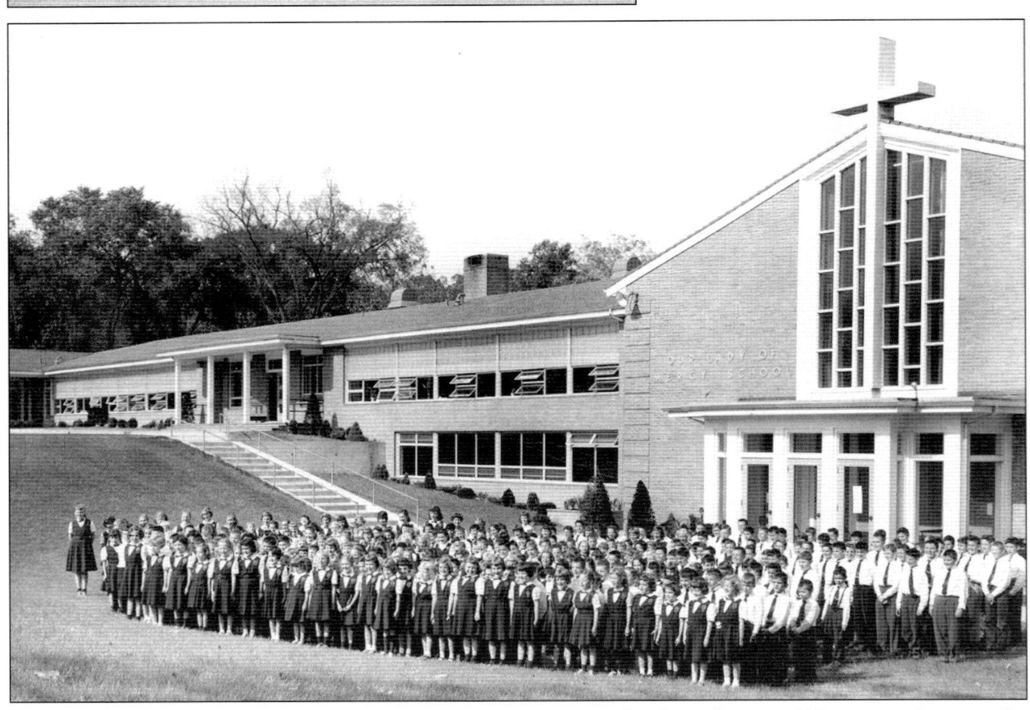

In 1956, the student body of Our Lady of Mercy poses on the front lawn, off Fremont Avenue. In 1955, the new school building was erected, and an eight-room addition was completed in 1958, followed by another addition in 1963.

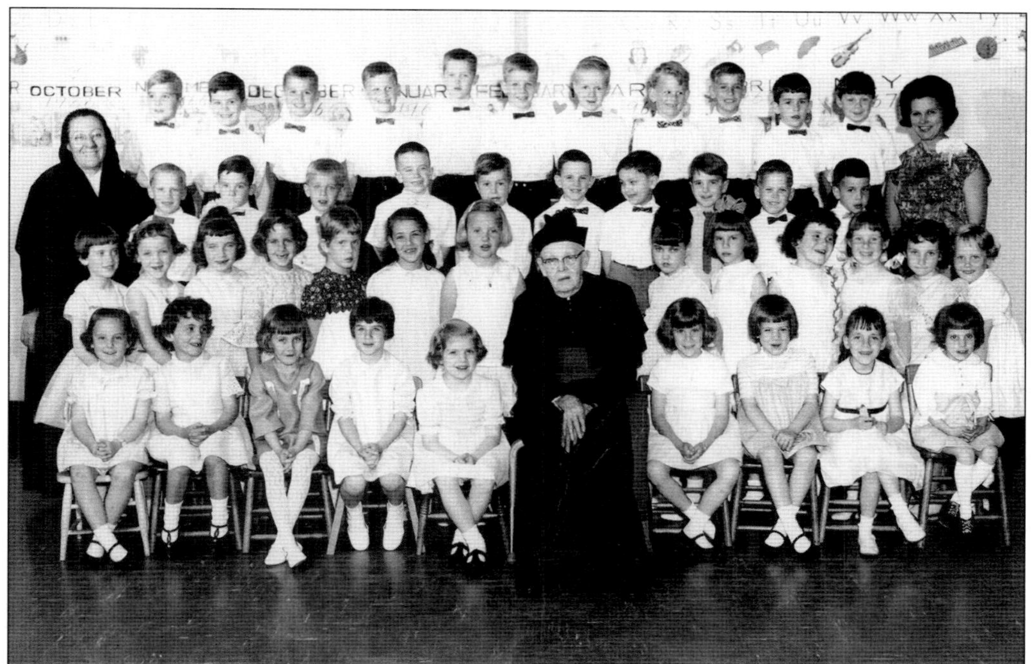


A class poses with Sister Anna, who served as the school's principal for many years, and with Mrs. Kuhn, who was a kindergarten teacher for many years and whose husband wrote the school song.

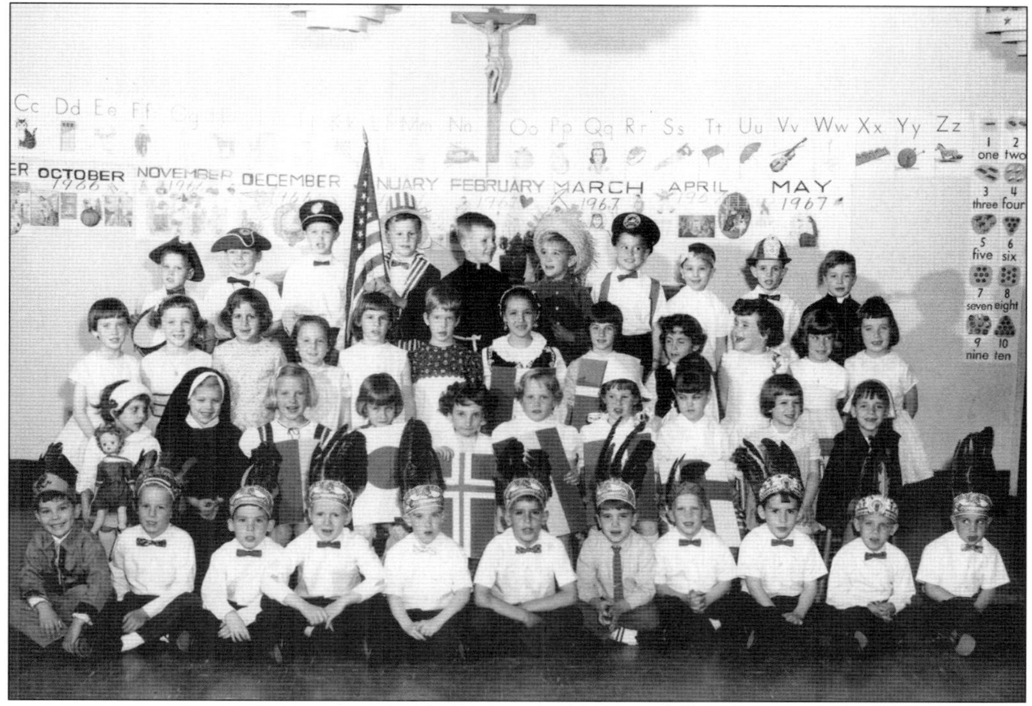


One of the pupils in the kindergarten class of 1965 was Eddie States, who many years later was piloting a flight of passengers on their way to South America when the plane crashed over Queens, New York.

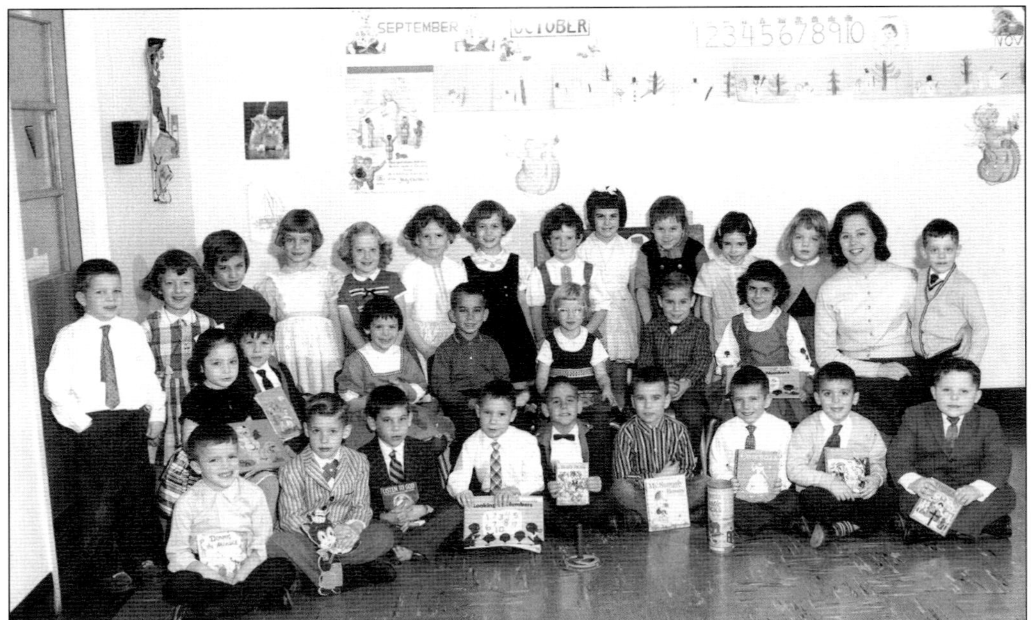


Members of an Our Lady of Mercy class display the books that they will have to read during the upcoming school year.

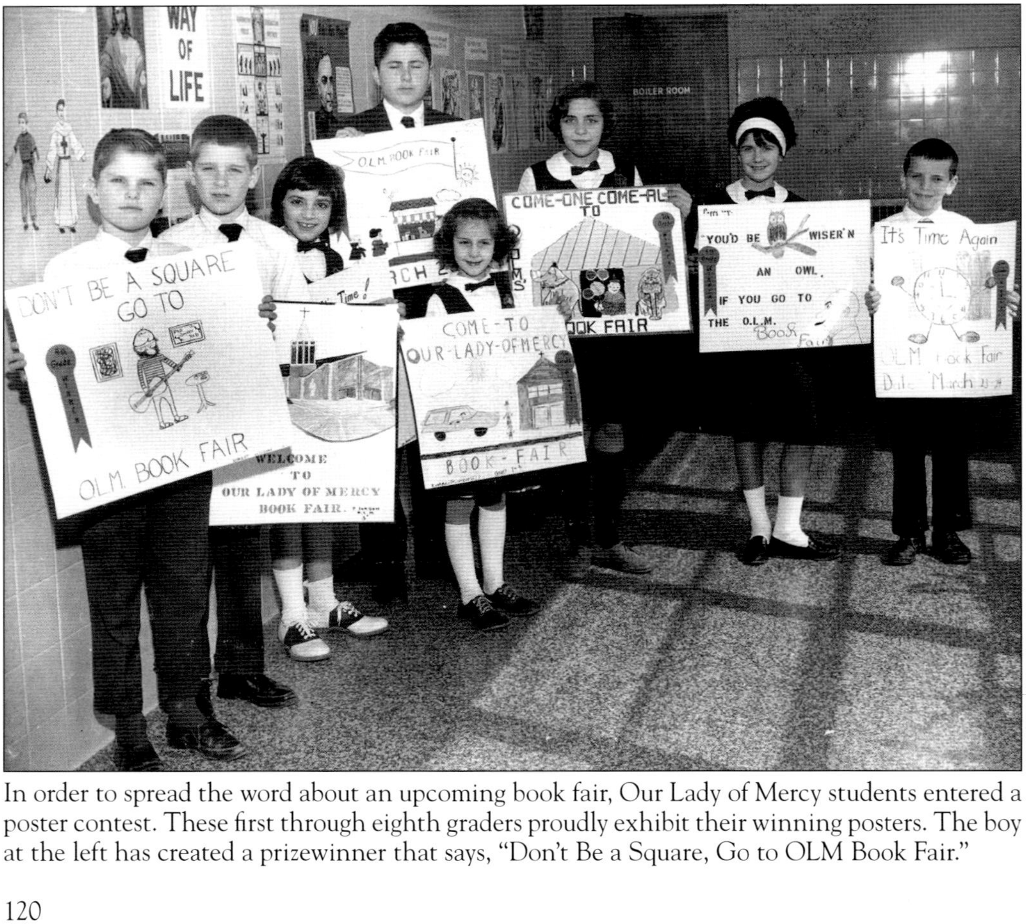

In order to spread the word about an upcoming book fair, Our Lady of Mercy students entered a poster contest. These first through eighth graders proudly exhibit their winning posters. The boy at the left has created a prizewinner that says, "Don't Be a Square, Go to OLM Book Fair."

# *Eight*

# Floods

A devastating flood occurred several years ago, causing damage in the borough that included a mud slide so severe that the police department did not open again in the same location. Many records were ruined, and the police temporarily relocated to a storefront on Kinderkamack Road, until moving in to the new headquarters on Willet Street and Park Avenue in 2006.

The history of flooding in the area predates that particular storm, however. There are records showing that back in the early 1900s there was a flood so severe that parts of the brand-new dam were washed away. The water at times may overflow, but the brooks, streams, and lakes of the area have long been, and continue to be, a source of good health and recreation in Park Ridge.

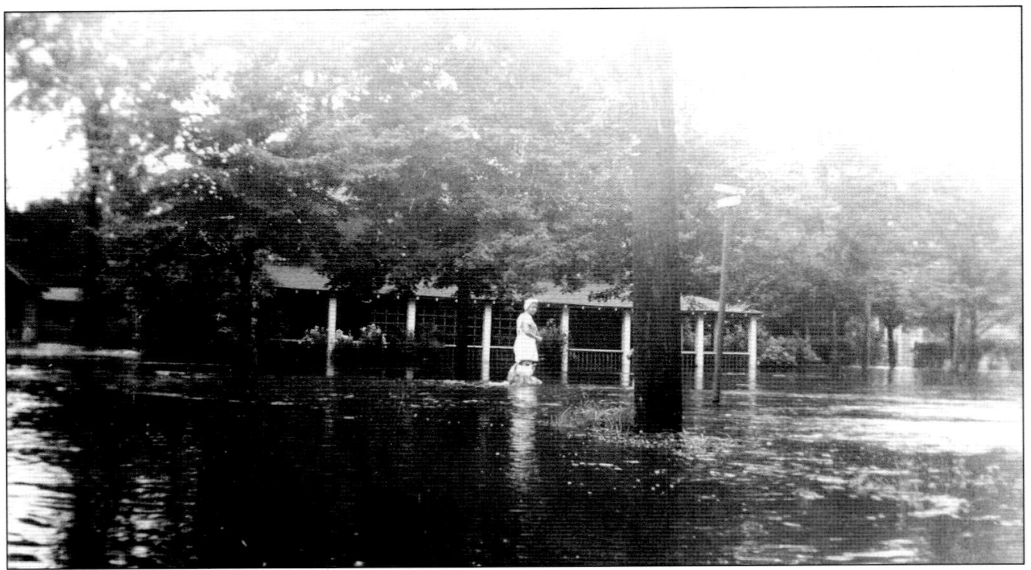

A woman can be seen in the center of this Park Ridge flood scene.

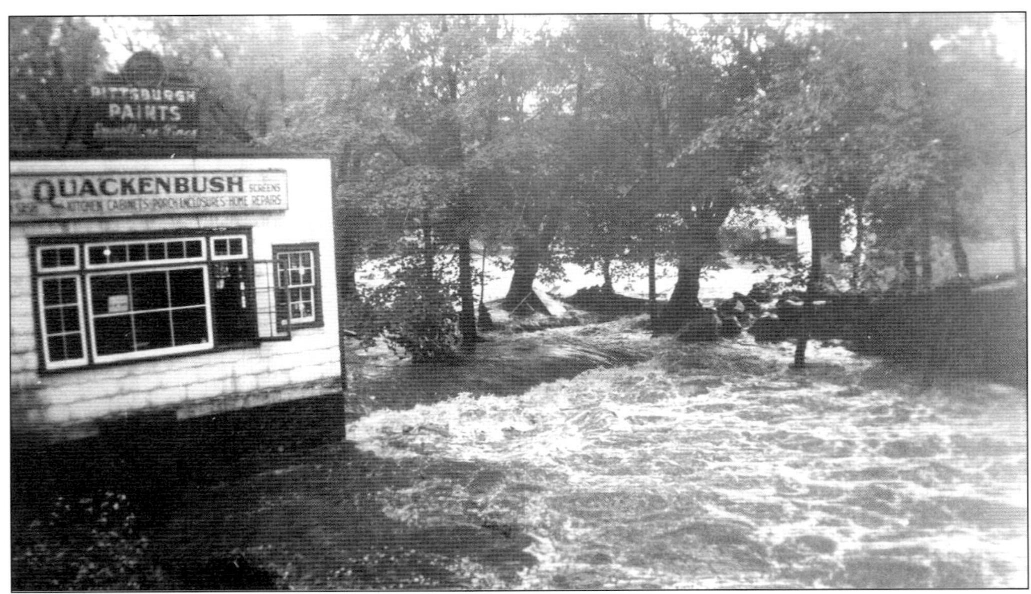


The waters of the Pascack Brook rise near the Quackenbush Lumberyard.

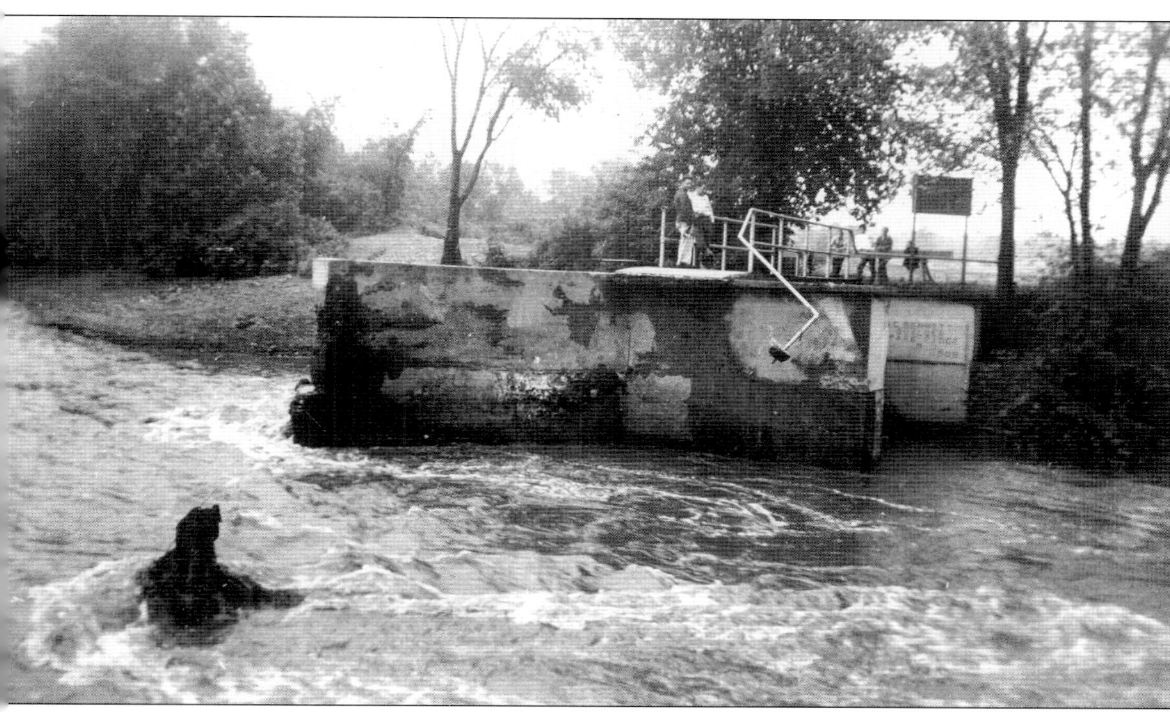

Here onlookers survey damage from the 1945 flood caused when the dam gave way at Electric Pond.

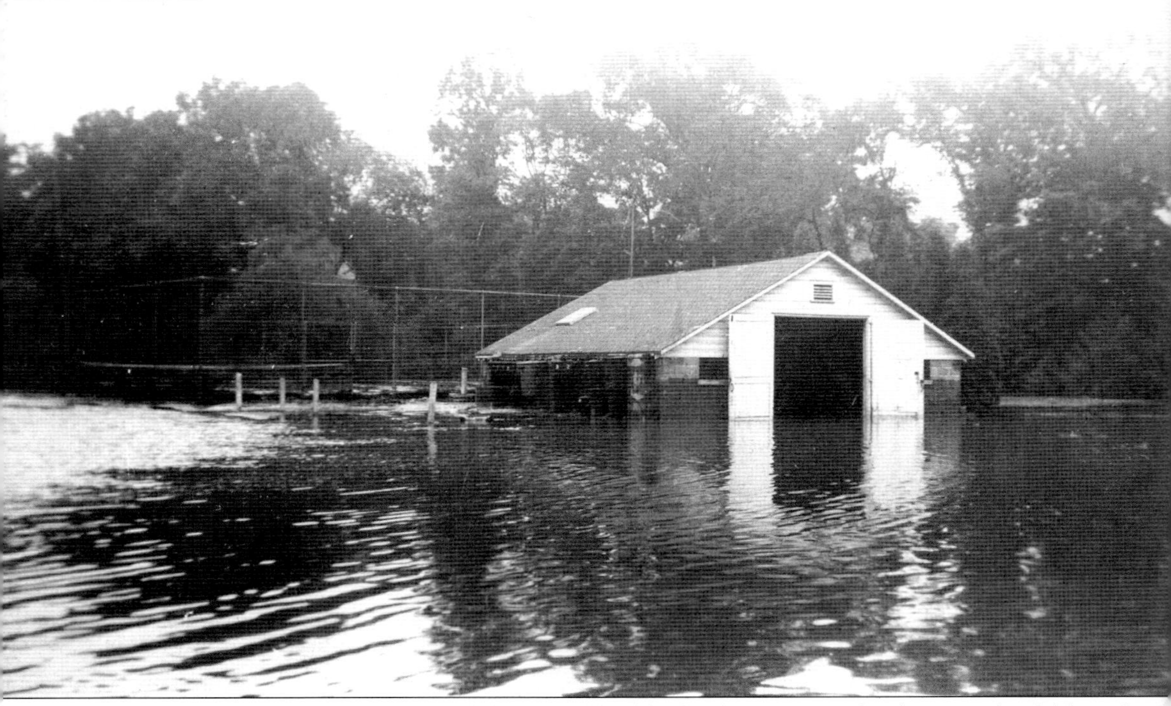

At Sulak Lane, where the borough has its ball fields, floodwaters completely cover the fields and rise high up the walls of the clubhouse.

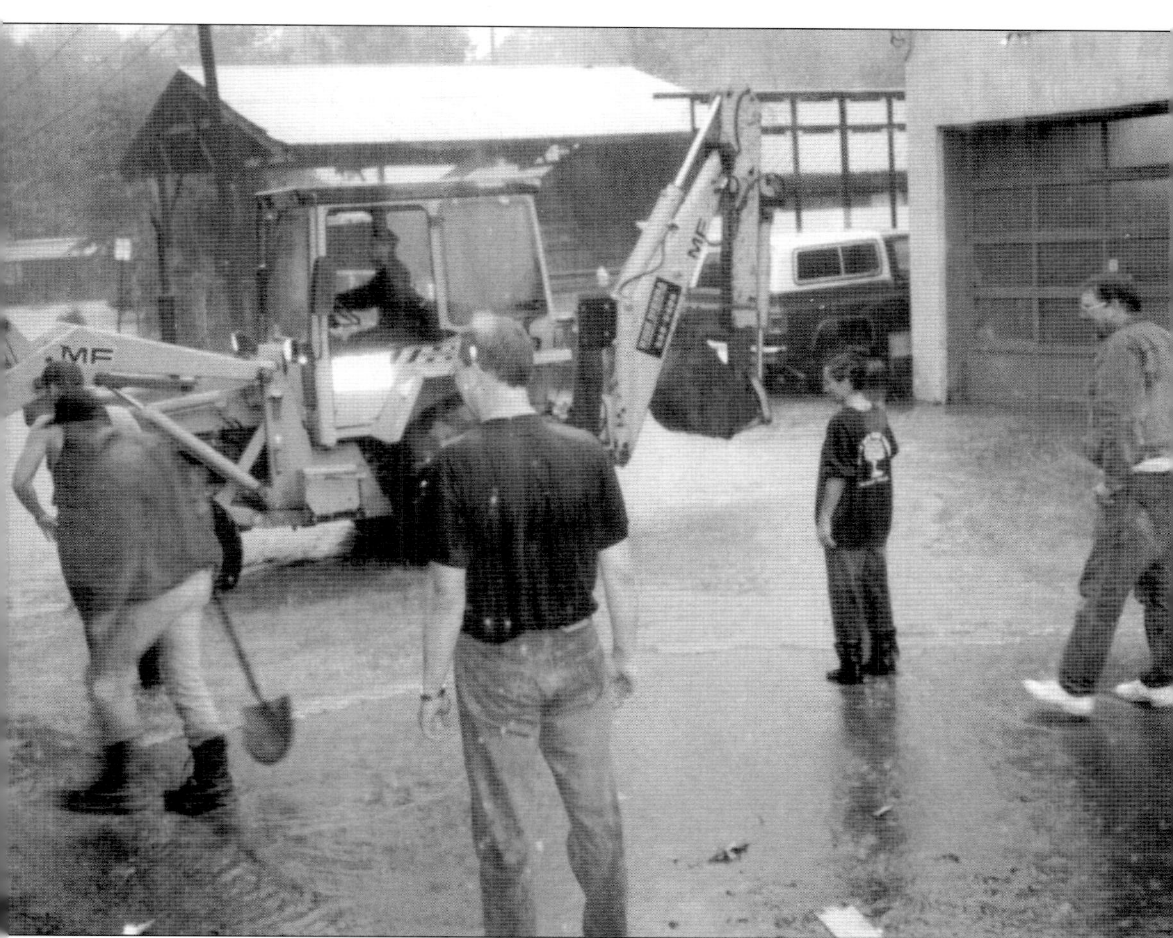


As floodwaters once again rush over the banks of the brook, residents armed with shovels and heavy equipment fight back.

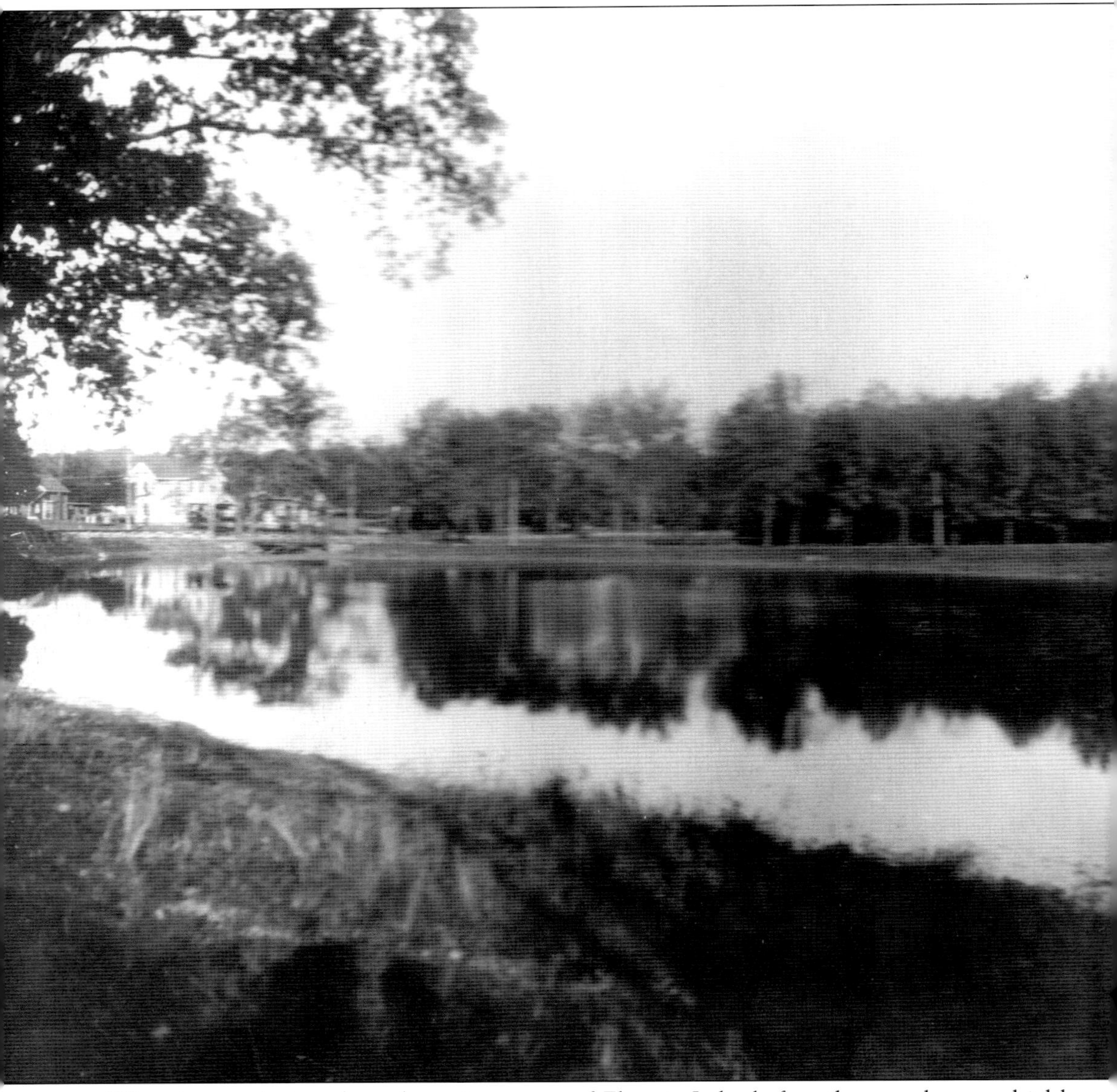

What better closing than the quiet waters of Electric Lake before the area became highly populated. The lake is still a quiet spot, although now it is in the middle of a lively and

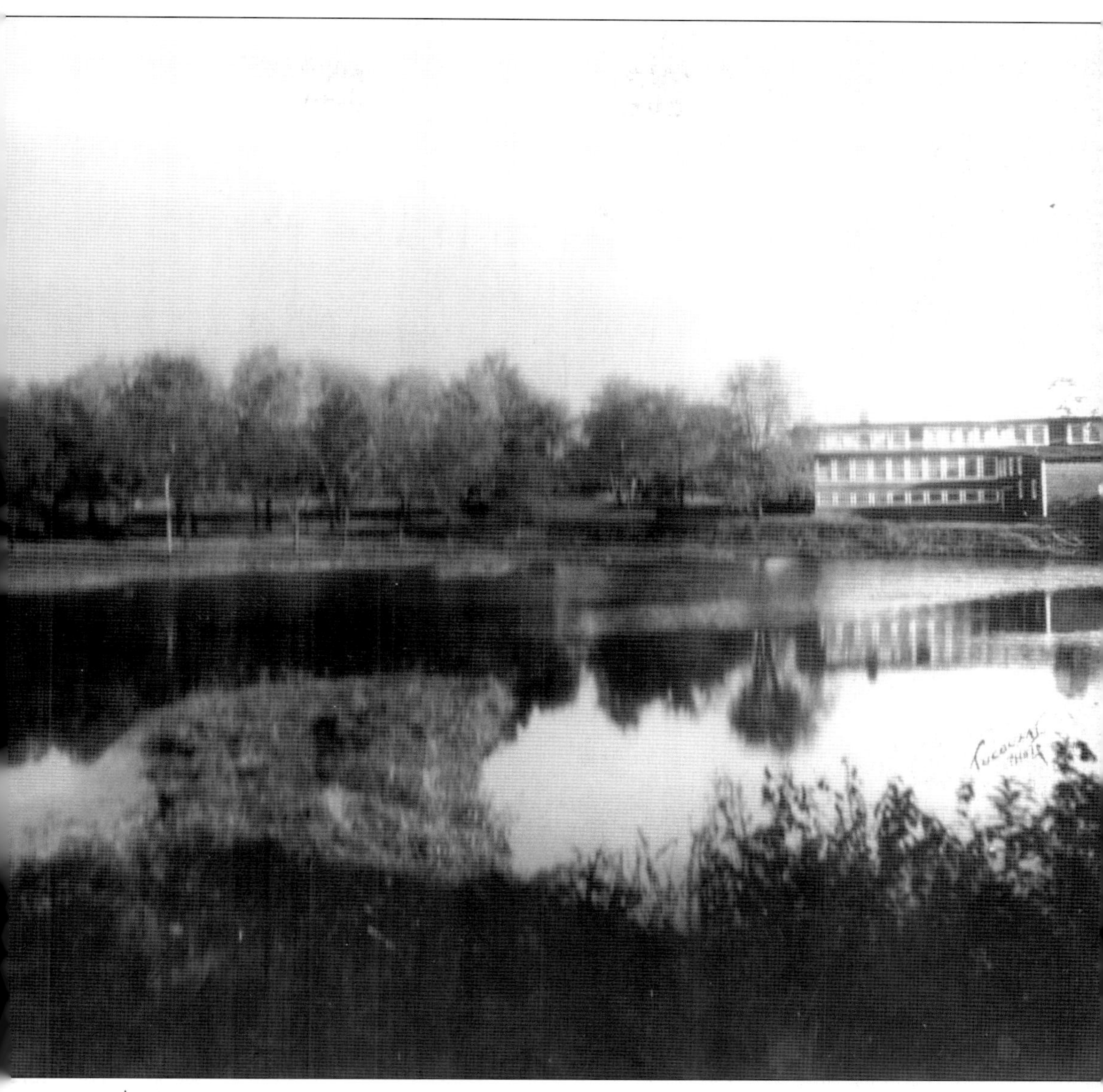

progressive town.

# ACROSS AMERICA, PEOPLE ARE DISCOVERING SOMETHING WONDERFUL. *THEIR HERITAGE.*

Arcadia Publishing is the leading local history publisher in the United States. With more than 3,000 titles in print and hundreds of new titles released every year, Arcadia has extensive specialized experience chronicling the history of communities and celebrating America's hidden stories, bringing to life the people, places, and events from the past. To discover the history of other communities across the nation, please visit:

www.arcadiapublishing.com

Customized search tools allow you to find regional history books about the town where you grew up, the cities where your friends and family live, the town where your parents met, or even that retirement spot you've been dreaming about.

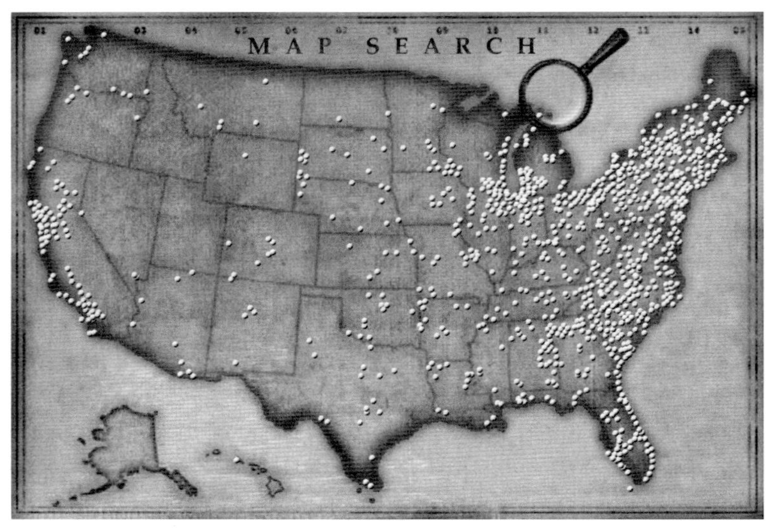